CHAMPION

JOE LOUIS
Black Hero in White America

CHAMPION

JOE LOUIS
Black Hero in White America

Chris Mead

CHARLES SCRIBNER'S SONS · NEW YORK

Copyright © 1985 Chris Mead

Library of Congress Cataloging-in-Publication Data
Mead, Chris, 1959–
Champion—Joe Louis, black hero in white America.
Bibliography: p.
Includes index.
1. Louis, Joe, 1914–1981.   2. Boxers (Sports)—United
States—Biography.   1. Title.
GV1132.L6M4   1985   796.8'3'0924 [B]   85-14440
ISBN 0-684-18462-1

Published simultaneously in Canada by Collier Macmillan Canada, Inc.—
Copyright under the Berne Convention.

1 3 5 7 9 11 13 15 17 19   F/C   20 18 16 14 12 10 8 6 4 2

Printed in the United States of America

CONTENTS

ACKNOWLEDGMENTS

I want to thank the people who work at the Library of Congress; National Archives; Yale University Library; the Michigan Historical Society Library, located at the University of Michigan, Ann Arbor campus; the Schomburg Center for Research in Black Culture, in New York; Howard University Library; American University Library; and George Washington University Library. I especially want to thank Dave Kelly, an expert in sports history at the Library of Congress.

Thanks also to the people who shared their memories of Joe Louis with me: Bob Pastor, Red Burman, Billy Conn, Truman Gibson, Colvin Roberts, Ted Jones, Shirley Povich, Barney Nagler, and Harry Markson. Prof. John Morton Blum of Yale University inspired and sharpened many of the ideas on this book and provided editorial guidance, especially on chapter 11. Thanks to Bert Sugar of *Ring* magazine and to Jules Tygiel, author of an excellent book on Jackie Robinson, *Baseball's Great Experiment*, who was kind enough to discuss his research with me.

Alan Hirsch edited portions of the manuscript, focused many of my ideas, and lent me some of his own. Tom and Jane Doeblin and John Eliasberg let me sleep in their apartment again and again on my trips to New York. Pete Deeb got me drunk in Pittsburgh. Benedict Sims Cohen put me up for several days in the middle of a snowstorm while I was in Chicago to conduct interviews.

Members of my far-flung family also housed me during my travels for research and interviews. My grandmother, Charlotte Burkitt, put me up in her house in St. Louis. My aunt and uncle, Karin and Alden Mead, sheltered me from the bitter cold in Minneapolis and translated Max Schmeling's memoirs and Nazi newspapers for me. My brother Andy made the extreme sacrifice of sharing a college dorm room at the University of Michigan. Andy also edited the manuscript with his usual sensitivity and smarts.

My editor at Scribner's, Maron Waxman, tightened and clarified the original manuscript and improved this book immeasurably.

I owe my parents more than words can express. They inspired, encouraged, and supported me during a very uncertain year. My father, a true professional, carefully edited the entire manuscript, reassuring his son as he went.

The year I took off to write this book would have been worthwhile if I had not produced a single word, because during that time I met my wife, Lauren. She made writing less lonely and makes all things possible.

If there is anything of value in these pages, all these people have had a hand in creating it. The faults are my own.

INTRODUCTION

Joe Louis's death, like so much of his life, was a media event. Newspapers, television, and radio marked Louis's passing with headlines, interruptions in regular programming, and phrases reserved for the famous—"Perhaps the greatest boxer of all time," "A great champion who restored integrity to boxing," "A man who, despite all his misfortunes, maintained his dignity and class." The words echoed an earlier generation of writers and broadcasters who had called Louis a "credit to his race."

Running through these obituary notices was a thread of condescension that wrapped Louis's memory in a cocoon of white warmth. Louis had become a pathetic figure, writers praised him without full respect because he had squandered his money and gone a little crazy in the end.

These tributes belittled a giant. Louis was the first black American to achieve lasting fame and popularity in the twentieth century. When he began to box professionally in 1934, there were no blacks who consistently appeared in white newspapers, no blacks who occupied positions of public prominence, no blacks who commanded attention from whites. Historians recognize W.E.B. DuBois and A. Philip Randolph as the most important black leaders of the 1930s; white Americans of that era would have been hard pressed to recognize their names, still less their faces. DuBois and Randolph simply did not appear in white newspapers.

A few black entertainers—Bojangles Robinson, Paul Robeson,

Louis Armstrong—occasionally made the back pages of the white press. No black athlete since Jack Johnson, the first black heavyweight champion of the world, had really made an impression on the white public, and the impression Johnson had made was entirely negative. Major league baseball was for whites only. Southern college football teams often refused to play northern teams with black players. Blacks had begun to make a breakthrough in track and field during the 1932 Olympics. No one had noticed.

By September 1935, after Louis had knocked out two former heavyweight champions in four months, the American public started to acknowledge him as the best fighter in the world. Louis became a sensation. Stories about his fights, his past, his training routine, his hobbies and personal habits, appeared in sports pages around the country. By 1936, Damon Runyon could write, "It is our guess that more has been written about Louis in the past two years than about any living man over a similar period of time, with the exception of Lindbergh."

The enormous popular interest in Louis was due in large part to his boxing skill. The United States was already undergoing the sports revolution that continues today; great athletes received more publicity than most statesman or artists. But Louis was more interesting than any other athlete the white public could imagine. Louis was an anomaly: he was black. The way white sportswriters wrote about Louis revealed how novel it was for a black to reach a position of prominence. White journalists, including the best and most sophisticated writers of the day, constantly wrote about Louis's color. Nor were they satisfied with simply identifying him as a "Negro." They gave Louis alliterative nicknames like "the brown bomber," "the dark destroyer," "the tan tornado," "the sepia slugger." They patronized him, stereotyped him, quoted him in darkie dialect, said he had "pin-cushion lips," implied that he was stupid and lazy, called him a "jungle killer." This was not critical comment; it was routinely included in even the most rapturous stories about the emerging champion.

Because Louis was the only black in the white world of fame and fortune, he became the symbol of his race to both blacks and whites. To blacks, Louis was the greatest of a pitifully small pantheon of heroes. Every time he stepped into the ring against a white opponent, Louis refuted theories of white superiority. Louis's victories touched off late-night celebrations in the black neighborhoods of northern cities. Extra details of white policemen watched, half indulgently, half uneasily, as thousands of blacks rejoiced in the streets.

Many people sensed that Louis was a symbol of his race to whites as well as to blacks. Black preachers and white sportswriters lectured Louis on his responsibility: the white public judged a whole people by his actions. That added up to a lot of pressure on a shy, uneducated young man, and the legacy of Jack Johnson compounded the pressure. Johnson had openly flouted the conventions of segregated America twenty years earlier by defeating white opponents and marrying white women.

With the help of a cooperative press, Louis and his managers carefully constructed a "well-behaved" public image. Louis bought his mother a house, modestly downplayed his victories, complimented his white opponents, and married a black "girl" of good family.

At first, the white press mixed patronizing and artificial praise of Louis's behavior with racist stereotypes. But as time went on, Louis won more and more acceptance. He began to relax with reporters and won a more human image. Louis lost his reputation for invincibility in 1936 when he suffered his first professional loss, to Max Schmeling of Germany. Louis won the heavyweight title from James J. Braddock in 1937, then defended his title in a rematch against Schmeling in 1938. Schmeling was the great white hope only of Nazi Germany. The American people embraced Joe Louis, a black, as their representative. In his greatest fight, Louis knocked out Schmeling in the first round. The war with Germany that followed confirmed the fight in America's collective memory as a symbolic defeat of Nazism and racism.

World War II whitewashed Louis in a wave of patriotism. He cheerfully entered the army, and risked his title twice in charity bouts for army and navy relief. The army used Louis as grist for the war propaganda mills, a symbol of U.S. unity, racial tolerance, and willingness to serve. Louis went on morale-boosting tours for the army throughout the war, fighting exhibitions in the United States, Alaska, and Europe. Just as Louis's "good behavior" as a boxer had reassured the white public, his patriotism and loyalty reassured whites who had wondered, at least to themselves, whether a people scorned by their country would nevertheless fight for it.

After the war, the white press's treatment of Louis changed. The alliterative nicknames disappeared, save the standard "brown bomber" and "dark destroyer." White journalists rarely identified him as a Negro; stereotyped references declined. Important newspapers praised Louis in editorials, and the praise had a more sincere and less condescending ring. The press found a word for Louis that would describe him for the rest of his life, and after— "dignity."

Louis retired for the first time in 1949. Of the forty-three men he had fought before the war, only one had been black. Now both leading contenders for his crown, Joe Walcott and Ezzard Charles, were black. Two years earlier, Jackie Robinson had become the first black to play in the major leagues. Louis had broken the ground. He had opened sports to blacks and made athletics a cutting edge of the civil rights movement.

1

"LET YOUR RIGHT FIST BE THE REFEREE"

One day in mid-June 1934, two black men walked into George Trafton's gym on Randolph Street in Chicago. They were the kind of men who dropped by the gym once in a while and didn't stay long. Flesh obscured the lines of their jaws and rounded their cheeks, and their stomachs bulged. They wore good clothes.

Jack Blackburn, a black trainer who worked with some of the boxers at Trafton's, recognized one of the men, Julian Black —the one with the darker, shiny skin and the straight hair greased back and parted on the left. Black introduced his balding friend with the polite mustache as John Roxborough. They had found a good heavyweight prospect in Detroit, Black and Roxborough told Blackburn, and they wanted Blackburn to train him. The young fighter's name was Joe Louis.

"Bring around this white boy and I'll look him over," Blackburn said.

Roxborough told Blackburn that Louis was a Negro.

"I won't have no truck with a colored boy," said Blackburn. "Colored boys ain't got much chance fighting nowadays—unless they just happen to be world-beaters."

Roxborough laughed and said a world-beater was exactly what they had. Blackburn said nothing. He had been around boxing too long to believe managers, but he needed work. Roxborough and Black left, saying they would bring in their fighter the next day.

Blackburn must have watched them go with some amusement

1

and disbelief. He had spent many evenings in Julian Black's speakeasy, the Elite Number 2, and knew that Black worked with Charlie and Dan Jackson. The Jackson brothers were morticians, and Dan controlled gambling and the numbers rackets on the South Side. In Depression-ridden black neighborhoods there were no surer ways to make money than funerals and the numbers; Julian Black was making plenty. His friend Roxborough smelled of money, too, though he didn't seem as street tough as Black. Such successful men should have known better than to back a black fighter, especially a heavyweight, because a black heavyweight wasn't going anywhere. Everyone in boxing knew that. And Jack Blackburn wasn't a person to hope for change. By nature he was a violent man of limited ambition; his life had given him no reason to be otherwise.

Blackburn was born in Versailles (pronounced Ver-sales), Kentucky, in 1883. As a teenager, he fled to Philadelphia and took up boxing. He was a lightweight, and while his record was not overly impressive, he often took on bigger men and earned a reputation as a smart boxer.

Like most fighters at the turn of the century, Blackburn just scraped out a living. Virtually every state in the union outlawed prizefighting. Boxers had to fight secretly in out-of-the-way places or rely on the local police force to look the other way. The American public regarded most professional athletes, and certainly boxers, as little better than hoodlums. Blackburn fit the part. He was an alcoholic and an angry, violent drunk.

During Blackburn's early years in boxing, several black boxers had achieved a measure of success and recognition, though they had difficulty making any real money. Boxing fans remembered Peter Jackson, the Australian black heavyweight who could not get a championship fight against John L. Sullivan or James J. Corbett. There was Joe Gans, and the original Joe Walcott and Sam Langford, the Boston Tar Baby. And Jack Johnson. Everybody remembered Jack Johnson.

Blackburn liked to tell about the day Johnson came into a gym in Philadelphia looking for a sparring partner. This was before Johnson became the first black heavyweight champion of the world in 1908. Jack Blackburn, the lightweight, got into the ring with Johnson and showed up the future champion, tagging Johnson several times and defending himself against Johnson's angry return punches. There had been bad blood between the two men ever since.

In 1909, Blackburn fatally stabbed a man during a bar fight in Philadelphia and was jailed for manslaughter. Blackburn was in prison when Johnson successfully defended his title against Jim Jeffries, the great white hope, in 1910. He was in prison while Johnson outraged white America with his arrogance, golden smile, boxing skill, and white wives. By the time Blackburn was released in 1913, Johnson had left the United States to escape a jail term for violating the Mann Act, and the racist anger against Johnson had reached such a pitch that no black fighter could hope for the same opportunity that Johnson had received.

But Blackburn knew no other profession. He boxed ten more years, then began teaching other fighters. He trained two world champions, Bud Taylor, a bantamweight, and Sammy Mendell, a lightweight. Both were white. Now fifty years old and bald, Blackburn was marking time, training several undistinguished white fighters. A deep scar, the badge of another knife fight, ran up the left side of his leathery face. His thin chest made the arms that hung out of his white t-shirt look longer than they were.

As promised, Julian Black and John Roxborough brought their fighter into Trafton's gym the next day. Blackburn quickly saw that this Joe Louis was no world-beater. Louis had just turned twenty. He was a handsome boy with a light complexion, and Blackburn probably shared the street-black's prejudice against the high yellows who dominated the thin ranks of the black bourgeoisie. Louis stood over six feet tall but weighed only 175 pounds. He had the big bones, the gangling build, and the awkward movements of a boy who had not fully matured. His body showed promise, but in the ring Louis was unpolished. He relied almost solely on his strength, which had been enough to defeat all but four of his amateur opponents. In the pros that wasn't enough; Blackburn had seen plenty of strong punchers lose to men who knew how to box. Blackburn watched Louis's slow footwork. Louis often threw himself off balance, he could not string his punches together, and his only defense was a good offense.

Standing near the ring with Black and Roxborough, Blackburn said, "If I take him—and I ain't saying I'm gonna—how much you gonna pay me?"

"Thirty-five dollars a week for four weeks. After that we'll see what's happened."

Blackburn laughed. "This will be the best job I ever had. Usually got to whip my man to collect my pay. I got to tell you, you'll never make a success of this kid, but I need the job. He ain't going to make no money worth shaking your finger at. Remember he's a colored boy."

The next day Blackburn initiated Louis into the daily routine that was to be the fighter's life rhythm for seventeen years. Black and Roxborough set Louis up in the apartment of Bill Bottom, a chef. Blackburn came to the apartment on 46th Street at 6:00 A.M. and got Louis out of bed. Together they walked five blocks to Washington Park. Once around the park was three miles. Louis ran around the park twice each morning, then returned to his apartment and slept until eleven. Bottom made him breakfast, and Louis would loaf around the apartment until it was time to go over to Trafton's gym in the afternoon.

For the first week in the gym Blackburn did not let Louis into a ring. Blackburn held the heavy punching bag, bracing it against his shoulder and leg, and had Louis hit it again and again, for hours. Blackburn stressed balance. He told Louis to plant his feet so that every punch would carry the full force of his body. He taught Louis always to lead with his left, to open his body so he would be ready to follow with a right.

Blackburn drove his new fighter hard. In response, Louis was very quiet, shy, and respectful. Too respectful. Blackburn called Louis "Chappie," a familiar name he used for everyone. Louis called the trainer "Mr. Blackburn." Blackburn had told Louis he would have to gain weight to succeed as a heavyweight, and several days into Louis's training Blackburn played on the boy's unquestioning obedience. "Starting tonight," he told Louis, "you'll have to go to the stockyards and drink two quarts of hot beef blood. You got to do that every day. That's the only way you'll put on weight. You hear?"

That night Louis went to Blackburn's apartment. "Mr. Blackburn," he said, "I've been thinking about drinking that blood. I just can't drink it, Mr. Blackburn, and I thought I'd better come 'round and tell you." Louis was too young and insecure to resent the joke. He desperately wanted the respect of this rough-talking man who knew so much about fighting.

At first, the unaccustomed routine wore at the young fighter. As a teenager in Detroit, boxing had been his recreation, something he was good at, something he could dream about. Now boxing was turning into work. Blackburn worried because Louis sometimes showed no enthusiasm for fighting; the trainer realized Louis possessed none of the inner anger or killer instinct so valuable in the ring. On the other hand, Louis learned quickly, and when he hit the heavy bag, Blackburn could feel it.

Blackburn taught Louis more than boxing. One day while Louis was resting between exercises, Blackburn said, "You know, boy, the heavyweight division for a Negro is hardly likely. The white man ain't too keen on it. You have to really be something to get anywhere. If you really ain't gonna be another Jack Johnson, you got some hope. White man hasn't forgotten that fool nigger with his white women, acting like he owned the world. And you got to listen to everything I tell you. You got to jump when I say jump, sleep when I say sleep. Other than that, you're wasting my time."

After a week on the heavy bag, Louis started to box. Blackburn sometimes sparred with Louis himself, throwing punches and teaching Louis to block them without ducking. If a fighter never made a mistake, Blackburn promised, he would never get hit. Anytime your opponent missed, Blackburn said, you should hit him. "And if you can throw one punch, you can throw two, you can throw three, because you're on balance."

Black and Roxborough also had a hand in training Louis. Roxborough, a cultured man who ran the numbers racket in the black neighborhoods of Detroit, told Louis, "To be a champion you've got to be a gentleman first. Your toughest fight might not be in the ring but out in public. We never, never say anything bad about an opponent. Before a fight you say how great you think he is; after a fight you say how great you think he was. And for God's sake, after you beat a white opponent, don't smile."

"That's what Jack Johnson did," Black added.

Roxborough went on. "Joe, you're going to get a lot of invitations to nightclubs. But you never go into one alone. And above all, you never have your picture taken with a white woman."

Roxborough and Black were neither Uncle Toms nor cowards, just successful businessmen who understood the implacable racism of Depression America. No black could safely offend whites.

"There's one more thing," Jack Blackburn said. "You never, never lose a fight." The trainer laughed.

Black and Roxborough scheduled Louis's first fight for July 4, 1934, against Jack Kracken, a mediocre club fighter, in the Bacon Casino on Chicago's South Side. A week before the fight Louis stretched out on a rubbing table while Blackburn massaged him after a workout. Blackburn told Louis never to forget that he was a Negro fighter, not a white fighter. His opponents would be white, and if Louis wanted to get anywhere, he would have to fight clean, stay out of clinches, and win decisively.

"You can't get nowhere nowadays trying to outpoint fellows in the ring," Blackburn said. "It's mighty hard for a colored boy to win decisions. The dice is loaded against you. You gotta knock 'em out and keep knocking 'em out to get anywheres." He reached for Louis's taped right hand. "Let your right fist be the referee. Don't ever forget that. Let that right fist there be your referee!"

2

BEGINNINGS

Appropriately enough for a man who was to become the symbol of his race, Joe Louis's early years were representative of the black experience in the United States during the first half of the twentieth century. Joe Louis Barrow was born May 13, 1914, in a sharecropper's shack in Alabama, the seventh of eight children. Two years later his father was committed to the Searcy State Hospital for the Colored Insane. Shortly thereafter, Louis's mother, the former Lillie Reese, a deeply religious woman, heard her husband had died. In fact, unknown to his family, Munroe Barrow lived another 20 years in the Searcy Hospital, a truly invisible man.

Lillie Barrow remarried while Joe was still very young, to a widower named Pat Brooks who had five children of his own. The Barrow family moved into the Brooks's small wooden house in the hamlet of Mt. Sinai in Alabama's Buckalew Mountains. The children slept three to a bed. They all worked to bring in the cotton crop and to raise food for the large family's table. Joe and the rest of the Barrow and Brooks kids walked barefoot to school, which was held in the Mt. Sinai Baptist Church.

In 1926, Pat Brooks joined the black migration north. He moved to Detroit, got a job working for Henry Ford, and sent for his large family. Joe was 12 years old when his family moved into a tenement on Catherine Street, in the heart of Detroit's black ghetto. A large boy for his age and already behind the Detroit kids because of his inadequate schooling in Alabama,

Joe was embarrassed when he was assigned to classes with much smaller children. He developed a stammer and retreated into a shell. Within a few years, the Detroit school system shunted him off to a vocational school.

The Depression threw Pat Brooks out of work, and the family went on home relief. Joe did odd jobs, carried ice with his friend Freddie Guinyard, and hung out with the Catherine Street gang. His mother, searching for something to keep him off the streets, scraped some money together for violin lessons. At the urging of friends, Joe used the money to pay dues at the Brewster Recreation Center so that he could box. He adopted the ring name Joe Louis so his mother wouldn't find out he was boxing. His fears that his mother would disapprove proved unfounded; when Lillie Brooks discovered her son liked boxing, she encouraged him to pursue the sport. Louis showed some promise as a boxer, largely because of a powerful punch, but he had little time for the gym. He quit school and got a job pushing truck bodies at the Briggs auto-body plant, exhausting work that left him too tired to train at the end of the day. In late 1932 or early 1933, Louis fought his first amateur match against a white boxer named Johnny Miler who had been on the 1932 Olympic team. Miler knocked Louis down seven times in two rounds.

Discouraged, Louis listened to his stepfather, who wanted him to concentrate on his job and forget about boxing. He stayed away from the gym for six months. But with his mother's support, Louis decided to quit his job and go back to boxing. Boxing was the one thing he was good at, and he dreamed of getting rich as a professional boxer. The next year Louis fought 54 amateur bouts as a light-heavyweight, winning 50, 43 by knockout. For winning, he received merchandise checks, which he used to buy the family groceries.

Louis's superb amateur record drew the attention of John Roxborough, the numbers king in Detroit's black ghetto. Like many black policy operators, Roxborough was a civic leader and a charitable man who helped many young people through college. With his family's permission, Louis moved into Roxborough's home. Roxborough put Louis on a proper diet and bought him some new boxing equipment. By June of 1934, Louis was ready to turn pro, and he asked Roxborough to be his manager. Roxborough went to his friend and business associate Julian Black for help in funding Louis's training.

Louis had chosen a difficult profession. Thousands of poor boys flooded inner-city gyms during the Depression. Dreaming of quick money, their parents played the numbers; these boys were entering a tougher lottery. Most wound up with little to show for their struggle. After a career in the ring, many moved slowly and slurred their speech, punch drunk from absorbing too many blows to the head. But a few did get rich, at least for a time. A top boxer could earn more money on a good night than the average American worker earned in a year; the heavyweight champion of the world could make more in one night than the president of the United States was paid in several years. And money was not the only reward. A popular heavyweight champion got almost as much publicity as the president and was held in higher esteem by a large percentage of the public.

In the 1930s the United States was in the middle of a sports revolution that continues today. Sport is a signpost of twentieth-century American society and has a peculiar and central role in our culture. To understand how important Joe Louis was about to become and why excellence in sports was a ticket to acceptance and admiration from the white public, it is necessary to understand the history of the rise of sport.

Sport was a radical departure from American traditions, reflecting the country's transition from a rural to an urban society. There were no organized spectator sports in early nineteenth-century America. Most Americans lived on subsistence farms, where they often worked from dawn to dusk. In the cities, small towns by today's standards, the average laborer worked a six-day, seventy-hour week. The vast majority of Americans did not have the time, money, or mobility to play sports or watch them.

Even if they had, the prevailing Protestant ethic frowned on recreation. Not only did work honor God, it also occupied mind and body. Many Protestant ministers thought leisure time was a temptation to sin.

That was not all. Most Americans worked six days a week,

and on the seventh day they rested. The religious mores of popular culture, reinforced by strict blue laws, prohibited organized recreation on Sundays.

But in the second half of the nineteenth century, the Industrial Revolution began to change the way Americans lived and thought. Improvements in transportation and communication, the growth of cities and an industrial work force, mass immigration—all helped create a vast market for organized recreation and break down the values of the old order.

The immigrants who helped fill the cities brought new games and customs with them. The Irish contributed strongly to boxing, the Scots to track, the Germans to bowling and gymnastics, and the Scandinavians to winter sports and Swedish gymnastics. Perhaps more important, Irish Catholics and German and Scandinavian Protestants did not observe the Sabbath so strictly. The German tradition of bowling on Sundays helped break down the strict American Sabbath observance in New York, Milwaukee, St. Louis, and Cincinnati.

The old strictures couldn't last in the cities, anyway. A farmer might be persuaded that his work, his religion, and his family life were one, but a factory worker was not likely to think so. He worked away from home, on a regimented schedule directed by someone else, and looked upon work as an unpleasant economic necessity. Moreover, in crowded urban neighborhoods, poverty, lack of education, and a mix of cultures combined to erode the mores of traditional American society. The new proletarians prized their time off and wanted to enjoy it.

The upper classes supported the beginnings of American sport, too, and throughout the nineteenth century had been in the forefront of the sports revolution. In the antebellum United States the most prominent sport was the "sport of kings." Horsemanship distinguished a gentleman, and many gentlemen bred racehorses, as they still do. Sailing, however, was the sport of the northern nouveau riche. America's new millionaires formed exclusive yachting clubs and tried to outspend each other on bigger and more lavish boats.

After the Civil War, middle-class athletes established sporting clubs in the northeastern cities, but soon it became fashionable to join an athletic club, and the middle class clubs could not resist the tide of rich new members and their money. The major clubs expanded quickly, building elaborate clubhouses, spending more money on dining rooms and bars than on actual sporting facilities.

Even baseball owes much of its present form to the upper classes. Children played the British games of rounders and town ball, forerunners of baseball, on both sides of the Atlantic in the early 1800s. In the 1840s a group of socially conscious men formed the New York Knickerbockers, a baseball club. A Knickerbocker, Alexander Cartwright, codified the rules in 1845, and on June 19, 1846, the Knickerbockers played the New York Nine in the first official game using Cartwright's new rules. The game and Cartwright's rules spread quickly. Northern and southern soldiers played the game during the Civil War, and when they returned home, they brought baseball with them. Unlike most other sports of the nineteenth century, baseball became a game of the masses: it required only a ball, a bat, and an open field. It was a game perfectly suited to rural communities, and after the Civil War virtually every town fielded its own baseball team.

Perhaps nowhere was the correlation of money and leisure with the growth of sport more obvious than on the college campus. Throughout most of the nineteenth century only the sons of the aristocracy could afford college—even as late as 1870 just 1.7 percent of eighteen- to twenty-one-year-olds attended. The universities had a strong religious orientation and a rigid curriculum that taught the classics of Western civilization in the original Greek and Latin. Recreation was not a value of traditional American culture, and it was not a part of any college administrator's vision of college life. But students left on their own discovered the new activities and values of the leisure society they would help create.

College sport began in the 1840s, when students at Yale and Harvard founded rowing clubs. In 1852 a resort owner organized the first intercollegiate sporting event when he promised to pay the expenses of the Yale and Harvard clubs if they would race on his lake in New Hampshire. The rowers accepted the free vacation but apparently did little training, and neither team seemed to care who won. After the Civil War, however, students began to organize teams in a host of sports and to compete in earnest.

While some college administrators denounced the trend toward greater emphasis on sports, others used sports to attract students and enhance the prestige of their institutions. American universities were growing quickly in number and enrollment; between 1890 and 1925 student enrollments grew four times faster than the overall population. In the competition for new students, a good football team was a great advertisement. Faced with the problem of trying to attract money and students for his brand-new school, President Harper of the University of Chicago hired Amos Alonzo Stagg to build and coach a good football team.

The rise of sport on America's college campuses inspired imitation in the secondary schools. Scholastic sport also got a push from the growing urban-reform movement. Concerned about poverty in crowded tenement districts, reformers like Jane Addams and Jacob Riis urged local governments and schools to provide organized recreation for the urban poor. They thought exercise would improve health and also hoped that sport might serve as a form of social control.

These urban reformers were not radicals—far from it. Their answer to the festering problems of industrial America was to spread middle-class values to the poor and to regulate the rich with the same values. Sports kept poor kids off the street and provided a bridge to middle-class values. Indeed, organized sport has been teaching those values ever since. Coaches preach subordination of the individual to the team, attendance, adherence to established procedure, obedience to a chain of command. Mixed with an open acceptance of competition and a win-at-all-costs philosophy, a team sport is a perfect introduction to American culture.

The revolution in communications also popularized sports. Railroad, telegraph, and telephone spread the news faster and wider, creating a national community. Between 1870 and 1900 the number of newspapers in the United States increased from

387 to 2,326. Their combined circulation rose from 3.5 million to 15 million. The new less religious, leisure-oriented, prosports urban culture naturally exerted a dominant influence on the communications industry.

The success of sports journals convinced even the most conservative newspaper editors that their new readers wanted sports news. After William Trotter Porter founded *Spirit of the Times* in 1831, other sports journals appeared. In 1877 Richard Kyle Fox took over the *National Police Gazette*, a magazine that attracted a large readership with its sensational stories on crime and sex. Fox soon realized that sport had even wider mass appeal. When the *Gazette*'s issue on the Paddy Ryan–Joe Goss prizefight sold 400,000 copies in 1880, Fox determined to make the *Gazette* the leading sports publication in the country.

Newspapers had devoted increasing coverage to isolated sporting events since the 1840s. By the 1880s they began to make conscious attempts to improve their sports coverage. In New York Charles A. Dana's *New York Sun* and Joseph Pulitzer's *New York World* competed for circulation by trying to outdo each other in sports coverage. Pulitzer established what was probably the first newspaper sports department. By 1892 most big-city papers had sports editors and separate sport staffs. When William Randolph Hearst took over the *New York Journal*, the battle for mass circulation in New York City heated up. Using the techniques of yellow journalism, the New York papers took aim at the reading public with sensational coverage of crime and disasters. But historians have often overlooked one of the most important components of the new journalistic style—increased sports coverage. It was William Randolph Hearst who first published a separate sports section, and newspapers around the country soon followed suit.

Around the turn of the century, participation in sports increased rapidly. The upper classes were eagerly participating in sports, and the lower classes were getting a chance to play, too, thanks to a rising standard of living, a reduced work week, and a pervasive prosports ideology.

American corporations also embraced and provided organized recreation for their workers. In the nineteenth century only a handful of companies had such programs. A 1913 survey by the U.S. Bureau of Labor Statistics revealed that half of the companies surveyed sponsored recreational programs for employees.

To be sure, sport had its detractors. Ministers criticized professional sport and its attendant vices—violations of the Sabbath, drinking, gambling. Thorstein Veblen, a critic of the upper classes that dominated sports participation in the nineteenth century, attacked sport as an example of conspicuous consumption in his *Theory of the Leisure Class*, published in 1899. Reformers criticized the growing commercialization of sport, especially in college athletics. They worked to restrict college games to the campuses instead of big-city neutral sites. In 1905 coaches and college administrators formed the National Collegiate Athletic Association (NCAA) to regulate football, which was becoming increasingly violent.

But the critics were fighting a rearguard action. Sport continued to grow before World War I, then exploded in the peace that followed. Major league baseball led the sports craze, behind the hulking and colorful figure of George Herman "Babe" Ruth. Ruth's prodigious athletic feats and his outgoing personality captivated the public. Soon the Yankees had to build a new stadium to hold all the fans who wanted to watch the Babe swing for the fences. Other sports prospered and had their own heroes. Between 1920 and 1930 the total seating capacity at 135 college football stadiums increased from less than one million to over two and a half million. Bill Tilden popularized tennis, Bobby Jones did the same for golf, and Jack Dempsey reawakened interest in boxing.

Newspaper coverage was overwhelming. Today's newspapers are sometimes criticized for devoting so much space to sports, but sports coverage now is trifling compared to that of the 1920s. In the final editions of the New York, Boston, Philadelphia, and Chicago papers, baseball coverage took up a third of the front page—not the lead sports page but page 1. *Editor and Publisher* magazine concluded that during the decade the *New York World* devoted 40 percent of its space to sports during the week; the *New York Herald-Tribune*, 60 percent.

Sport also got a boost from the new movie industry. News-reels brought rushed and jerky images of athletes into movie houses all over the country, and Hollywood producers capital-ized on the fame of sports stars such as Ruth and Dempsey by casting them in low-budget films. Radio, another new medium, could cover sporting events as they happened. In 1927 the World Series was broadcast for the first time.

The tone of sports coverage during the 1920s was openly adulatory, a reflection of the naïveté and forced optimism of the era. Sportswriting was not only uncritical but also almost uni-versally bad and overwritten. The purple prose of the sports pages made athletes and their victories seem larger than life.

By the 1920s most of the barriers against sport had been trampled. Strict observance of the Sabbath was no longer an issue in most cities. The American public had accepted profes-sional athletics and bestowed a special status on athletes. In a society that worshiped wealth, prominent athletes made a lot of money; in a new media age, athletes won instant fame for their accomplishments; in an era of bland politicians, athletes were colorful and exciting; and in an emerging corporate order that often made people feel insignificant, athletes reaffirmed the yearning for individual accomplishment. Athletes also benefited from the now-accepted division between work time and leisure time. People played or watched sports in their time off; they pleasantly associated great athletes with their own leisure time.

American society had elevated athletes to a unique status, and in turn it created a set of expectations for its new hero class. Sportswriters reminded the public that wide-eyed boys were watching the athlete's every move, so the athlete had to be a "good influence." Sport was supposed to teach competitiveness, toughness, sportsmanship, leadership; a sports hero was supposed to embody those ideals. The values of sport now became the standards by which American society judged not just its ath-letes but everyone. Sport became the Esperanto of male culture and the test of masculinity. Frank Merriwell, the fictional ath-letic hero, replaced Horatio Alger's fictional poor boy who got rich as the idol of red-blooded American youth. Sport took on a reality and meaning to millions of Americans uncommitted in politics and unmoved by the intellectual and artistic currents of the day.

Like many American sports, boxing was a British import. England was the first country to experience the Industrial Revolution, and by the late eighteenth century brutality and poverty were facts of life in the working-class neighborhoods of British cities. Violence had a compelling attraction to the violent extremes of British society—the lower and upper classes. Huge crowds turned out to watch public executions. Boxing matches also drew large crowds and evoked the same spirit. Early bouts under London Prize Ring Rules were bloody, bare-knuckle fights "to the finish." A round ended when either fighter's knee touched the ground, and the fight went on until one fighter failed to "toe the mark" for the next round.

Boxing owes its beginnings in America to aristocratic sponsorship. The sons of southern planters who went to England for an education brought boxing home with them. Some plantation owners taught their slaves to box and matched them against slaves from other plantations. The first two noted American boxers, Bill Richmond and Tom Molineaux, were slaves who won freedom through their prowess in the ring. That was in the first decade of the nineteenth century, before there was any public following for boxing in the United States. To pursue their profession, Richmond and Molineaux had to move to England.

In the United States, boxing found its first public support in the natural constituency of sport, the growing urban populations along the eastern seaboard. Sailors on shore leave and Irish immigrants occasionally disobeyed the laws against prizefighting, fighting by London Prize Ring Rules in the back rooms of taverns, on barges, islands, or in secluded parts of the countryside.

Tom Hyer and Yankee Sullivan fought the first recognized bout for the American heavyweight championship in 1849, at Still Pond Creek, an out-of-the-way site near Baltimore. Hyer won. The creation of an American title generated public interest in fights between America's leading boxers. Sports journals and newspapers began to cover the most important fights.

More than any other sport, boxing had to fight the forces of traditional American culture. Its brutality aroused the wrath of religious leaders. Though it had taken root in America with the help of at least some members of the southern planter aristocracy, by the mid-nineteenth century boxing lacked the upper-class support that most other American sports enjoyed. Most boxers and boxing fans were lower-class immigrants who committed the additional sins of gambling and drinking around boxing matches. *Turf, Field and Farm* magazine, which tried to appeal to the upper classes, announced, "[This] paper denounces pugilism, and all low, disgusting sports."

Even the newspapers that covered boxing matches felt obliged to echo the sentiments of "proper" opinion. The *New York Times*, then the *Daily Times*, editorialized after a heavyweight championship fight between Yankee Sullivan and John Morrissey in 1853:

> With all the benefits of a diffused education; with a press strong in upholding the moral amenities of life; with a clergy devout, sincere, and energetic in the discharge of their duties, and a public sentiment opposed to animal brutality in any shape; with these and similar influences at work it is inexplicable, deplorable, humiliating, that an exhibition such as the contest between Morrissey and Sullivan could have occurred.

Horace Greeley published six columns on the Morrissey–John C. Heenan fight in 1858 and then wrote, "The thing is whereby in its natural gravity of baseness it stinks. It is in the grog-shops and the brothels and the low gaming hells." The sport may have driven Greeley to incoherence, but Greeley and other newspaper editors were paying attention. So was the public.

Boxing in the United States received another infusion of public interest when the American titleholder, John C. Heenan, went to England and challenged Tom Sayers, the British champion. On April 17, 1860, Sayers and Heenan fought the first international heavyweight championship match. In the thirty-seventh round, Heenan rushed Sayers and tried to strangle the English boxer against the ropes. A riot ensued; the crowd surged into the ring, and the fight eventually ended in a draw, with Heenan running to a train pursued by angry fans. The Sayers-Heenan fight, and the riot it caused, capped a growing public sentiment against boxing in England. Leading British boxers had to emigrate to America, and the United States became the boxing center of the world.

Boxing's modern era began when John L. Sullivan, the son of Irish immigrants, won the heavyweight title in 1882. Sullivan reigned as champion for a decade and popularized boxing as no champion had before him. Outgoing, personable, and ruggedly handsome, Sullivan had a flair for self-promotion. He went on a national tour offering $1,000 to any man who could last four rounds with him. Sullivan fought far more frequently than past champions, keeping his name before the public and adding to his aura of invincibility. He cashed in on his great popularity, earning over $900,000, a huge fortune in those days, appearing in vaudeville tours and acting in melodramas during a stage career that lasted until 1915.

Sullivan's dominating presence gave boxing a new excitement and an air of legitimacy. Many municipalities either legalized prizefighting or stopped enforcing their anti-boxing laws. Sullivan and his opponents rarely had to hide from the police. Sullivan also fought many of his bouts under the new Marquis of Queensbury Rules, which mandated gloves and eliminated many of the wrestling, fouling, and delaying tactics permissible under the old London Prize Ring Rules. Sullivan's seventy-five-round knockout of Jake Kilrain in 1889 was the last bare-knuckle fight for the heavyweight championship.

When James J. Corbett knocked out Sullivan in New Orleans, September 7, 1892, most boxers were using the Marquis of Queensbury Rules, and boxing had won a measure of public acceptance. Corbett and the two heavyweight champions that followed him, Bob Fitzsimmons and Jim Jeffries, were able boxers but could not match Sullivan's popularity. By 1904 Jeffries had eliminated all the top heavyweight contenders. He retired, naming Marvin Hart and Jack Root the leading contenders for his vacant title. Jeffries refereed a bout between Hart and Root in Reno, Nevada, on July 3, 1905. Hart won the fight but never won much of a following; he lost his title to Tommy Burns a year later. Burns was hardly bigger than a middleweight and was not widely respected.

The decline of talent in the heavyweight division, coupled with several suspicious bouts held in New York, sent boxing into eclipse. New York repealed its Horton Law, which had temporarily legalized boxing in the city. Only California and Nevada officially tolerated prizefighting during the first decade of the century.

After defending his title several times on the West Coast, Tommy Burns left the United States to fight in Europe. The American public paid little attention, but one man, Jack Johnson, followed every move Burns made, pursuing the champion to England and demanding that Burns fight him for the championship. Johnson had established himself as the top contender for the heavyweight title. Burns didn't want to fight him and wasn't expected to, because Johnson was black.

Since John L. Sullivan had ducked Peter Jackson, the great black heavyweight from Australia, no black had had a chance to fight for the heavyweight title. Several blacks, including George Dixon and the original Joe Walcott, had won championships in the lighter weight classes, but the public followed only the heavyweight division.

Johnson wasn't the only good black heavyweight of his era. Joe Jeannette, Sam McVey, and Sam Langford were excellent fighters, at least the equal of any white boxers of the day. Denied a chance at the championship, often ducked even by leading white contenders, black boxers were left to fight among themselves. Because their fights drew little attention or money, they had to fight frequently.

Not that boxing was more segregated than any other sport. After the Civil War blacks had entered sports in increasing numbers, but in the 1880s organized sport joined the rest of the country in setting up a system of segregation. Blacks had played in organized baseball as early as 1872, but in 1887 Adrian "Cap" Anson, later elected to the Hall of Fame, led his Chicago White

Stocking teammates in a boycott of a scheduled exhibition with the Newark club of the Eastern League because Newark's starting pitcher was to have been George Stovey, a black who had won thirty-five games the year before. Anson's prejudice set a precedent. White baseball players and club owners banned blacks from baseball for the next sixty years. From 1875 to 1904 black jockeys won the Kentucky Derby thirteen times. In 1904 the Jockey Club of New York took over the licensing of jockeys. The club let established black riders keep their licenses but denied licenses to young blacks. No black riders appeared in the Derby after 1911.

Neither Jack Johnson nor Tommy Burns cared much for social theories. Johnson wanted the championship both for his own pride and for the money. Johnson was a superb defensive boxer. He stood 6 feet 1½ inches tall and weighed close to 200 pounds. He outweighed Burns by twenty pounds and knew he could beat the champion. Johnson's manager, Sam Fitzpatrick, bargained endlessly with Burns, making more and more concessions in hopes of getting Burns into the ring. Though Burns shared the racism of his time and had been ducking the black challenger for over a year, he was not afraid of Johnson, and money finally swayed him. Fitzpatrick offered him $30,000 guaranteed, a fantastic sum for those days. Johnson was so confident and so desperate to get Burns into a ring that he settled for a $5,000 guarantee and even agreed to let Burns's manager referee the fight. Fitzpatrick arranged the match for December 26, 1908, in Sydney, Australia.

Burns's decision to fight Johnson aroused little public disapproval or interest. Boxing had sunk to such a low estate that the American press hardly noticed the signing of the contracts. John L. Sullivan denounced Burns, saying, "Shame on the money-mad champion! Shame on the man who upsets good American precedents because there are Dollars, Dollars, Dollars in it." The "good American precedents," of course, were those separating blacks and whites.

Johnson's fourteen-round victory over Burns got scarcely any press attention. Most papers used wire-service accounts of the fight, because they could not afford to send correspondents to

Australia. For the most part, the papers briefly noted Johnson's victory, mentioned that he was the first black man to win the title, and left it at that.

Johnson returned to the United States, and during 1909 he successfully defended his title five times against the best white challengers the country had to offer. As Johnson got more and more press coverage and as the public came to know him, white antipathy toward the black heavyweight champion grew. Johnson was an arrogant boxer; press accounts of his fights could not help but reveal this trait. Johnson was not content to defeat his opponents; he humiliated them. During a fight Johnson kept up a steady stream of chatter, making fun of his opponent's attempts to hit him, adding commentary for the reporters at ringside. He smiled often when he fought, flashing a mouthful of gold fillings. Such immodesty and poor sportsmanship would have been almost as offensive in a white champion.

Out of the ring, Johnson also rubbed people the wrong way. His behavior was typical of sudden celebrities. A poor boy grown rich, Johnson delighted in spending money. He was an ostentatious dresser, fond of diamond rings and stickpins. He loved big cars and drove them at suicidal speeds. Johnson reveled in fame and attention. He was the life of the party, a fixture of the late-night bar scene in any town he happened to be in.

But it was Johnson's refusal to obey the conventions of black behavior, to stay in his place as a black man in the segregated United States, that most aroused white hatred. At a time when southern blacks were lynched for looking the wrong way at a white woman, Johnson openly cavorted with white prostitutes. Later, in his autobiography, Johnson claimed that bad experiences with black women "led me to forswear colored women and to determine that my lot henceforth would be cast only with white women." The truth was that Johnson used white women for effect. While sparring, Johnson played further on white sexual insecurities by wrapping his penis to make it look bigger.

None of the active white challengers was a match for Johnson, so the white press and public turned to Jim Jeffries, the retired champion, who had been out of boxing for five years. Jeffries refused at first, because he was out of shape and because he didn't want to break the color line, but public pressure and interest built to irresistible levels. In December of 1909, Tex Rickard, a gambler who had started promoting fights in Alaska during the gold rush there, finally signed Jeffries to fight Johnson, offering the two fighters the largest guaranteed purse in history: $101,000. Rickard scheduled the fight for July 4, 1910, in San Francisco.

Rickard immediately ran into bitter opposition. Religious leaders and moral reformers still strongly condemned boxing. They had succeeded in shunting boxing off to the obscure corners of the West, but this fight was attracting national attention. Disgust with Johnson, fear of racial disturbances, and fear that Johnson would win added to their determination to stop the fight. Church organizations wired their protests to President Taft, members of Congress, and Governor J. N. Gillette of California. Gillette caved in, announcing on June 23 that he would not allow the fight to be held in San Francisco. The resourceful Rickard shifted the fight to Reno, Nevada, where Gov. Denver Dickinson welcomed the revenue the fight would bring his state. Besides, the governor wanted to see the fight.

The black press denounced the hypocrisy of white ministers who opposed boxing so loudly, yet were silent about lynchings. Most blacks rooted for Johnson, who had done much to increase black pride and was rapidly becoming a black folk hero. Other blacks feared the possible consequences of Johnson's actions. One black reader of the *New York Times* wrote the paper:

> It is clear that [the Johnson-Jeffries fight] is coming rapidly to be regarded as a racial test . . . and it is White versus Black. Herein lies the evil and the danger in the proposed contest. It is even now increasing a tension already stretched to the snapping point, namely, the race or anti-negro tension, and in this view incalculable harm is likely to result.

The public openly viewed the fight as a battle for racial superiority, and Rickard pitched his promotion on that raw, racial test. It was smart business. The Jeffries-Johnson fight attracted more attention than any sporting event previously held in the United States. On the day of the fight the *Chattanooga Times* editorialized: "Whether or not we admit it, and however much its truth may be deplored, the interest of the majority of the ninety-odd millions of people in these United States is centered on Reno today." Black churches held special services and prayed for Johnson's success. Thirty thousand people gathered outside the Times building in New York to hear news of the fight, while large crowds gathered outside the offices of other newspapers around the country.

Johnson completely outclassed a washed-up Jeffries, talking, jeering, and smiling for fourteen rounds before knocking out the former champ in the fifteenth. The next day newspapers played up the fight on page 1. The *New York Times* devoted several columns of the front page to the fight and all of pages 2 and 3.

Next to stories about the fight itself appeared stories on race rioting all over the country. In Uvalda, Georgia, a white gang fired on blacks who were celebrating Johnson's victory at a construction camp on the outskirts of town. Three blacks died, and five were wounded. Charles Williams cheered Johnson's victory too loudly in Houston, Texas; the wire services reported that a white man "slashed his throat from ear to ear." Thirty people were hurt in a Pueblo, Colorado, race riot. A black man was beaten to death in New York City. In Washington, D.C., blacks fatally stabbed two whites. All told, at least eight blacks died in the racial disturbances that followed the fight.

Johnson returned triumphant to his home in Chicago. He was a hero to blacks, who sang:

> *Amaze an' Grace, how sweet it sounds,*
> *Jack Johnson knocked Jim Jeffries down.*
> *Jim Jeffries jumped up an' hit Jack on the chin*
> *An' then Jack knocked him down again.*

> *The Yankees hold the play,*
> *The white man pull the trigger;*
> *But it makes no difference what the white man say;*
> *The world champion's still a nigger.*

Johnson was temporarily flush with money, as well. He had earned over $70,000 from the Jeffries fight, and he commanded top dollar as a vaudeville attraction. Never a restrained man, Johnson felt that riches and fame freed him completely from social convention. He drove like a maniac, wrecking cars and ignoring the litter of speeding tickets he accumulated. He got one ticket for parking seven feet from the curb. He maintained a hectic schedule, traveling constantly on vaudeville tours, drinking heavily, living on three or four hours sleep a night. After a trip to Europe he failed to report a $6,000 diamond necklace he had purchased abroad for one of his lady friends. The government confiscated the necklace and prosecuted him for evading customs duties. Johnson got off with a stiff fine.

Johnson routinely traveled with two or three white prostitutes at the same time. He set them up in separate hotels and visited each of their rooms briefly. When the women complained too loudly about his inattentiveness, Johnson beat them.

In 1911 he married Etta Duryea, a white woman who had been a traveling companion for several years. Etta was not a prostitute in the fullest sense—she had been a mistress to men in the racetrack crowd before she met Johnson. Johnson kept the ceremony from the press, which was under the impression that he was already married. Johnson had always introduced whichever prostitute he happened to have on his arm as "Mrs. Jack Johnson."

Marriage did not alter Johnson's life-style. After defending his title successfully against Fireman Jim Flynn on July 4, 1912, Johnson opened a nightclub, the Cabaret de Champion, in Chicago. He decorated the bar with gaudy cuspidors and marble fixtures. As patrons entered, they were greeted by a huge portrait of Johnson embracing his white wife. The cabaret was one of the few spots that allowed free mixing of the races. Johnson led the drinking and carousing there late into the night. The champion sometimes joined the band to sing, "I Love My Wife," a popular song of the day.

Johnson had affairs with Ada Banks, a mulatto singer at the Cabaret, and Lucille Cameron, a white prostitute whom Johnson employed as his personal secretary. His wife, depressed by his infidelity and by the recent death of her father, felt increasingly isolated. Etta was an exile from white society, and she thought that Johnson's black friends disliked her, as well. On September 11, 1912, Etta shot herself in the temple with one of Johnson's guns.

The world was coming down on Johnson. White journalists took Etta's suicide as proof that the mixed marriage had been a mistake. Her death did not stop Johnson's womanizing; his relationship with Lucille Cameron, who was only eighteen years old, continued without interruption. Because of Johnson's unpopularity and his refusal to obey racist convention, federal authorities were very receptive when Mrs. F. Cameron-Falconet, Lucille's mother, stormed into Chicago, demanding Johnson's arrest and claiming that he had abducted her daughter. On October 18, 1912, federal officials arrested Johnson and charged him with violating the Mann Act by abducting Lucille.

The Mann Act, passed in 1910 and aimed at "white slavers" who were supposedly smuggling foreign prostitutes into the United States, forbade the transportation of women in interstate or foreign commerce "for the purpose of prostitution or debauchery, or for any other immoral purpose." The act's broad language made it a federal crime for a man to travel across a state line with and make love to any woman not his wife, whether or not he paid her or intended to put her to work as a prostitute, and left individual U.S. attorneys with considerable discretion.

The government brought charges against Johnson first and asked questions later. Johnson knew the charges were groundless, for Lucille had come to Chicago on her own and had been working as a prostitute there for several months before she met Johnson. He bragged to reporters that he had too much money to stay in jail long. The next day he was out on bond. In the meantime, the government locked Lucille in jail, hoping that she would eventually give in and testify against Johnson.

On October 22 the government brought Lucille before a grand jury to testify about her relationship with Johnson. Lucille admitted she was a prostitute. The government tried to prove that prostitutes working for Johnson had recruited her

from Minneapolis to service Johnson, but Lucille denied the
government's story and went into a "hysterical fit." The grand
jury did not vote an indictment; the government had no case.
U.S. Attorney James H. Wilkerson put Lucille back in jail to
hide the truth from the public.

Wilkerson and other federal officials in Chicago were in an
embarrassing position. They had acted too soon on Mrs.
Cameron-Falconet's charges because of their prejudice against
Johnson. Like white men everywhere, they considered Johnson
a threat to racial order and thought he should be jailed, for
something. The white public also wanted Johnson in jail. It
would be a political disaster to drop the case, but there was no
indictment. Meanwhile, the press was digging into Lucille's past,
and several papers had already reported that Lucille was no
virgin before she met Johnson.

Department of Justice officials met with agents of the Bureau
of Investigation, the forerunner of the FBI. The bureau had
been unable to turn up evidence that Johnson had anything to
do with Lucille's trip from Minneapolis to Chicago. In a politically vulnerable position and determined to get Johnson, the
Department of Justice and the Bureau of Investigation decided
to search Johnson's past for evidence of other Mann Act violations.

The government quickly found what it was looking for in
the person of Belle Schreiber, a prostitute who had traveled with
Johnson off and on from 1909 to 1911. She was one of the
women often identified in news photographs as Mrs. Jack Johnson. Belle had a remarkably clear and detailed memory, and she
was willing to testify against Johnson. The government was
particularly interested in one phase of her relationship with
Johnson. In the summer of 1910, after one of their frequent
fights, Belle had left Johnson and gone to work in a Pittsburgh
brothel. In August she wrote Johnson and told him that she had
been fired. Johnson wired her seventy-five dollars and told her
to come to Chicago. When she arrived, Johnson set her up in an
apartment so that she could practice her trade as an independent.
He remained a favorite nonpaying customer.

When Johnson paid for Belle's trip to Chicago, he violated the letter of the Mann Act. Ordinarily, the government would not have prosecuted such a case. Johnson had not violated the spirit of the act because he did not share in the profits of Belle's business and the trip occurred as part of an ongoing sexual relationship. This was no ordinary case, however; the government was already committed to prosecuting Johnson.

On November 7 Belle told her story to the grand jury, which voted an indictment. Judge Kenesaw Mountain Landis, who later became the commissioner of baseball, issued a warrant for Johnson's arrest. Johnson spent a week in jail before he could arrange for the $30,000 bond Judge Landis imposed. Several weeks later the government released Lucille Cameron and dropped the charges against Johnson relating to her "abduction."

Lucille went straight to Johnson. On December 4 Johnson added fat to the fire by marrying Lucille in a quiet ceremony at his house. The white press suggested that Johnson had married Lucille to prevent her from testifying against him.

During this series of events white hatred of Johnson intensified. Southern politicians condemned the boxer. On the floor of Congress, Rep. Roddenberry of Georgia said, "In Chicago, white girls are made the slaves of an African brute." The reaction against Johnson was not limited to the South. Northern and national publications were hardly more restrained. Frank Force of the *Police Gazette* wrote that Johnson

> is the vilest, most despicable creature that lives. . . . In all sporting history, there never was a human being who so thoroughly deserved the sneers and jeers of his fellow creatures. . . . [H]e has disgusted the American public by flaunting in their faces an alliance as bold as it was offensive.

The black press, while careful to point out the racist basis for much of the reaction against Johnson, found it difficult to defend the champion. The *Philadelphia Tribune* ran the headline "JACK JOHNSON, DANGEROUSLY ILL, VICTIM OF WHITE FEVER." The *Baltimore Afro-American Ledger* wrote that Johnson had "proven himself anything but a credit to his race." The *New York Age* wrote, "As a black champion he has given the Negro more trouble by his scandals than he did in twenty years as a black tramp."

Johnson's trial began May 7, 1913. Government officials rejected Johnson's offer to plead guilty if he could get off with a substantial fine. They wanted him in jail. An all-white jury, after hearing five days of testimony about Johnson's woman beating and his travels with a host of white prostitutes, returned a guilty verdict. Asst. Atty. Gen. Harry Parkin revealed the government's motives for prosecuting Johnson when he said after the trial:

> This verdict . . . will go around the world. It is the fore-runner of laws to be passed in these United States which we may live to see—laws forbidding miscegenation. This negro, in the eyes of many, has been persecuted. Perhaps as an individual he was. But it was his misfortune to be the fore-most example of the evil in permitting the intermarriage of whites and blacks.

Several weeks later Judge George Carpenter sentenced Johnson to a year in prison. Johnson had two weeks to appeal the verdict. In the meantime, he was free on bail. Johnson knew an appeal was hopeless, and he made plans to flee the country rather than serve his sentence. Federal officials were in touch with paid informants close to Johnson and almost certainly knew he was fleeing, yet they did nothing when Johnson boarded a train and crossed the Canadian border. There was some question whether under the conditions of Johnson's bail the government had any authority to stop him; perhaps the government preferred that Johnson leave the country for good. Johnson and several members of his family later claimed that Johnson had bribed federal agents to let him escape.

Now an exile, Johnson defended his title twice in France and toured the Continent with a vaudeville troupe until World War I cut short his travels. He wound up in London, where Jack Curley, an American fight promoter, approached him with an offer of a $30,000 guarantee to fight Jess Willard. Willard,

6 feet 6½ inches and 250 pounds, from Pottawatomie, Kansas, was the leading "white hope." Johnson agreed to fight Willard, and Curley finally set up the fight in Havana, Cuba, for April 5, 1915.

The two men fought in the middle of the day, under a bright sun, with the temperature over a hundred degrees. Willard knocked Johnson out in the twenty-sixth round. Johnson later claimed that he had thrown the fight, that Curley had promised him that if he lost the title, he would be able to return to the United States without having to go to prison. Johnson also claimed that Curley paid Johnson's wife, Lucille, an extra percentage of the gate proceeds just before the twenty-sixth round in return for Johnson's promise to take a fall.

No one is sure whether the fight was fixed. Mrs. Johnson did leave ringside just before the twenty-sixth round, and one thing is sure from films of the fight—Johnson let himself be knocked out. Johnson might have quit from exhaustion and not because he was paid off, but he did quit. During the twenty-sixth round Johnson lowered his guard and stuck out his chin toward Willard. Willard hesitated, not sure of what was happening, then threw a right-hand lead to Johnson's chin. Johnson made no attempt to block the punch and fell flat on his back.

Johnson did not move while the referee counted ten. A famous picture of Johnson lying on his back, his hands resting on top of his forehead, has led many fight fans to conclude that Johnson was shading his eyes from the sun—proof that he was conscious and staying down intentionally.

Johnson returned to the United States in 1920 and served a year in Leavenworth Prison for his Mann Act conviction. Lucille divorced him in 1924 on the uncontested charge of infidelity. Johnson remarried a year later, once again to a white woman. He worked in vaudeville, circuses, and any other odd entertainment jobs he could find before he died in an automobile accident in 1946, at the age of sixty-eight.

During the 1960s Jack Johnson became something of a cult hero. Muhammad Ali's brashness, and his difficulties with the law and with white public opinion, invited comparisons to John-

son. Howard Sackler portrayed Johnson as a tragic hero in a
popular play about his life, *The Great White Hope*, and influ-
ential sectors of American society came to accept and admire
black militants. There is no question that Johnson was a victim
of racism, but to lionize him for it is a fantasy of martyrdom
that denies the realities of Johnson's character. Certainly it was
racist and unfair of American society to condemn Johnson for
sleeping with white women, much less for marrying them, but
that aside, Johnson was egotistical, selfish, and irresponsible.
Moreover, Johnson had an entirely negative impact on the cause
of civil rights. Segregation and racial hatred were on the rise in
American society during the first fifteen years of this century,
and Johnson greatly aggravated the trend. In the spring of 1913,
as Johnson awaited the trial that would result in his Mann Act
conviction, newly inaugurated Pres. Woodrow Wilson reim-
posed segregation in government facilities and fired many black
civil servants. Wilson was a hardened racist long before he ever
heard the name Jack Johnson, but Johnson had so inflamed
white hatred that hardly anyone dared protest Wilson's policies.

The political reaction against Johnson took even more obvious forms. Only twenty-seven days after Johnson's last title
defense in the United States, Congress prohibited interstate
transportation of fight films. During the anti-Johnson furor of
1912–13, bills banning interracial marriage were introduced in
at least half of the states that did not already have such laws.

Johnson's impact reached further than antimiscegenation bills
and lasted longer than Pres. Wilson's lifetime. Johnson confirmed the worst stereotypes of black behavior and provided
the perfect justification for segregation. His reign as heavyweight champion had resulted in race riots and increased racial
tension. He convinced many people that greater opportunities
for blacks were dangerous and would have to wait. For thirty
years the few black celebrities who followed Johnson had to
live down his unpopular image and fight those racist attitudes.

Johnson also hurt boxing. From 1910, when he defeated Jim
Jeffries, to 1915, when he lost to Jess Willard, interest in boxing
declined. Johnson's unpopularity fueled traditional opposition to
the sport. After Willard's victory, Grantland Rice wrote:

The Big Shadow over the fight game has been lifted at last. When Jess Willard wrested the chaplet of apple blossoms from the sable brow of Jack Johnson, he did something more than restore the heavyweight championship to the Caucasian caravanserie. For beyond this, he swept away the big barrier which had clogged the game's popularity for five lagging years.

Rice and other sportswriters approved Willard's declaration that he would redraw the color line in boxing; barring blacks was seen as an act of virtue.

The American public greeted Willard like a Roman general returning from a successful campaign. Willard got rich on theatrical tours, but he did not retain the public's esteem for long. He did not enjoy boxing or the people associated with the sport, and he defended his title only once between 1915 and 1919.

In the interim the United States joined the rest of the world at war. The U.S. Army taught boxing as part of its physical training program, and boxing was popular with many servicemen who returned home after 1918. With Johnson gone and the nation eager to forget the war, the time was right for a renewal of interest in boxing. But opposition to the sport remained strong. In 1919 an alliance of churchmen, social reformers, and rural bluenoses succeeded in enacting Prohibition. The same people also fought the growing acceptance of boxing. When Jess Willard signed to defend his title against a young contender named Jack Dempsey in a fight to be held July 4, 1919, in Toledo, Ohio, the ministers of Toledo objected, the lower house of the Ohio legislature passed a resolution deploring the fight, and Rep. Charles H. Randall asked the U.S. House of Representatives for a resolution "to protect the Nation's birthday against desecration by a prize fight."

Neither moralists nor Jess Willard could stop Dempsey. The former hobo knocked Willard down seven times in the first round. Willard somehow kept swinging for two more rounds before he had to quit, his face battered beyond recognition and his jaw broken. Sportswriters hailed Dempsey as a great talent, and his savage ring style captured the imagination of the public.

In 1920 New York State legalized boxing. Tex Rickard, who

had promoted the Jeffries-Johnson fight, shifted his operation to New York and soon established the Madison Square Garden Corporation as the controlling force in boxing. Rickard and boxing still faced a few more hurdles. Dempsey had avoided military service during World War I and had to clear his name in court in early 1920. Rickard used Dempsey's bad-boy image to his financial advantage, promoting a bout between Dempsey and Georges Carpentier, a handsome French war hero. Rickard cast Dempsey as the villain and Carpentier as the good guy. His little morality play, held July 2, 1921, was boxing's first million-dollar gate, grossing over $1,700,000. Dempsey knocked Carpentier out.

One year later Nat Fleischer founded *Ring* magazine, which became the leading boxing publication in the country. One of Fleischer's first acts as editor was to name Harry Wills, a black fighter, the number-one contender for the heavyweight title, and to demand that Dempsey fight Wills. Dempsey was not afraid of Wills, but he had announced the day after he won the championship that he would not fight black challengers. And Tex Rickard, shaken by the aftermath of the Johnson-Jeffries bout, had sworn that he would never promote another interracial heavyweight championship fight.

Dempsey made people forget about Wills, at least temporarily, by defending his title twice in 1923. In July he won a fifteen-round decision from Tom Gibbons in Shelby, Montana, a town so small and remote that it has gone down in history as perhaps the most incongruous location ever for a major sporting event. The 1920 census reported that Shelby had a population of 537 souls, with men outnumbering women twenty to one. In March 1922 the Kevin-Sunburst oil field was discovered nearby, and it became apparent that Shelby was sitting in the middle of one of the richest oil fields in the nation. Some of Shelby's leading citizens, buoyed by sudden prosperity and optimistic about Shelby's future, decided to host the fight to promote their town, but the fight had the opposite effect. Dempsey's $300,000 guarantee far exceeded the gate receipts; four Shelby banks failed. Gibbons did not get paid for losing the fifteen-round decision.

In September, Dempsey and Luis Angel Firpo, the "wild bull of the pampas," hooked up in the most explosive heavyweight championship fight of all time. Dempsey knocked Firpo down nine times in two rounds, finally knocking the South American out, but not before Firpo had knocked Dempsey out of the ring during the first round. The Firpo fight cemented Dempsey's image as a brawler and made him a national hero. He became one of the most famous men in America and the richest athlete of his era. In 1924 Dempsey earned over $500,000 from boxing exhibitions and movie roles. In the 1920s, $500,000 was the equivalent of more than ten million dollars today.

When Dempsey didn't defend his title in 1924, sentiment built for a Dempsey-Wills fight. Rickard twice faked arrangements for bouts between the two men, but he still had no intention of going through with the match. In 1925 the New York Boxing Commission banned Dempsey from boxing in New York because of his failure to meet Wills. The commission's three members were political appointees. Politicians in New York were feeling pressure from a growing block of black voters in the city.

That merely shifted Dempsey's next title defense from New York to Philadelphia. On September 23, 1926, Dempsey met Gene Tunney in Sesquicentennial Stadium before 120,757 spectators. Tunney outpointed Dempsey in ten rounds and went on to hold the title for two years. During that time Wills, thirty-seven years old in 1926, lost several fights and slipped out of the heavyweight picture.

Jack Dempsey fought for the last time on September 22, 1927, trying to recapture his lost title from Gene Tunney. That fight perhaps best symbolized the sports revolution that had come to fruition in the twenties. Held in Chicago's Soldiers Field, the fight drew 104,943 spectators, who paid $2,658,660. The fight was broadcast nationwide by radio. Dempsey received 5,000 letters a day in the weeks preceding the fight.

Tunney outpointed Dempsey through the early rounds, but in the seventh round Dempsey caught Tunney against the ropes and knocked him down. Dempsey stood over the fallen champion, just as he had stood over fallen opponents throughout his career. But boxing had changed. It had become a mass spectator sport, thanks largely to Dempsey himself, and much of the sport's old brutality was now against the rules. The referee refused to start the count against Tunney until Dempsey moved to a neutral corner. Given this reprieve, the famous "long count," Tunney got up and went on to win. Dempsey retired afterward, but he had won boxing permanent acceptance and had made it the number-two professional sport behind baseball.

3

"NEW YORK
AIN'T READY FOR HIM"

By late 1934, Joe Louis had a growing reputation in boxing circles. From July 4, when he knocked out his first professional opponent, Jack Kracken, in the first round, until October 30, when he knocked out Jack O'Dowd in round two, Louis won nine straight fights, seven by knockouts. Mushky Jackson, a fight manager at the time, recalled:

> I handled nothin' but heavyweights. I had heard of a prelim boy, a colored boy from Detroit who was knocking everybody out. Scotty Monteith, a Detroit matchmaker, called me and said he could set up a fight for me with my fighter Reds Barry. "I'll give you six rounds with this Joe Louis." I said I don't want to fight him, I don't want no part of him. . . . I had a fighter, Stanley Poreda. He had a reputation, but he was going backwards. I asked [Chicago promoter Benny] Ray how much we could get to fight Louis. They offered a $1,000 guarantee, a week's expenses, the hotel bill, plus two round-trip tickets.
>
> But the boxing commission insisted that Poreda would have to work out, show that he was in shape. I agreed only to have him limber up. We're in the same gym where Louis is, and he's knocking his sparring partners all over the place. Julian Black, the manager, is there too. I says to Poreda, "Don't look over there." I put up a punching bag with a swivel, and I tells Poreda to hit it. The bag flies off, and I say, "What a puncher. That's enough, you'll break the

bag." Black's new in the business, and I figure they won't catch on.

The fight itself was something nobody ever heard of. My fighter took a count of thirty-nine in one round. The first punch from Louis put him down for nine, the second punch for another nine. The third punch knocked Poreda out of the ring, and the referee kept counting until he got back. He got up to twenty-one.

When I got back to New York, I tell everybody what a fighter that Louis is. But nobody paid any attention. He was colored, and colored fighters were a dime a dozen.

The fight with Stanley Poreda was one of Louis's easiest, but none of his early fights was really tough. Managers Roxborough and Black and trainer Blackburn brought Louis along carefully, matching him against fighters a notch lower in talent. Louis's skills improved with constant training and frequent fights. He filled out to over 190 pounds. Most important, Louis learned in his early fights that other boxers could not match his hand quickness or strength. Adding to his natural advantages, Jack Blackburn drilled into Louis the fundamentals that most other boxers never learned, and Louis was in better shape than his opponents. Louis gained a confidence as total as it was silent. He expected to win every fight by a knockout, and boxing held little fear for him. He began to call Blackburn "Chappie."

Louis was happy. The check for $59 he received from his first fight made him feel rich. He sent most of it home to his family in Detroit but kept enough so he could go bowling and eat junk food with his friend Freddie Guinyard. And the checks kept getting bigger: $62, $101, $125, $250, $300, $450. At the age of twenty Louis was providing for his family, and everyone from his old neighborhood was enthusiastic about his boxing career. Because this success was so unexpected, Louis felt a special pride. No one, certainly not Louis himself, had imagined that a black boy from the Detroit ghetto would make so much money during the Depression.

Louis continued to send money home, and he enjoyed spending what was left over. He bought striped suits with wide lapels and broad-brimmed hats. He bought a black Buick with white-wall tires. When he visited home during infrequent breaks in training, Louis and his boyhood friends would cruise the neighborhood in the shiny Buick and invite girls to go for rides. After a while mothers told their daughters, "I better not see you get in Joe Louis Barrow's car."

Louis's managers decided it was time for tougher competition. They signed Louis to fight Charlie Massera, who had been the eighth-ranked contender in the *Ring* magazine ratings at the end of 1933. On November 30, 1934, at Chicago Stadium, Louis knocked Massera out in the third round. Louis received $1,200 for the fight. Two weeks later he fought Lee Ramage in the same ring. Like Louis, Ramage was a heavyweight on the rise. He was fast on his feet and a skillful defensive boxer. During the early rounds Ramage boxed circles around Louis, and Louis became increasingly frustrated at his inability to punch through Ramage's guard. Between rounds Blackburn told Louis to keep punching, to hit Ramage on the arms if he couldn't punch him in the stomach or head. Louis's pounding took its toll; by the eighth round Ramage could not hold his arms up. Louis trapped him against the ropes and knocked him out.

Some experts estimated that over 50 percent of black families in America's major cities were on relief, but Joe Louis was prospering. He brought expensive presents home to his family for Christmas. His first year in boxing had been a successful one. *Ring* magazine now rated him the ninth-ranking contender for Max Baer's heavyweight title.

John Roxborough thought Louis was ready for the big time: New York, Madison Square Garden, a fight with one of the leading contenders. "Yeah, he's ready for New York," Jack Blackburn said, "but New York ain't ready for him." Accounts differ as to why Roxborough and Jimmy Johnston, the man who had been running boxing promotions for the Garden since Tex Rickard's death, could not reach an agreement. Barney Nagler, a Louis biographer and one of the leading boxing writers in America, believes Johnston called Roxborough, not knowing Roxborough was black:

"I can help your boy," Johnston said.

"We can use your help. We think Joe is ready for big things," Roxborough said.

"Well, you understand he's a nigger, and he can't win every time he goes into the ring."

"So am I," Roxborough answered, and hung up.

In his autobiography Louis said that Roxborough and Julian Black had called Johnston: "His answer went something like this: 'You're a colored manager, and so's your fighter—you're not going to make the same money as the white boys, and your boy is going to have to lose a few.' In the end he turned the deal down."

Blackburn, who had never believed that Louis would get a chance, laughed at Roxborough and said, "I told you so."

Johnston was following the dictates of what passed for common wisdom in boxing. Throughout boxing history promoters had generally excluded black fighters from big fights and big money. Jack Johnson had inflamed the white public and roused tremendous antagonism. But even after the furor over Johnson had subsided, Tex Rickard, the most important promoter of the 1920s, thought that interracial matches might touch off racial hostilities. Because boxing had always operated on the fringes of respectability, promoters had some reason to fear a negative public reaction to interracial fights.

As discrimination hardened into custom, another rationalization developed for excluding black fighters. Without the backing of the major promoters and without title fights to generate public interest, black boxers naturally had trouble drawing crowds to their fights. So promoters like Jimmy Johnston concluded that white fans would not pay to see black fighters.

In 1935 the idea of promoting a heavyweight fight between a leading white contender and a black man was a venture into the unknown, a social gamble and a financial risk. Johnston felt that Louis and his managers should take a smaller cut to lessen the financial risk and should throw some fights to avoid a white backlash like the one Jack Johnson's success had unleashed.

Not that Johnston regretted his decision. He shared the general prejudice of his time. Barney Nagler said of the promoter,

"Jimmy Johnston was a friend of mine, but he was a bigot." Besides, Johnston was operating with the arrogance of monopolistic power. He controlled Madison Square Garden, and the Garden had controlled boxing since Tex Rickard tied up the heavyweight championship in the early 1920s.

But Johnston was making a fatal miscalculation. Garden promotions were not making enough money, and Johnston's monopoly was getting shaky. Johnston's problems began as soon as he took over boxing promotions for the Garden after Tex Rickard's death in 1929. Under the best of circumstances Johnston would have been hard-pressed to match Rickard's successes, and Johnston did not inherit the best of circumstances. His first difficulty was the absence of a charismatic heavyweight champion to draw big gates. Gene Tunney had defended his title only once after winning his epic rematch with Dempsey and had retired undefeated in 1928. Tex Rickard had arranged an elimination tournament among the four leading heavyweight contenders to fill Tunney's vacant title, but while Johnston was finishing the tournament, the Great Depression hit.

Boxing proved resilient at first. On June 11, 1930, Jack Sharkey and Max Schmeling fought the final bout of the elimination tournament for the world's heavyweight championship. Nearly 80,000 fans filled Yankee Stadium, paying a total gate of $749,935. Sharkey took an early lead on points, but in the fourth round he threw a right that landed well below Schmeling's belt, and Schmeling collapsed in pain, unable to continue. Under the rules then in effect, the judges awarded the fight, and the title, to Schmeling on a foul. The fight's sour conclusion was an omen.

Johnston's first champion, Max Schmeling, was the best fighter of the era, but he was too methodical in the ring. Besides, he was German. Schmeling won one title defense before losing a rematch to Jack Sharkey on a questionable decision. Sharkey in turn lost to Primo Carnera, a plodding, mob-controlled Italian giant. And in June of 1934, Carnera lost his title to Max Baer, an unpredictable and unpolished fighter who spent far more time partying in Hollywood and New York than he did in training. None of the heavyweight championship fights drew million-dollar gates in the early 1930s. The heavy influence of organized crime and a series of controversial fouls and decisions shook faith in the sport.

Johnston and the Madison Square Garden Corporation also faced competition for control of boxing—competition created partly, although accidentally, by the Garden itself. For several years Mrs. William Randolph Hearst's Free Milk Fund for Babies, a New York charity, had promoted boxing shows at the Garden and had been given a cut from other Garden boxing cards. The arrangement worked to everyone's benefit; babies got free milk, and Garden boxing got good publicity from William Randolph Hearst's two New York newspapers. Three Hearst newspapermen—Damon Runyon, columnist and famous short story writer; Edward J. Frayne, sports editor of the *New York American*; and Bill Farnsworth, sports editor of the *New York Journal*—promoted boxing for the milk fund.

Then, in 1933, the Garden decided to raise the rent on milk fund shows. If the Garden could be greedy, so could Runyon, Frayne, and Farnsworth, who saw a chance to make money for themselves in the name of charity. They secretly decided to form their own corporation to promote boxing in competition with the Garden. They would continue to give the milk fund a percentage of the proceeds in order to enlist the support of the Hearst publicity mill, which, of course, they could rev up to maximum speed, since they were its principal writers and editors.

For help in their tawdry plot, the three journalists turned to Mike Jacobs, which, as Runyon, Frayne, and Farnsworth later discovered, was like getting into bed with a rattlesnake. Jacobs grew up in absolute poverty and devoted his life to a single-minded, almost fanatic pursuit of money. His parents, Isaac and Rachel, were Eastern European Jews who emigrated first to Dublin and then to New York. They settled in an Irish neighborhood on the West Side, where they lived in a two-room tenement behind Isaac's tailor shop. Mike began hustling at an early age. He sold newspapers and worked as a "digger," a boy who bought theater or opera tickets for scalpers. Soon Jacobs figured out the business and went into scalping himself. By the age of sixteen Jacobs had saved $1,000. He bought the refreshment concession on the excursion boat *Dreamland*, which ferried tourists and couples from Battery Park to Coney Island. Jacobs had to provide a free lunch to the customers—that came with the ticket—but he sold salted peanuts cheap, which cut down his customers' appetites and stimulated thirst for his more expensive lemonade. He dropped candy on the laps of women as though it were free, then collected later from their dates, who were too embarrassed to refuse payment. In the off-season Jacobs waited tables at Tammany Hall.

But Jacobs devoted most of his energies to scalping. He pounded the pavement so hard finding buyers for his scalped tickets that his feet bled. His wife, Josie, told writer Budd Schulberg, "As I'm sittin' here, it was sweat 'n' blood. You c'n forget about the tears. Win or lose, up or down, I never saw the boss cry in his whole lovin' life." Jacobs arranged theater tours for Enrico Caruso, the great singer, and for British suffragette Emmeline Pankhurst, and cleaned up. By World War I, Jacobs was already moderately wealthy. He greatly increased his fortune by securing the refreshment concession for a string of army camps during the war and then selling out months before the Armistice.

During the war Jacobs also got involved in boxing. He advanced Tex Rickard money for the Willard-Moran heavyweight title fight in 1916 and in return got a block of choice tickets to scalp. He cemented his alliance with Rickard in 1921, when Rickard promoted the Dempsey-Carpentier fight. Rickard had guaranteed Dempsey $300,000 and Carpentier $200,000, staggering sums that scared off some of Rickard's financial backers. Jacobs stuck by Rickard, advancing him money and forming a syndicate of ticket scalpers to raise even more. The fight grossed $1,700,000. From then on Jacobs had an inside track with Rickard for the choicest tickets to boxing matches. Jacobs was a hidden power at Madison Square Garden, working out of an obscure office hardly as big as a closet. Rickard relied on Jacobs's advice and the scalper's expertise in selling tickets. When Rickard died in 1929, Jacobs expected to be named promoter for the Garden. The Garden chose the better known, more flamboyant Jimmy Johnston instead.

When Runyon, Frayne, and Farnsworth approached him, Jacobs eagerly seized the opportunity to compete against Johnston and the Garden. The three reporters met with Jacobs in the Forrest Hotel on West 49th Street, across the street from Jacobs's ticket brokerage, and drew up the papers for the 20th Century Sporting Club. All the stock was in Jacobs's name, since the reporters could not publicly acknowledge ownership in an organization they would be writing about. The 20th Century Club began to run boxing cards at the old Hippodrome at Sixth Avenue and Forty-fourth Street. Jacobs kept his eyes open for any big fights he could arrange on the side.

In the meantime, Louis was still winning, and his managers were still frustrated at their inability to arrange a big money fight. On January 4, 1935, Louis won a ten-round decision from Patsy Perroni, the sixth-ranked heavyweight contender. A week later he knocked out Hans Birkie in Pittsburgh's Duqesne Gardens.

At this point Mike Jacobs began to hear about Louis. Nat Fleischer, the editor of *Ring* magazine, did some publicity work for Jacobs. Fleischer had followed Louis's career since the fighter's amateur days and recommended Louis to Jacobs. Sam Pian and Art Winch, comanagers of Barney Ross, the junior middleweight champion, also told Jacobs about Louis. In early 1935, Jacobs conferred with his Hearst partners. Runyon, Frayne, and Farnsworth had also heard about Louis. They advised Jacobs to go ahead and sign Louis, even if he was black.

Jacobs himself was not an astute judge of boxing talent, but he searched out good advice. And he was in a position to gamble. A sensational young fighter was just what he needed to break Madison Square Garden's monopoly on the heavyweight division. No sensational white heavyweight was in sight, and Jacobs apparently did not share Jimmy Johnston's prejudice. Joe Louis remembered of Jacobs, "Mike had no prejudice about a man's color so long as he could make a green buck for him."

Jacobs went to Los Angeles to see Louis fight a rematch

against Lee Ramage, on February 21, 1935. This time Louis knocked Ramage out in the second round. Joe Louis was now the best fighter in the world, a once-in-a-generation talent, and he must have been electrifying to watch for the first time. His shoulders and back were massive, his chest and stomach flat. His muscles were solid but deeply buried. In the ring Louis's legs moved slowly, cautiously, and his feet were always planted. But his hands were incredibly fast. He threw short, jolting punches with both hands in quick sequences. In a fight, Louis always seemed to occupy the center of the action.

Jacobs was impressed. He met with Roxborough and Black and reached a tentative agreement to bring Louis to New York that summer for a big fight. When Roxborough cautiously asked what Louis would have to do in the ring to fulfill his contract, Jacobs told him, "He can win every fight he has, knock 'em out in the first round if possible. I promise if Joe ever gets to the top, he'll get a shot at the title." Jacobs was promising something he could not guarantee because he did not control the heavyweight championship, but it would be in Jacobs's interest for his new fighter to win the title. And Jacobs knew that if Louis was even suspected of throwing a fight, he might never become a top gate attraction.

Jacobs had told Roxborough and Black what they wanted to hear. Joe Louis would do his fighting for the 20th Century Sporting Club.

Louis and his entourage stayed on the West Coast to fight Mushky Jackson's fighter, Donald "Reds" Barry. Louis knocked Barry out in the third round on March 8, 1935, then returned to Detroit for a fight against Natie Brown scheduled for March 28. Meanwhile, Jacobs went back to New York to find a match for Louis and to begin selling his new fighter to the press. Jacobs's secret partners, Runyon, Frayne, and Farnsworth, readily pitched in, and the sports pages of the Hearst national newspaper chain sang Louis's praises.

Jacobs wooed sportswriters from other papers. For the Natie Brown fight Jacobs hired a private railroad car, stocked it with food and booze, and invited twenty or thirty New York sportswriters to travel to Detroit with him to see Louis fight.

This was the first fight in which Louis got any significant press attention, and he knew he had to impress the writers. Brown was a tough, experienced fighter, the eighth-ranked heavyweight boxer. Louis knocked him down in the first round, and Brown quickly realized he was out of his depth. From then on Brown just tried to survive and managed to stay on his feet for the rest of the ten-round fight. Louis outscored Brown by a wide margin, but he was overanxious. After the fight Louis felt that he had failed.

But even on an off night Louis was something to watch. Caswell Adams of the *New York Herald-Tribune* expressed a typical reaction in his story about the fight:

> Louis . . . can punch with terrific power. He can move with lightning speed. He can feint a foe out of position. And his timing on the defense is so perfect that blows usually miss him and never land squarely. . . . He is cold as ice and when he moves, he does so as would a tiger or a lion.

At a victory celebration, Louis apologized to Jacobs for looking so bad, but Jacobs brushed the apology aside. He knew Louis had impressed the New York writers and made his sales pitch to Louis. As Louis remembered it:

> He told me there was a kind of silent agreement between promoters that there would never be another black heavyweight champion like Jack Johnson. He told me how Jack Dempsey had run all over the country to avoid fighting Harry Wills. . . . If I could fight, he'd get me a shot at the title, and he'd make a lot of money for me.

Louis knew his managers wanted to sign with Jacobs, and Louis rubber-stamped their decision. To get away from the noisy party, Jacobs, Roxborough, Black, and Louis went into the bathroom to sign a contract that bound Louis to the 20th Century Sporting Club.

Mike Jacobs had his fighter. The outsider in heavyweight promotion had teamed up with the outsider among heavyweight contenders. Jacobs soon found Louis the perfect opponent for a fight in June—Primo Carnera, the six-foot-six-inch giant from Italy who had held the world's heavyweight championship for a year before losing it to Max Baer in 1934.

Despite his size and impressive record, Carnera was little better than an average fighter. A French fight manager named Leon See had discovered Carnera working in a carnival as a strongman and a wrestler. See knew that Carnera's size was a marketable commodity even if his boxing skills were not. See's connections in the European underworld took care of Carnera's fighting deficiencies. After a year of boxing in Europe in which he won a series of fixed fights by early-round knockouts, Carnera came to the United States at the end of 1929.

Owney Madden, a New York racketeer, murderer, and bootlegger, bought out Leon See's interest in Carnera. Madden owned the famous Cotton Club in Harlem, where the best black entertainers in the United States performed before all-white audiences. Under Madden's guidance Carnera toured the United States, fighting twenty-three matches and winning twenty-two times by knockouts in a total of forty-six rounds. Carnera won the other fight on a foul. Two Carnera victims, Ace Clarke and Leon Bombo Chevalier, later testified that their fights with Carnera were fixed. Chevalier had stubbornly insisted on beating Carnera up, but between rounds his seconds rubbed Vaseline in his eyes and nose and warned him that he would be shot if he had the gall to win. Chevalier tried to continue, half blind from the Vaseline. His seconds were stubborn men. They threw in the towel with Chevalier still in no danger of being knocked out. The fight was so obviously fixed that the California State Athletic Commission lifted Carnera's license.

After a few losses to fighters that Madden could not buy, Carnera's reputation soared when he fought Ernie Schaaf on February 10, 1933. Schaaf was a legitimate contender, but he had suffered a terrible beating from Max Baer several months before and apparently sustained brain damage. Against Carnera, Schaaf collapsed in the thirteenth round. He died several days later. Schaaf's death earned Carnera a title shot against heavyweight champion Jack Sharkey, who had convincingly beaten Carnera two years before. Only 10,000 fans showed up to watch the fight. Sharkey was well ahead on points, but in the sixth round Carnera threw a long right hand to Sharkey's chin. Sharkey went down and stayed down for a count of ten.

Carnera returned home to Italy, the owner of a questionable title. Italian dictator Benito Mussolini welcomed Carnera with an extra-large black shirt, the uniform of the Italian fascists. While in Italy, Carnera won a fifteen-round decision from Paulino Uzcudun, then successfully defended his title against Tommy Loughran in Miami before losing it to Max Baer in June 1934. Baer knocked Carnera down eleven times before the referee stopped the fight in the eleventh round.

Though he had lost his title, Carnera was still well known. If Louis could beat him, it would be a big step toward the championship. Carnera was at least big and strong, and he had acquired a degree of boxing skill. He would be a good test for Louis.

4

"SOMETHING SLY
AND SINISTER"

In the spring of 1935, Mike Jacobs announced that Joe Louis would fight Primo Carnera that summer. The buildup to the Carnera fight catapulted Louis into public prominence. He was twenty-one years old and unlettered, but he quickly became the most famous black in America.

He had little competition, even in sports. No black had fought in an important heavyweight fight since Jack Johnson lost his title in 1915. Baseball, the only professional sport more popular than boxing, had barred blacks since the late nineteenth century. The fledgling National Football League also excluded black players. Some northern colleges allowed a token black on the football or basketball team, but in October 1934 Georgia Tech refused to play a scheduled football game against Michigan unless the Wolverines benched their black star, Willis Ward. Despite petitions from Michigan students and professors demanding that Ward be allowed to play, the Michigan administration did not even allow Ward to dress. He had to watch the game from the press box. The game was played at Michigan.

Segregation in sports reflected the unthinking racism of society at large. In the South blacks could not vote, could not go to school with whites, could not use the same drinking fountains or bathrooms. Segregation was almost as rigid in the North. Blacks were hemmed into crowded slums, and most restaurants and nightclubs refused to serve them. In the nation's capital even St. Elizabeth's Hospital for the Insane was segregated. Employment discrimination was open and blatant; most unions barred blacks, and skilled jobs were reserved for whites. Whites hired blacks for menial work but otherwise considered it inappropriate for blacks to intrude upon their world. Segregation and overt discrimination were taken for granted; they were not subjects of interest or discussion.

Blacks were not active in politics and were not on the political agenda, even with Franklin D. Roosevelt in the White House. To be sure, Roosevelt had a few token black advisers, and unlike the last Democratic president—Woodrow Wilson—he did not bar blacks from civil service. Some New Deal money trickled down to blacks, but the government never considered targeting relief programs to help blacks, even though the Depression was hitting them much harder than whites. One of the New Deal's proudest creations, the Tennessee Valley Authority, displaced black tenant farmers. Roosevelt even refused to lobby for a federal antilynching law, though in the South whites lynched hundreds of blacks every year and were never punished. The only black member of Congress, Oscar DePriest of Chicago, was a Republican.

To most white Americans, blacks were invisible. Red Burman, one of Louis's white opponents, remembered growing up in Baltimore during the Depression: "At that time the only blacks in existence were in back alleys." Bob Pastor, who fought Louis twice, was asked whether he had any black neighbors when growing up in the Bronx: "No, no, no way. It was an all-white country at that time, white city in 1914, that's when I was born. It was all white, everybody was white, there was no black people around at all. And then later on they came in." One reason black problems rarely surfaced was the near-total segregation of the American media. White newspapers, from the *New York Times* to the *New Orleans Times-Picayune*, covered whites only. They printed pictures of white brides, white politicians, white athletes, white clergymen. Blacks rarely appeared except as perpetrators or victims of crime.

Shirley Povich, who began to write for the *Washington Post* in the 1920s, remembered:

Very often when covering a crime and you came upon a stabbing, you came upon a murder, the city editor would say, "White or . . . white or nigger?"—I'm sorry that's the expression they used—and you would say, "Nigger," and they'd say, "Forget it, not worth recording." You had the sense that nobody really cared what went on in the black world.

Perhaps the most famous black in America before Louis came along was Father Divine. Divine was a religious mystic who was running a noisy commune on Long Island when his white neighbors complained. Judge Lewis J. Smith convicted Divine of maintaining a public nuisance, and Divine told reporters, "Pity the judge; he can't live long. He's offended Almighty God." Four days later Judge Smith died of a heart attack, and Divine was on his way to establishing a cult that won many poor black converts with its ascetic life-style. The white press gave Divine front-page coverage for a while, writing about him in a tone of bemused ridicule.

The white press ignored more substantial black leaders. Historians regard A. Philip Randolph and W.E.B. DuBois as two of the most important black leaders of the 1930s, but in their time they were almost unknown to the white public. Randolph, a black political activist and president of the Brotherhood of Sleeping Car Porters, was mentioned in the *New York Times* three times between 1935 and 1940, only once on the front page. DuBois, editor of the NAACP's *Crisis* magazine and a leading black writer, appeared just as infrequently. Walter White appeared in the white press somewhat more frequently in his role as head of the National Association for the Advancement of Colored People (NAACP). But neither White nor the NAACP made the front page of the *New York Times* from 1935 to 1940.

Blacks appeared rarely in the movies or on radio, and then always in stereotyped roles. Dancer Bill "Bojangles" Robinson got rich playing the dancing fool; his picture never appeared in white papers without his broad smile. The other leading black movie actor of the period assumed the stage persona Stepin

Fetchit, a name that said a great deal about the roles he played. An occasional mammie rounded out black appearances in the movies. On the radio Amos 'n' Andy and Jack Benny's foil Rochester also played humorous, stereotyped roles.

A few black athletes won fleeting fame. In 1932, Eddie Tolan won two gold medals in the Los Angeles Olympics for the 100- and 200-meter dashes. His teammate Ralph Metcalfe, also black, finished second in the 100 and third in the 200. Tolan made headlines for a few days, but he won no lasting fame with his gold medals. The Olympics were not as important then.

Paul Robeson became famous as an All-American football player at Rutgers and later as an actor and singer. A brilliant and initially popular man, Robeson might have shattered stereotypes about blacks, but he drew the scorn of white America for his visits to the Soviet Union and his public advocacy for leftist causes. By the 1930s *The New York Times* ran only an occasional back page story on Robeson, often concentrating on his radical politics.

The journalistic style of the day revealed how unusual it was for whites to write or think about blacks. When white papers mentioned blacks, they always identified them as Negroes. They did not just give this information once and then dispense with it, like a first name. White papers constantly referred to blacks as "Negroes." If "Negro" was too prosaic, they called blacks "dusky," "tanned," or "dark."

To white sportswriters and their white readers, the color of Louis's skin was his most salient characteristic. Louis was "the Detroit Negro," "the dusky challenger," "the colored pugilist." Sportswriters during the 1930s had an inane passion for alliterative nicknames, and Louis's race inspired their most imaginative work. Besides the well-known nicknames "Brown Bomber" and "Dark Destroyer," various writers also called Louis "the sepia slugger," "the mahogany maimer," "the dark dynamiter," "the dusky David from Detroit," "the sable cyclone," "the tawny tiger-cat," "the saffron sphinx," "the dusky downer," "Mike Jacobs's pet pickaninny," "the shufflin' shadow," "the saffron sandman," "the heavy-fisted Harlemite," "the coffee-colored kayo king," "the murder man of those maroon mitts," "the tan-skinned terror," "the chocolate chopper," "the mocha mauler," and "the tan Tarzan of thump."

The dynamic of white meeting black worked both ways. When Louis arrived in New York four weeks before the Carnera fight, promoter Jacobs scheduled a press conference for him in the offices of the 20th Century Sporting Club. Louis was twenty-one years old, uneducated, and shy. He had to deal with a large crowd of reporters for the first time, and he was unequal to the task. He managed only monosyllabic responses to the rush of reporters' questions; his managers and Jacobs did most of the talking. White reporters took Louis's silence and his wooden expression for hostility and stupidity. For years after Louis broke into the big time, reporters described him as sullen and commented frequently that it was difficult to get him to talk. Roi Ottley, a black writer in New York, had no difficulty getting Louis to talk and wrote later, "The white sportswriters were making much of Louis' impenetrable silence. Actually, before he got into the important money, he had had little contact with white people and was very shy of them."

To prepare for Carnera, Louis and his entourage set up training camp in Pompton Lakes, an hour's drive from the city in upstate New York, on the estate of Dr. Joseph Bier, a dentist. The Ku Klux Klan threatened Bier, but he stood firm; in the middle of the Depression, he needed the rental income.

While Louis trained, Mike Jacobs and Louis's managers, Roxborough and Black, went about the business of selling their fighter to the public. Jacobs hired press agents to work at the training camps of both Louis and Carnera and had another press agent working out of his offices in New York. They turned out daily releases for newspapers all over the country.

New York was the sports and newspaper center of the country. In the Depression, few out-of-town papers could afford to send reporters of their own to cover the training camps. New York sportswriters had syndicated columns that were reprinted as far away as Seattle. In addition, sportswriters in other cities read the work of the New York writers, borrowed information from them, and emulated their clichéd and hyperbolic styles. The combination of Jacobs's press releases and the widespread reprinting and imitation of New York writers ensured that press coverage of Louis was basically uniform throughout the rest of the country and remarkably repetitious.

Boxers fight only a few times a year, and so much of the publicity about them focuses on their character and personality. This helped Louis become a real person to the white public, more so than any other black. Jacobs's press agents, and Roxborough and Black in their contact with New York sportswriters, spread a kind of "official" image of Louis's character that strongly influenced public perceptions of Louis for the rest of his career. They wanted to dissociate Louis from the memory of Jack Johnson. John Roxborough told reporters he had laid down seven rules for Louis to follow. Many papers printed Roxborough's commandments with approving comments:

1. He was never to have his picture taken along with a white woman.

2. He was never to go into a nightclub alone.

3. There would be no soft fights.

4. There would be no fixed fights.

5. He was never to gloat over a fallen opponent.

6. He was to keep a "dead pan" in front of the cameras.

7. He was to live and fight clean.

The rules themselves were apocryphal, though Louis commented later that Roxborough had given him similar advice. It is clear that Roxborough aimed these rules at Johnson's negative image.

Jacobs, Roxborough, and Black portrayed Louis as a model of middle-class virtue. The official explanation of Louis's reticence with white reporters was that he was modest and unassuming. Roxborough and Black taught Louis to compliment his opponents and never to brag. Jack Blackburn, Louis's trainer, kept Louis on the same rigorous schedule they had maintained for a year. Louis ran five or six miles in the morning, did exercises every afternoon, and sparred four times a week. He impressed reporters as a hard worker. Jacobs's publicists emphasized that Louis did not drink or smoke.

At the prompting of a press agent, Louis's mother sent him a huge Bible, and press releases from Louis's camp said that he read the good book every night before going to sleep. The day before the fight with Carnera, pictures of Louis holding his Bible appeared in newspapers all over the country. Another fictional element of Louis's official image was that he was saving his money for the future, like a good capitalist.

Roxborough and Black were so conscious of Louis's public image that they hired him a tutor. For several years Russell Cowans, a black sportswriter and college graduate, was at every one of Louis's training camps. For two hours a day he taught Louis the rudiments of grammar, geography, history, and math. These sessions probably did little to bridge the cultural gap between Louis and white reporters, but the approving press stories on Louis's continuing education helped build his "official" image.

Louis reinforced the image when he bought his mother a house in April 1935. The press delighted in telling and retelling the story of how Louis had taken his mother for a drive and surprised her by pulling up in front of her new house. Louis's mother, Mrs. Lilly Barrow Brooks, made good copy. She had raised seven children in a sharecropper's cabin in Alabama, lost her first husband, married Pat Brooks, a widower with six children of his own, and moved with Brooks and their considerable brood to Detroit. She was fat and friendly and religious and talkative, a comfortable stereotype for white writers. "Joe always was a good boy," Mrs. Brooks reassured reporters.

The press and the public might greet such an image with skepticism today, but the reporters of Louis's time ate it up and asked for more. To be sure, the descriptions of Louis contained elements of truth. Louis really didn't drink or smoke and refused to endorse cigarettes until late in his career. He was truly modest, and generous to a fault. On the other hand, Louis played around considerably and did not restrict himself to black women. He was just "discreet," in his own words. And money ran through his hands like water.

Times were different. Sportswriters were more inclined to

make heroes of athletes than to expose their faults. As an indication of the journalistic custom of looking the other way, sportswriters never made an issue of the backgrounds of Roxborough, Black, or Blackburn, although they knew that Louis's managers were numbers men and that Blackburn had served time for manslaughter. In their own patronizing way, white sportswriters were aware of Louis's potential social significance and wanted to avoid creating another Jack Johnson as much as Louis and his entourage did.

So reporters wrote countless stories about how "well behaved" Louis was. Many of these testimonials included explicit comparisons to Johnson. Jack O'Brien, a popular, if ungrammatical, columnist, wrote:

> Joe Louis is a non-pretentious, self-effacing lad and a credit to his race. Unlike Jack Johnson, Joe is as clean as a hound tooth. One can get an insight to his character when they remember he stated the other day that his favorite book is the Bible.

Richards Vidmer of the *New York Herald Tribune* wrote:

> Joe Louis is as different a character from Jack Johnson as Lou Gehrig is from Al Capone. It seems to me that the Brown Bomber is just what the doctor ordered to restore life in the business of boxing. He is a God-fearing, Bible-reading, clean-living young man, to be admired, regardless of creed, race, or color. He is neither a showoff nor a dummy. Modest, quiet, unassuming in his manner, he goes about his business, doing the best job he can every time he climbs into a ring.

The common concern of Louis's entourage and the press about the behavior of a young black boxer rested on a common assumption: that Joe Louis, the only black making news in a segregated society, was the symbol of his race to millions of white Americans and that the white public would judge all blacks by the way they judged him. Jacob's publicists, and John Roxborough especially, pushed Louis as an ambassador of goodwill from the black race to the white, and Louis's role as a symbol became an integral part of his press image.

Roxborough claimed that he had sponsored Louis with the idea that the young boxer would someday become champion and that Louis's good behavior would bring about better racial understanding in America. It is doubtful that anyone, John Roxborough included, could have looked at a black amateur boxer as a racial ambassador in 1934. Truman Gibson, Louis's lawyer and adviser late in the fighter's career, said:

> I don't think John really had those ideas. All they thought of in the early days was that they had a good fighter and wanted to bring him along carefully. I don't think John had any notion of the ambassadorial role for Joe, or any idea how far Joe would go, because in those days black fighters were decidedly limited.

But it is easy to see why Roxborough pushed the idea so hard. Roxborough came from an educated, solidly middle class background. His father was a doctor, his brother a lawyer and a member of the Michigan state legislature. Roxborough, though, dropped out of the University of Detroit to become a bail bondsman and a numbers operator. He told reporters that he was a lawyer and a graduate of the University of Michigan. Creating a racial ambassador would confer status and legitimacy on Roxborough.

Louis got many letters testifying to his importance as a racial ambassador, and the publicists were quick to pass them on to reporters. Newspapers all over the country reprinted the letters, like this one from Gov. Frank D. Fitzgerald of Michigan, written three days before the Carnera fight:

> Dear Joe:
> Don't be too greatly impressed by this stationery. I happen to be Governor of Michigan but I'm talking to you as a man more than twice your age just to give a little advice to a young fellow who has a real chance to do something for his people. . . .
> Destiny seems to have pointed you for a high rank in pugilism. Your ability to overpower others by skill and physical force is something of which you may be proud. It's going to make you a lot of money too; more money

than is made by those who excel, let us say, as artists or surgeons, or poets. You'll have world prominence and money.

They will mean little, Joe, if you do not use them as God intended that gifts bestowed by Nature should be used.

Your race, at times in the past, has been misrepresented by others who thought they had reached the heights. Its people have been denied equal opportunity. Its obstacles and its handicaps have been such that it has been saved only by its own infinite patience and its ability to endure suffering without becoming poisoned by bitterness.

The qualities which may soon make you a world champion should call to the attention of people the world over, that the good in you can also be found in others of your race, and used for their own welfare, and the welfare of humanity at large.

So, Joe, you may soon have on your strong hands the job of representative-at-large of your people.

Louis publicly accepted his symbolic role in *Joe Louis' Own Story*, a pamphlet-size biography written by his literary ghost, Gene Kessler:

I realize the Negro people have placed a big trust in me. I can't throw my race down by abusing my position as a heavyweight challenger. It is my duty to win the championship and prove to the world that, black or white, a man can become the best fighter and still be a gentleman.

This sense of responsibility stayed with Louis and his managers for the rest of Louis's career. The pains they took to ensure that Louis did not offend the white public may seem exaggerated today, but in their time they certainly were not. Neither Louis nor his managers would have dreamed of criticizing whites for their racism, nor would they dare any political statements beyond an occasional mild appeal for equal opportunity.

But even if Louis and his managers dared not offend the white public, they did not play Uncle Toms. Louis remembered in his autobiography:

One time we were talking about these little black toy dolls they used to make of fighters. Those dolls always had the wide grin with thick red lips. They looked foolish. I got the message—don't look like a fool nigger doll. Look like a black man with dignity.

It was not a lesson Louis needed to learn. For all of his lack of education and his embarrassed silences around white reporters, Joe Louis possessed a natural sense of self-worth and dignity. Harry Markson, a sportswriter then who went on to become a publicist and promoter for Madison Square Garden, remembered a picture-taking session with Louis before the Carnera fight:

All the photographers were out there, and one of the guys went into Pompton Lakes and he came back with a sliced watermelon. And he gave it to Joe Louis. Blackburn wasn't around, Roxborough wasn't around, because they were just going to take fighting pictures of him. One of them tried to have Joe Louis pose with this watermelon. "Great shot, Joe. Make a great shot." And Louis wouldn't do it. Now nobody told him not to, but instinctively he knew that this was a racist kind of a thing and he wouldn't do it. And they kept saying, "Well why not, Joe. Make a great shot, Joe, great shot."
"I don't like watermelon."
Well, he loved watermelon.

Press awareness of Louis's role as ambassador of his race increased because of the symbolic implications of the Carnera fight. By the summer of 1935 Carnera's homeland, Italy, under the fascist dictatorship of Benito Mussolini, was threatening to invade Ethiopia. In an era of widespread colonialism, Ethiopia was one of the few independent black countries on earth. American blacks felt a deep sympathy with Ethiopia. Black historian John Hope Franklin wrote of the period, "Even the most provincial of American Negroes became international minded. Ethiopia was a Negro nation, and its destruction would symbolize the final victory of the white man over the Negro." Ethiopian Emperor Haile Selassie became a hero to black Americans.

Two white columnists, Westbrook Pegler of the Scripps-Howard newspaper chain and Arthur Brisbane of Hearst,

warned that the Louis-Carnera fight might spark race riots between black and Italian spectators. Half of the families in
Harlem were on relief, and blacks there had rioted in March
when a false rumor spread that a white shopkeeper had killed
a young black shoplifter. Pegler hinted at the fight's "dangerous
possibilities" and went on:

> The principals in this prizefight are Joe Louis, a young
> American Negro, and Primo Carnera, the Italian military
> reservist. The Yankee Stadium lies just across the Harlem
> River from the greatest Negro city in the world, where
> riots have flared twice in recent weeks.

Brisbane, a virulent racist, wrote:

> A 20-year-old Detroit Negro, Joe Louis, with some white
> blood, will fight the Italian giant, Carnera. . . . [W]hat
> might cause excitement, possibly a fight bigger than the
> scheduled fight, is the fact that this heavyweight prize fight
> between an American colored man and an Italian comes at
> a time when the Abysinnian [Ethiopian] question creates
> feeling between Italians and Negroes in New York. The
> crowd at this Italian-Negro prizefight will be composed
> largely of Italians, all enthusiastic about their giant country-
> man, and Negroes from New York's Harlem section.

These columns had a familiar ring. For years whites had used
exaggerated fears of racial violence as an excuse for excluding
blacks from full participation in American life. After all, the
segregationists liked to point out, race riots had erupted after
Jack Johnson beat Jim Jeffries in 1910.

William Randolph Hearst, whose wife ran the Free Milk
Fund For Babies, the charitable sponsor of the fight, apparently
was so disturbed by the talk of riots that he wanted to call off
the Louis-Carnera fight. Fortunately for Louis, Mike Jacobs
paid no attention to Hearst. Louis also found an ally, if a patronizing one, in New York Police Commissioner Edward P. Mul-
rooney, who reassured reporters, "There won't be a Harlem
disturbance. The American Negro is by nature law-abiding,

kindly, well-behaved. He is also happy and fun-loving. If Louis wins, there will likely be singing and shouting and dancing in the streets of Harlem."

Public interest in the Louis-Carnera fight ran higher than for any fight in years. Although a former champion, Carnera had never been a big drawing card; it was curiosity about Louis that generated the attention. Certainly Louis's record—twenty-two straight wins, eighteen by knockout—interested boxing fans. Louis was the best prospective fighter to come along since Jack Dempsey.

Just as certainly, Louis's color interested the general public. Louis was an anomaly, if a well-behaved one. He was a black invader in the white world of fame and fortune, and whites wanted to see what would happen when Joe Louis stepped across the color line. Mike Jacobs had unerringly built his pre-fight promotion around Louis's race, and his publicity efforts worked. More than 60,000 paying customers and 400 sports-writers, the biggest press delegation to attend a fight since Dempsey fought Carpentier in 1921, filled Yankee Stadium the night of June 25. It was Louis's first appearance in New York.

Ring announcer Harry Balogh walked to the center of the ring, waited for the microphone, then said to the crowd, "Ladies and gentlemen, before proceeding with this most important heavyweight contest I wish to take the liberty of calling upon you in the name of American sportsmanship, a spirit so fine it has made you, the American sporting public, world famous. I therefore ask that the thought in your mind and the feeling in your heart be that, regardless of race, creed, or color, let us all say, may the better man emerge victorious. Thank you."

With less than a minute left in the fifth round Louis threw a short right, and when Carnera tried to clinch, Louis threw him sideways into a corner. Carnera, who was five inches taller than Louis and outweighed him by sixty pounds, opened his eyes wide in surprise. He told Louis through bloody lips, "I should be doing this to you." Caught in the corner, Carnera tried a jab. Louis moved his head to the side to slip the jab and delivered a right hook to the head that bounced Carnera off the ropes. Louis landed a left and then another right that started Carnera down, but the Italian giant held on to Louis, and the two boxers spun around. Louis pushed Carnera away. Carnera jabbed and waved his left hand in the air. Louis jabbed, threw a left hook and a right cross that Carnera blocked. They clinched, and Louis walked Carnera backward into the ropes. Referee Arthur Donovan broke them.

Louis missed an overhand right, and Carnera clinched again. Carnera tried another jab, and Louis countered with a right cross that staggered Carnera. Both fighters jabbed, then clinched and broke. Louis blocked a left, slipped a jab, landed a left hook that made Carnera hop away, then threw an overhand left to the head, and Carnera's legs buckled briefly.

Carnera jabbed twice, nervous jabs that belied his size. Louis jabbed, Carnera jabbed, and Louis landed a left to the body, but Carnera blocked the right cross that followed. Louis jabbed and was short with a long right and a long left. Carnera jabbed, then blocked a Louis left hook. Louis tried again with his left hand, missed, missed a jab and a right to the body, and the bell rang.

Urged on by his handlers or false bravado, Carnera rushed out for round six. Louis calmly circled him. Carnera tried a jab, but Louis sidestepped. Suddenly, alone with Louis in the ring again, Carnera's brief burst of confidence evaporated. Louis walked into Carnera, and Carnera tried to jab him away. Louis threw a left and ducked as Carnera threw a slow left of his own. Carnera hitched up his trunks and backed away. Both fighters jabbed. Louis ducked a left hook and a jab. Carnera feinted twice, and Louis covered up and clinched. They broke. Louis jabbed, then jabbed again, the second punch landing solidly. Carnera missed a left-right combination.

Louis swung a wild right and missed but followed instantly with a left that hurt Carnera. Carnera tried to hold on, but Louis threw an overhand right to the head. Now wobbling on his feet, Carnera tried a feeble jab, but Louis ducked under it and came up swinging a right to the head. Carnera pitched forward on his knees, and his face hit the canvas. As Carnera tried to get up, he fell backward on his rear end. Carnera rolled over and got up at the count of four. He staggered backward. Louis walked in quickly, his eyes locked on Carnera and his face expressionless. Louis missed a right and a left, missed another right, ducked a jab, and landed an overhead right to the head that dropped Carnera to his knees. Again Carnera got up at four, his mouth smeared with blood.

Louis came out of his neutral corner and threw an overhand right and a left hook. Carnera's arms splayed out behind him as he tried to back away. Carnera regained his balance, but Louis hit him with a right hook and a left. Carnera tried to hold on to Louis. The referee broke them, and as Carnera stepped away, he quickly rubbed his mouth with his right hand.

Louis swung a right and then a left, and Carnera went down to one knee. Carnera got up quickly and took a weak step backward, arms at his sides. Carnera was displaying considerable courage and an ability to absorb punishment, but that was all he had left. He put his left hand on the top strand of the ropes, lost. Referee Donovan stepped in front of him and waved his arms, stopping the fight.

Joe Louis, who was standing behind the referee, waiting to hit Carnera again if necessary, began to walk past Carnera with his head down. As Donovan led Carnera away, Louis turned and touched Carnera on the arm. Carnera, probably only half conscious, didn't notice Louis's gesture. Still expressionless, Louis put his head back down and walked toward his corner where his handlers were waiting, their arms outstretched to hug him. Policemen quickly filled the ring. Louis put on his robe; then Harry Balogh brought him to the center of the ring. Balogh raised Louis's right hand in victory and turned Louis to face all four sides of the crowd. Louis circled stiffly with small steps. He had a pained look, as if he were anxious or embarrassed. In fact, Louis was happier than he had ever been. He said twelve years later:

> This was my first night in New York and this was the night I remember best in all my fighting. If you was ever a raggedy kid and you come to something like that night you'd know. I don't thrill to things like other people. I only feel good. I felt the best that night.

Many Americans saw something very unusual on the morning of June 26, 1935—a black man's name in the headlines across the front page of their newspapers. Louis's performance against Carnera had been utterly convincing. Most sportswriters who covered the fight wrote glowing praise of Louis's boxing skills.

What they wrote about Louis the man was less flattering. Few sights in sport are more brutal than a knockout. Reporters had often called great white boxers cruel or savage because of the way they mercilessly attacked their opponents. The color of Louis's skin added a deeper resonance to such descriptions. White reporters wrote that Louis was savage, animalistic, endowed with instinctual prowess. They carried this image to absurd lengths, suggesting something of the prejudice and fear with which white Americans looked at their fellow black citizens. Davis Walsh's lead for the International News Service account of the fight read: "Something sly and sinister and perhaps not quite human came out of the African jungle last night to strike down and utterly demolish the huge hulk that had been Primo Carnera, the giant."

Grantland Rice, one of the best-known sportswriters of the day, helped spread the image of Joe Louis as a "jungle killer." By 1935 Rice's column, "the Sportlight," was syndicated all over the country, and he had somehow acquired a reputation as a great writer, a reputation that survives in some measure today. Sportswriting during the 1930s was uniformly hyperbolic, clichéd, and addicted to inane puns and nicknames, but for dreadful writing Rice stood out even among his peers. He was also a racist. Barney Nagler remembered, "Grantland Rice used to talk about Joe Louis as 'the nigger.' Don't you ever believe anything else, because there was the ultimate bigot. I never thought much of Grantland Rice."

Rice wrote this poem about Louis after the Carnera fight:

> For he is part of years long lost, back on an age-old
>   beat,
> Where strength and speed meant life and love—and
>   death ran with defeat

For those who slugged the dinosaur, or lived on
   mammoth's meat.

There was a day when brawn and might were all they
   cared to know;
There was a day when fang and claw made up the
   ancient show—
And so today we slip our cash to Bomber Joe.

Let politicians have their howl in this infested land;
Let cock-eyed thinkers bore us stiff each time they
   take a stand—
The world still seeks its vanished thrill—a punch in
   either hand.

Rice called Louis a "bushmaster" and a "Brown Cobra" and referred to his "blinding speed," "the speed of the jungle, the instinctive speed of the wild." Rice used another animal image to describe Louis in the ring: "Joe Louis was stalking Carnera, the mammoth, as the black panther of the jungle stalks its prey." The subconscious workings of clichéd minds would make Louis, like Jack Johnson before him, a panther in print many times.

When writers weren't implicitly denying Louis's humanity by calling him a jungle animal, they did it another way. Louis was naturally impassive, and around reporters he was shy and restrained. White reporters rarely saw his expression change. As a result, writers often described him as a heartless, merciless engine of destruction. Shirley Povich of the *Washington Post* wrote:

> No killer with the ferocious scowl of Dempsey or the fiendish leer of [Max] Baer is this Joe Louis, but a killer nevertheless. Like some machine, a methodical, mechanical destroyer, geared for destruction, did he attack the gargantuan specimen who opposed him with a 64-pound weight advantage, and was cut down for the finish.

Povich's colleague on the *Post*, Bill McCormick, referred to "a cruel, destructive fighting machine trade-marked Joe Louis."

Louis's stare of concentration in the ring added to his machine-like image. Davis Walsh described the crowd's ovation after the Carnera fight: "And high above the clamor of the knockout, Joe Louis, the strange, wall-eyed, unblinking Negro." Syndicated columnist Haywood Broun wrote of Louis's "icy, deadpan determination."

Because blacks had been excluded from most top-flight competition for many years, there was little tradition of black athletic excellence in 1935. Nevertheless, many journalists explained Louis's success in terms of race. In an editorial, the *New York Daily Mirror* suggested that "[i]n Africa there are tens of thousands of powerful, young savages that with a little teaching, could annihilate Mr. Joe Louis." The *New York Sun*, in an editorial entitled "Negro Boxers," said, "[t]he American Negro is a natural athlete. The generations of toil in the cotton fields have not obliterated the strength and grace of the African native." In a column on Jack Blackburn, "the great teacher," Grantland Rice wrote that Blackburn's own boxing skill "was a matter of instinct with him, as with most of the great Negro fighters. . . . The great Negro boxer is rarely a matter of manufacture, like many white boxers. He is born that way."

Whatever the source of his ability, sportswriters generally agreed that Louis was the best young heavyweight since Dempsey. It was obvious that he would be in the upper ranks of the heavyweight division for years to come and, if given a chance, would probably become the world champion. Thus, his race, and his role as a symbol of his race, seemed more important than ever. Under the headline "Stick To Your 'Ma,' Joe" and a subhead that read, "More Than a Fighter—a Symbol?" Bill Corum of the *New York Evening Journal* wrote:

You saw for yourself Tuesday night that everybody means to play fair with you. They'll keep on being that way if you give 'em the chance. Don't get big headed. Don't think when you get a bad break—and you'll get some; the game calls for it—that you got it because of your race. That's the bunk in sports.

The people who make race feeling are the people who

keep harping on it. Those who do most to kill it are those who don't think about it one way or the other. Be that way, Joe. Be yourself, behave yourself. Be an example to your race as well as a champion.

Joe Louis was on his way to becoming the most-written-about man in America. Sportswriters repeatedly said that Louis was popular with both whites and blacks. These estimates of Louis's popularity were not based on public-opinion polls; the reporters were writing off the tops of their heads. They took Louis's popularity among blacks for granted, and they sensed that Louis was popular with whites because so many white fans paid to see him fight. The Louis-Carnera bout drew the biggest fight crowd in New York since 1930, and reporters agreed that Louis was reviving interest in boxing and was the greatest gate attraction since Dempsey.

Joe Louis was not the only man turning boxing upside down in the summer of 1935. Only twelve days before Louis fought Carnera, challenger Jimmy Braddock outpointed heavyweight champion Max Baer. It was one of the biggest upsets in boxing history. Braddock, the new champion, had lost twenty-six fights in his career. Like everyone else, Madison Square Garden promoter Jimmy Johnston had assumed that Baer would beat Braddock, and he had committed a fatal contractual mistake. Johnston had signed Baer and Braddock to the standard championship fight contracts, with a clause in each fighter's contract that if he won, he would fight his next title defense under Garden promotion. Because he lost, Baer had no further contractual obligation to Johnston or the Garden. He was free to sign with Mike Jacobs and the 20th Century Sporting Club. Baer might have been able to get a rematch with Braddock, but the new champion was in no hurry to risk his new title in a fight with a top-flight contender. Besides, the Baer-Braddock fight had drawn fewer fans than the Louis-Carnera fight. Joe Louis had emerged as the top gate attraction in the heavyweight division; a Baer-Louis fight would make a fortune. The title could wait. Baer signed with Jacobs to fight Louis in September.

In the meantime Jacobs scheduled Louis against Kingfish Levinsky, who had been the fifth-ranked heavyweight the year before. Over 50,000 fans filled Chicago's Comiskey Park to see Louis fight Levinsky on August 7, 1935.

Less than an hour before the fight was to start, Jacobs stopped by Levinsky's dressing room. Levinsky was clearly afraid; he was one man who had read enough about Joe Louis. Jacobs gave orders to start the fight half an hour early, worried that Levinsky might not make it into the ring if he had more time to think.

"Why? It's too early," an Illinois Boxing Commission official said.

"It's gonna rain," Jacobs said. The official looked up into a clear sky.

As Louis and Blackburn walked toward the ring, Blackburn said, "Man, I don't feel so good; been drinking too much."

"You just walk up the steps with me one time; that's all you have to do," Louis said. Then Louis had an idea. "Chappie, if I knock him out in the first round, would you quit drinking for six months?"

"Okay, okay."

Louis knocked Levinsky down three times in the first two minutes of round one. After the third knockdown Levinsky got up quickly but staggered backward into the ropes, helpless. Louis hit him with two lefts, and Levinsky sat down on the middle strand of the ropes. Louis stood over him, waiting for Levinsky to fall, but still Levinsky sat. Louis shuffled, light on his feet, readying punches but not wanting to hit the defenseless boxer. Finally, the referee stepped in front of Louis to give Levinsky a standing count. But two seconds later the ref, indecisive, motioned Louis back toward Levinsky.

"Don't let him hit me again," Levinsky begged. The referee stepped back in front of Louis and called the fight. Back in the dressing room, Blackburn said to Louis, "Chappie, about that drinking, would you let me off the hook?"

The next day Mike Jacobs announced that Louis would fight Max Baer on September 24 in Yankee Stadium. Although Jim Braddock was now champion, the Louis-Baer fight was billed—

quite correctly—as a match between the world's two best heavy-weights. Baer had all the tools to be a great fighter. He was 6 feet 2½ inches tall and weighed 210 pounds. He had a murderous right hand and could take a punch himself. He had knocked out former champions Carnera and Max Schmeling of Germany. But Baer never learned to box and never took conditioning seriously. When he lost to Braddock, he had been badly out of shape.

Louis-Baer generated more prefight publicity than any boxing match since Dempsey met Tunney in 1927. With the aftermath of one fight merging into the buildup for another, Louis became even more the celebrity—and a racial curiosity. Although Louis had shown mercy in the final seconds of the Levinsky fight, his devastating performance reinforced impressions of him as a "jungle killer"; to the writers, that was just too good an image to let go.

Paul Gallico of the *New York Daily News* took Louis's animal image even further than his colleagues. Gallico came from a cultured background, a rarity for sportswriters in those days. His father was a concert pianist, and Gallico himself graduated from Columbia University. In 1923 he became the sports editor of the *Daily News*, and from 1924 to 1936 Gallico's popular sports column was syndicated nationwide. Television was not yet born, and network radio was in its infancy—in influence, Gallico was his era's equivalent of a Howard Cosell or a Brent Musberger.

As a sportswriter, Gallico had been sympathetic to black athletes, and more than one black writer complimented him on his fairness. But watching Louis train, even this liberal and cultured New Yorker could not shake off the overwhelming prejudice of his day:

> I felt myself strongly ridden by the impression that here was a mean man, a truly savage person, a man on whom civilization rested no more securely than a shawl thrown over one's shoulders, that, in short, here was perhaps for the first time in many generations the perfect prizefighter. I had the feeling that I was in the room with a wild animal.

On the eve of the Louis-Baer fight Gallico wrote:

> Louis, the magnificent animal. He lives like an animal,
> untouched by externals. He eats. He sleeps. He fights. He
> is as tawny as an animal and he has an animal's concentra-
> tion on his prey. Eyes, nostrils, mouth, all jut forward to
> the prey. One has the impression that even the ears strain
> forward to catch the sound of danger. He enters the arena
> with his keepers, and they soothe and fondle him and stroke
> him and whisper to him and then unleash him. When the
> leash slips, he fights. He prowls from his corner cruelly and
> stealthily, the way the lion prowled into the Roman arena
> when the bars were raised and stood blinking in the light
> for a moment and then headed for the kill.
>
> He lives like an animal, fights like an animal, has all the
> cruelty and ferocity of a wild thing. What else dwells
> within that marvelous, tawny, destructive body? The cow-
> ardice of an animal? The whipped lion flees. The animal
> law is self-preservation. Is he all instinct, all animal? Or
> have a hundred million years left a fold upon his brain? I
> see in this colored man something so cold, so hard, so cruel
> that I wonder as to his bravery. Courage in the animal is
> desperation. Courage in the human is something incalculable
> and divine. It acquits itself over pain and panic.

Another image, just as stereotypical, shadowed stories about
Louis. Journalists repeatedly wrote that Louis slept and ate a
lot, read the comics, rooted for the Detroit Tigers, and liked
to play baseball and golf. Coupled with the habit of quoting
Louis in Uncle Remus dialect, these stories began to shape an
image of Louis as a typical "darkie."

There was no truth to any of these generalizations. Even in
the ring, much less outside it, Louis did not exhibit cruelty. He
did not foul or eagerly attack his opponents when they were
hurt or show pleasure at their pain. Nor was he indolent; Louis
trained hard, and any writer who covered his training camps
knew it. As far as his mind went, Louis was no intellectual, but
what boxer was? All this imagery arose from one thing and one
thing only: Louis's race.

Far from being limited to southern newspapers or to a few racist writers, these stereotypes appeared regularly in the work of the most urbane and sophisticated newsmen of the day. Gallico was one; another was John Kieran, the intellectual dean of sportswriting and brain of the "Information, Please" radio quiz show. Kieran then had the *New York Times*'s prestigious "Sports of the Times" space, and he devoted several columns to Louis's sleeping habits. Kieran nicknamed Louis "Shufflin' Joe" and rarely called him anything else; he was still using the nickname ten years later.

Newspaper coverage leading up to the Baer fight centered on Louis, and its sheer volume overshadowed other fighters. Ed W. Smith of the *West Coast Sports Digest* wrote:

> James J. Braddock is the new heavyweight champion of the world and should be in the very center of the stage and in the full flare of the flood light. But he isn't. That precious and financially luscious spot is occupied by a colored man, the astonishing Joe Louis.

Even southern papers, which traditionally paid little attention to black athletes, used wire service copy on Louis and sent their sports columnists to see him fight.

Unfazed by all the attention, Louis went through the familiar motions of training for another fight. He had other things on his mind, as well. In December 1934 he had met Marva Trotter, a beautiful nineteen-year-old secretary at the *Chicago Defender*, a black newspaper. Louis shyly courted her during his brief vacations from training, and he more than made up for his lack of boldness by rapidly becoming rich and famous. By the summer of 1935 Louis was the most celebrated black man in America; women sought him. He did not hesitate to take advantage of his new status, but while enjoying other women, he fell in love with Marva Trotter. Julian Black encouraged Louis to marry her. Black and John Roxborough both had reasons to approve the match. Marva Trotter was smart, ambitious, well-spoken, and came from a middle-class family. Most important, she was black. As Louis remembered wryly in his autobiography, "No Jack Johnson problem here." Louis proposed to Marva over the phone from his training camp, and Black and Roxborough made arrangements for the wedding. At first they planned the wedding for the day after the fight, but Louis insisted on marrying beforehand—he wanted to come home to a bride after the fight.

On the morning of September 24, 1935, Joe Louis got to the offices of the New York Boxing Commission before Max Baer. After waiting for Baer a few minutes in a roomful of babbling reporters, Louis sat down, pulled a newspaper over his head, and went to sleep. He didn't wake up until Baer touched him on the shoulder and said, "Come on, Joe, let's go down and see what we weigh." Baer weighed in at 210½, Louis at 199½.

At six in the evening Louis woke up from another nap in the apartment of a friend at 381 Edgecomb Avenue, on Harlem's Sugar Hill. He put on a gray suit and a white shirt without a tie and went downstairs to a bigger apartment for his wedding ceremony. The streets outside were jammed with fans waiting to cheer Louis as he left for the fight; Marva Trotter and her sister came into the building through a fire escape to avoid the crowd. Julian Black and his wife witnessed the signing of the marriage license. The wedding started at 7:45. Marva Trotter's brother, a minister, conducted the ceremony. Julian Black was best man. John Roxborough, Jack Blackburn, and a few of Louis's close friends watched. At 8:00, Louis left for the fight.

The new Mrs. Joseph Louis Barrow had a ringside seat when announcer Joe Humphreys introduced the two fighters:

> We'll be brief because you want action, and I'm here for that poipose to give it to ya. Main event. Fifteen rounds. Principals. Presenting . . . the sensational . . . Californian and former world's . . . heavyweight . . . champion, Max . . . Baer! [Cheers].
>
> His worthy opponent, the new . . . sensational . . . pugilistic product. Although . . . colored . . . he stands out in the same class with Jack Johnson . . . and Sam Langford. The idol of his people, none other . . . than Joe . . . Louis!

By the fourth round Max Baer was on his last legs. He had been bleeding and confused by the second round; he hit Louis with two punches after the bell. Louis just stared at him. In the third round Baer went down for a nine count. At the end of the round Louis knocked him down again, but the bell saved Baer at the count of four. Radio announcer Clem McCarthy, broadcasting to 130 stations over the NBC-WEAF-WJZ network, tried to keep up with Louis's punches in the fourth round:

> Max straightened up, and Louis gives him another left. Now Louis is in close, and Baer ties him up. And Louis is backing away, but he comes in on Baer. They're right above me as I talk now, Baer with his back to me, and Louis gives him two left jabs. But Baer wants more. Louis leads with a left, and Baer has got his hands back close against him. Now and then he sticks out—he ducks his head back that time, and he got a left, ah, good stiff left jolt on the chin. And now he missed with a left that, ah, Louis ducked and went under. Louis gave him a left full in the face, a left over the eye. Louis another left, another left, and Louis is ready with that right at any instant. Now they are out there in the middle of the ring, fiddling; neither one has made a move for about five seconds, and then Louis jabbed him with a left. Now Louis is following up another left; aw, these lefts are like—but there came a fast right, a right swing right across that got Max high on the jaw, and Max went into a clinch. The referee orders them to break. They're over here against the rope. Max has got his back [oohhhhh!] and he took an awful right and then a left to the jaw, and he has gone to his knees. He's down, and the count is four . . . five . . . six. Baer's on one knee, seven, eight, nine. Baer is not up [booo!], and Baer is on his knee at the count of ten. Your fight is all over; your fight is all over. The boys are coming into the ring with the speed of a Buick. Of a new Buick, and I'm going up to see these fighters if I can.

When asked about taking the final count on one knee, Baer told a reporter, "I could have struggled up once more, but when I get executed, people are going to have to pay more than twenty-five dollars a seat to watch it."

Bill McCormick of the *Washington Post* wrote a typical account of the fight:

> Stalking like a panther on the hunt from the first round, in which he tasted madcap Maxie's most powerful punch, then stood toe-to-toe with the former titleholder, pounding his face into a bloody mess, the dusky detonator twice drove Baer to the canvas in the third round in which the bell saved him.
>
> Baer's instinct for the spectator stayed with him even in the third round as he sank to the canvas for the first time in his ring career and waved a careless hand, covered with his own blood, toward the corner from which the sensational Negro was eying him with an impassive face, eyes filled with blood lust.

That Louis had said his wedding vows only hours before made his victory over Baer seem even more violent. Paul Gallico wrote a syndicated column entitled "Husband-Executioner":

> He went from tenderness to terror, and there is no figuring, or knowing, or even believing a man like that. . . . Here was the coldest concentration ever a man displayed. And I wonder if his new bride's heart beat a little with fear that this terrible thing was hers. She must still remember his glances, and the pressure of his arms and his silky voice, so few hours before.
>
> There is no more wonderful moment for a woman than when she faces what she believes is her god and takes to herself her man. "I now pronounce you man and wife."
> Br-r-r-r-r!
> The thing is macabre. . . . If Baer had offered more resistance, and there had been no rules, or referee, Louis would have killed him with his hands and never so much as blinked an eye, or altered the shape of his half-parted lips.

By demolishing the former heavyweight champion, Louis firmly established himself as the greatest fighter in the world. Baer had been the last white fighter thought to have a chance against Louis; Braddock, the champion, was considered a pushover. Sportswriters revealed an awareness of the fight's racial implications. More often than they had when writing about

Louis's previous opponents, white reporters identified Max Baer as "white."

Before the fight Shirley Povich of the *Washington Post* reported a widespread rumor: "They say [Baer] will surpass himself in the knowledge that he is the lone White Hope for the defense of Nordic supremacy in the prize ring." After Baer's failure, several reporters, remembering a previous time when a black man had been the best heavyweight in the world, announced the dawn of a new "white hope" era. Simon Burick of the *Dayton Daily News* wrote, "The Brown Bomber has struck again, and a new hunt for 'White Hopes' is already under way." Gregory Kirksy of the United Press wrote, "A new white hope epoch was ushered in today on the fist of Brown Man Joe Louis." These white reporters assumed that the white public would react negatively to Louis and would prefer a white champion. Shirley Povich remembered in an interview nearly a half-century later:

> To me it was apparent in terms of the times that people insisted that the good thing was a white champion and a bad thing was a black champion. Simple as that. All people have natural prejudices, this is a prejudice of the American scene.

But in a column written the day after the fight, Povich noted:

> In the case of Joe Louis, though, it is obvious that the reaction has softened. There has been no great umbrage, no severely ruffled pride among the great body of whites. Never did the public as a whole show a greater tolerance for the black man. If it did not care to see Joe Louis beat Max Baer and thus pave the way for the return of the title to the black race, then, at least, it did not kick up a great fuss about it. . . .
> At Yankee Stadium the other evening, the cheers that greeted Louis almost shamed in volume the applause that greeted Baer's introduction. It seemed that the crowd wanted the better man to win. Twenty-five years ago, even less, it would not have been a question of skill or conduct, but color. Baer had not been a popular fellow. A consummate braggart, a playboy and clown, he had profaned the

popularity that was his after his conquest of Carnera. Yet, he was white. But it seems that didn't make any difference.

But Jonathan Mitchell of the *New Republic* saw beyond this. Mitchell reacted against the popular perception of Louis, seeing him as a man who could undo black stereotypes. Of Louis, he wrote:

> He reeks of study, practice, study. Any romantic white person who believes that the Negro possesses a distinctive quality ought to see Louis. He suggests a gorilla or a jungle lion as much as would an assistant professor at the Massachusetts Institute of Technology.

Mitchell then asked the real question: Would Louis make more than a superficial breakthrough in race relations?

> Baer must have meant something to many people. He made wisecracks and went to parties and was a harbinger of the return of the old days. He was Broadway, he was California and Florida, he represented the possession of money once more and spending it.
>
> This saddle-colored, dour-faced, tongue-tied, studious youth, who is punishing Baer, . . . what does he represent?

5

"THE FINGER OF GOD"

After the Baer fight Mike Jacobs, John Roxborough, and Julian Black began laying plans to make Joe Louis the world's heavyweight champion. They would have to deal with Jimmy Johnston and the Madison Square Garden Corporation, which controlled heavyweight champion Jimmy Braddock. The championship was Johnston's last bargaining chip in the battle for control of big-time boxing, and Johnston was determined to make Jacobs sacrifice the independence of the 20th Century Sporting Club in exchange for a title fight.

But Mike Jacobs had cards of his own to play. The most important was his control of Joe Louis. The public now considered Louis the best fighter in the world, and he drew crowds. No one took Jimmy Braddock very seriously as a champion, and Braddock lacked Louis's box-office appeal. Louis could continue to make money fighting lesser lights, but Braddock would need a fight against a legitimate contender to draw a big gate. Besides Louis, only one fighter in the world could possibly be considered a legitimate contender.

Max Schmeling of Germany came to America in 1928, where his strong right-hand punch and facial resemblance to Jack Dempsey drew favorable comparisons to the Manassa Mauler. After winning the heavyweight championship in 1930 on a foul by Jack Sharkey, Schmeling defended his title successfully against Young Stribling in 1931 before losing a questionable decision to Sharkey in a rematch. Schmeling beat Mickey

Walker in September of 1932, then fell into an inexplicable slump. Max Baer knocked Schmeling out in ten rounds, and Schmeling then lost a decision to Steve Hamas, a mediocre American fighter, in February 1934. Schmeling returned to Europe and at first fared no better, drawing a match with Paulino Uzcudun, a Spanish heavyweight he had previously defeated. But Schmeling then proceeded to knock out Walter Neusel in August of 1934 and kayoed Steve Hamas in a rematch on March 10, 1935. In July, Schmeling won a twelve-round decision against Uzcudun.

Schmeling put out feelers for a return to America. He wanted a championship match with Braddock. Jimmy Johnston surely would have liked to deal with Schmeling rather than with Mike Jacobs, but Louis's knockouts of Carnera, Levinsky, and Baer had put Louis first in line for a shot at the title. The New York Boxing Commission informed Schmeling that he would have to fight Louis before he could fight Braddock. Schmeling agreed to face Louis the following June. Mike Jacobs was delighted with the prospects for the bout; he expected another big gate, and with Schmeling out of the way, Braddock would have to fight Louis.

To build up interest and to invite comparisons between Louis and Schmeling, Jacobs offered Paulino Uzcudun $19,000 to come to the United States and fight Louis. Jacobs scheduled the Louis-Uzcudun fight for December 13, in Madison Square Garden, significantly concluding the deal with Col. John Reed Kilpatrick, chairman of the board of the Garden corporation, not with Jimmy Johnston. The Garden corporation had never before leased its arena to a rival boxing promoter, but Kilpatrick showed an early willingness to deal with Jacobs; the handwriting was on the wall, and the Garden could not afford to ignore Uncle Mike. Jacobs agreed to pay the Garden a flat rental fee plus a percentage of the profits.

On December 6, Max Schmeling sailed into New York Harbor on the S.S. *Bremen*. Schmeling had come to America to watch Louis fight Uzcudun, to sign a contract with Mike Jacobs, and to help publicize his upcoming fight with Louis. Schmeling also came on a mission for his government. The International Olympic Committee had awarded the 1936 Olympic Games to Berlin in 1932, a year before Adolf Hitler became chancellor of Germany. After Hitler consolidated his dictatorship, suppressed civil liberties, and began his persecutions of Jews, some Americans called for a boycott of the Olympics, led by Jeremiah T. Mahoney, who headed the Amateur Athletic Union. Mahoney wrote an open letter in October 1935 to Dr. Theodor von Lewald, president of the German Olympic Committee, accusing the Nazis of excluding Jewish athletes from participation in Germany's Olympic program.

The American boycott movement disturbed Hitler and the Nazis, who were planning to use the Olympics as a showcase for their new regime. To forestall criticism, Hitler allowed a few token Jewish athletes to participate in German Olympic trials. Dr. Lewald contacted Schmeling, Germany's most prominent and popular athlete, before the boxer left for America and asked him to carry a letter to Avery Brundage, then a young official on the American Olympic Committee. In a meeting with Brundage and other American Olympic officials in a New York hotel room, Schmeling delivered the letter from Lewald and promised Brundage that German athletes would guarantee fair treatment of Jewish athletes, Americans, and others. Brundage was already disposed to send the American Olympic team to Berlin, and most of the Olympic Committee members agreed with him.

Schmeling then went to work publicizing his fight with Louis. He gathered an entourage of reporters and paid a visit to the New York Boxing Commission to act out a decision that had actually been made weeks before. Schmeling asked for permission to fight Jimmy Braddock for the title, and the commission told him it would not sanction the match because Joe Louis was the more deserving challenger. "I will fight Joe Louis, then," Schmeling said, and he marched the reporters over to the offices of the 20th Century Sporting Club, where Mike Jacobs announced that Schmeling would fight Louis on June 18, 1936, in Yankee Stadium.

Schmeling went out to Pompton Lakes to see Louis train and had a ringside seat in sold-out Madison Square Garden on December 13 when Louis fought Paulino Uzcudun. Louis's professionalism impressed Schmeling. Louis and his handlers carried themselves with an air of utter confidence. The preparations in Louis's corner were precise; no one spoke. Between rounds Jack Blackburn would say a few soft words in Louis's ear, and Louis would go out and hammer his opponent for another round. Schmeling could not help but notice Louis's power and quickness, but he thought he saw a weakness in Louis's style. Louis brought his left hand back too low after a jab, leaving himself open to a right-hand counterpunch. Schmeling was a strong right-hand puncher.

Others watching the fight saw no weaknesses in Louis, only strength. By 1935, Paulino Uzcudun had passed his prime. His only remaining claim to respectability was that he had never been knocked out. Against Louis, Uzcudun's sole concern was trying to stay on his feet for the full fifteen rounds. Uzcudun came out in a crouch, bent forward at the waist, with his arms held across his face, forearms parallel to the ground. Harry Markson, who covered the fight for the *Bronx Home News*, remembered:

Louis kept popping away, popping away, but his [Uzcudun's] arms were always there. Finally, in the fourth round, Louis sort of stepped back and Uzcudun separated his arms like this to see where the hell Joe was and in that infinitesimal fraction of a second Louis lashed out with a right-hand punch that lifted this 200-pound Uzcudun right off his feet and deposited him on the other side of the ring. His head bounced off the lower rope. And when he finally climbed to his feet, at eight or nine, his face was smashed and Art Donovan had to stop the fight. I can't begin to describe that punch. I still see that after all these years. When they talk about a devastating blow, this was the hardest punch I've ever seen thrown.

The punch drove two of Uzcudun's teeth through his lower lip. After sitting in his dressing room for twenty minutes, Uzcudun got up to take a shower and fell over.

Mike Jacobs had already scheduled a fight for Louis against Charley Retzlaff, a competent young boxer, on January 17, 1936, in Chicago just two and a half weeks after the Uzcudun fight. Jacobs wanted to cash in while the public's enthusiasm for the new heavyweight sensation still ran high. Blackburn had trained Retzlaff a few years before and warned Louis to be careful, but his only real concern was that Louis might be overtrained from such a busy year in the ring. Blackburn kept Louis's sparring down to a minimum but made sure that Louis ran five miles each morning. As always, Louis would be in excellent shape.

Early in the first round, Charley Retzlaff made several offensive passes at Louis but took wicked counterpunches as he charged in. Ready to try again, Retzlaff dropped his left hand to his waist for a left hook, his weight coming forward as his hand swung in an arc for the right side of Louis's head. Louis leaned back and was quick enough to get his right hand inside Retzlaff's punch, pushing Retzlaff's arm so that the punch harmlessly passed Louis's head. Retzlaff was now leaning forward, the left hand, which had missed, straight out and useless around Louis's waist and his right hand down. Joe Louis cocked his own left with his elbow bent, his arm at a right angle to his body, and drove it around with his shoulder. As he delivered the punch, he was falling back with the momentum of Retzlaff's charge, but his right foot was down and solidly planted even as his left foot was coming off the floor in a step backward.

Louis drove his whole shoulder and back across with the punch, and Retzlaff's head jerked sideways when it landed. Retzlaff fell in the direction he had started his punch, toward Louis's right side, and Louis leaned away to let him fall.

Retzlaff landed on his hands and knees, then got up on his haunches to wait for the referee to count nine, trying to take all the time he could to clear his head. As the referee counted, Retzlaff lost his balance and fell backward, catching himself with his left hand. He got up in time, wobbling. Joe Louis came out of his neutral corner.

Louis feinted with his left and started to bring up his right, but Retzlaff held him off with a left jab that was really just a stiffarm. Retzlaff tried to follow with a right brought up from the floor, but Louis smothered the punch with his left arm and shoulder. Now in close, Louis landed a left uppercut, a punch that traveled a foot at most but nevertheless jerked Retzlaff's head and shoulders up. Retzlaff moved to Louis's right, and Louis turned to face him.

Retzlaff came in again, swinging a left hook that landed on Louis's forehead, moving Louis's head back slightly, but Louis simultaneously threw a left hook, a real roundhouse, arm extended at his side and whipping around in a full arc. It landed on Retzlaff's face, and Retzlaff leaned precariously over his left leg before recovering his balance.

Louis circled around to Retzlaff's left and threw a right hook around Retzlaff's outstretched left arm, leaning forward on his left foot as he threw the punch, then stepped forward with his right foot and threw a shorter left, with his elbow bent. Retzlaff, who had his left arm extended trying to block the first right, now tried to bring his right glove up to block Louis's left. He was too late. Louis's left glove moved inside Retzlaff's right arm and hit Retzlaff squarely in the stomach, lifting Retzlaff up on his toes and backing him up as he tried to hold Louis with both arms. Louis threw another short right to the body as Retzlaff hugged him, then pushed Retzlaff away easily with both hands.

In a characteristic move, Louis put his left glove out to touch the side of Retzlaff's jaw, as if to hold it in place or get the range for the right hook he was readying at waist level. Retzlaff, groggy and reacting on instinctual fear, raised both hands to block. Louis threw an uppercut under Retzlaff's arms that snapped Retzlaff's head back, and Retzlaff's arms waved comically in the air. Retzlaff backed away, rising up on his toes and cringing against the ropes as his right arm and leg touched them.

Louis feinted with his left, and Retzlaff balled up and put both hands out to protect against a left that never came. Louis brought a roundhouse right around to the side of Retzlaff's head, driving him back against the ropes and spinning him around so that Retzlaff's back was turned to Louis. Louis took a step back as Retzlaff half turned to face him. Retzlaff's right arm was tangled in the ropes. Louis hit him with a glancing left uppercut, a right hook to the ribs, then a left and a right to the head.

Retzlaff's head and shoulders sagged on the ropes, his back again turned to Louis. Retzlaff tried to move away to the side, Louis threw another left hook, and Retzlaff bounced off the ropes into a right uppercut. Louis stepped aside as Retzlaff fell.

The referee pushed Louis toward a neutral corner. Louis took a step, looked down at Retzlaff, then turned his back and jogged to the neutral corner, a twenty-one-year-old who had been fighting for less than two minutes and was still frisky. When Louis got to the corner, he jumped and spun around in the air to look back at Retzlaff, who was sitting up with the referee standing over him. The timekeeper was standing at the side of the ring, a fat white man with a round face, his right arm moving rhythmically up and down.

Retzlaff rolled over, put his right hand out, and got to his knees. He toppled over as the count reached ten and the referee waved his hands over the fallen fighter, then grabbed Retzlaff around the arms to help him up.

Louis, who had watched the end of the count with his arms resting on top of the ropes on either side of the corner post, came forward with his arms dragging behind him like wings, bowing his head but bouncing as he moved toward the man he had just defeated. Louis reached down with his right arm and helped Retzlaff up, lifting him under the left arm. Jack Blackburn came running up, grabbing Louis's arm and leaning into the crowd around Retzlaff to see if Retzlaff was all right. Retzlaff's handlers sat their fighter on his stool, and Blackburn turned away, pulling Louis with him. Cops and cameramen and officials were climbing into the ring.

A clause in the contracts Louis and Schmeling signed forbade either man to fight again before their match in June. Louis welcomed the chance for a vacation. He had been in almost constant training for two years. Already the pressures of being a leading heavyweight contender and a symbol of his race, coupled with the temptations of his new wealth and fame, were producing a kind of schizophrenia in Louis. While in training he was under constant scrutiny, and his managers expected him to restrain his emotions and work to create an inoffensive public image. That meant trying to get along with white reporters, people who were alien to him and made him feel uncomfortable. Louis also resented the things white writers were saying about him, calling him catlike and a killer, but his managers told him never to argue with or challenge whites. Blackburn, Roxborough, and Black ran every detail of his life in training camp. They told him when to wake up, when and what to eat, what exercises to do, told him to rest when he wasn't working out, forbade him to make love, and sent him to bed early.

Outside of training camp, though, Louis had the world at his feet. He was the most famous black in America, a handsome man whose athletic prowess gave him an irresistible aura of physical attractiveness. Women flocked to Louis. Few men could have resisted such temptation, and Louis was not inclined to try. Because he had to abstain from sex while in training, Louis felt he was entitled to enjoy himself between fights. Louis was a true believer in the double standard. He did not seem to care how much his playing around hurt his wife but expected Marva to remain faithful to him. In the spring of 1936 Louis went to Hollywood to make a movie. *The Spirit of Youth* was a low-budget film, loosely based on Louis's life, about a dishwasher who becomes champion of the world. Louis took Marva along, but her presence did not prevent him from having affairs with many starlets, white and black. When he wasn't in Hollywood, Louis had his pick of Harlem showgirls or camp followers. He developed a serious case of physical vanity, dressing sharply and occasionally bragging about his sexual exploits to close friends.

Louis had met Marva after his boxing career was in full swing. They never established a regular home life together. Louis's training schedule kept him away for months at a time, and when he wasn't in training, Louis had too much free time and too many opportunities to enjoy himself. He didn't have to wake up for work in the morning and had plenty of money to spend and women to meet. He didn't want to sit home with his wife. At first, Marva Louis liked sharing Louis's hectic schedule, traveling with him to make personal appearances and sampling the night life in various cities. But Louis often preferred to go out with a gang of his buddies and wanted his wife to stay behind. Eventually, Marva tired of traveling all the time and wanted her husband to settle down and spend more time with her.

Marva didn't like the people her husband associated with, either. She came from a solidly middle class family and had visions of elegance. She wanted a social life to go along with her status as the first lady of black America. Her husband accommodated her interests only rarely, when they fit his desires, as well. He liked to ride horses, so the Louises sponsored several horse shows for the black aristocracy.

But apart from his physical vanity, Louis was a man free of pretensions, social or any other kind. He came from a poor background, and he felt most comfortable in the presence of people from similar backgrounds. He kept up with some of his boyhood friends, including Freddie Guinyard. He employed his stepbrother, Pat Brooks, as his chauffeur. Louis liked to go to bars or nightclubs with a group of his friends. He was quiet. He didn't drink, partly out of concern for his public image but largely because he didn't need to. He didn't need to fit in with any crowd; he was always the center of attention. He sipped on a ginger ale or some orange juice and listened to the conversation around him, signed autographs for fans who approached him, always picked up the check, and picked up a woman when he wanted to. He laughed easily.

Perhaps as a reaction to being scrutinized by an alien culture, Louis often disappeared into black neighborhoods for days at a time, out of the sight and reach of white reporters and his wife and managers, as well. He was welcome everywhere, and he had many cronies or lady friends he could hole up with.

Part of being a heavyweight contender, and a vital part of Louis's self-image, was being rich. Louis's family never had had enough money, and to a poor kid money is for spending—there are too many pressing wants to think of postponing gratification. Louis never shook his childhood conception of money, never saved for the future or wondered how he would make money when his boxing career was over. His role models were the flashy spenders in the Detroit ghetto, in boxing circles, and in Harlem nightclubs. When he ran out of money, he borrowed against future purses from Mike Jacobs.

There was a charming side to Louis's fiscal irresponsibility—most of the money went to other people. Everyone who knew Louis has a story about some stranger who approached Louis and asked him for money and walked away with more than he or she asked for. Louis was a big tipper. He bought his wife and his many lady friends expensive gifts. He supported his brothers and sisters and a shifting entourage of hangers-on. He bought his mother a house and supported her, as well. Louis contributed to every black cause—that, too, was part of his self-image. In the summer of 1935 Louis visited home and was distressed to see that many of his boyhood friends did not have jobs and were going nowhere. He bought them a bus and uniforms, christened them the Brown Bomber softball team, and gave them the money to start touring the country. He promised to help them draw fans by playing with them when he could.

While Louis played, Max Schmeling went home to Germany. American reporters had laughed after the Louis-Uzcudun fight when Schmeling told them, "I see something." But Schmeling was a serious man. He took films of Louis's fights home to study.

When he got back to Germany, Schmeling lunched with Adolf Hitler in Munich. Hitler asked Schmeling about his meeting with the American Olympic Committee and thanked Schmeling for helping to prevent a boycott. Hitler also asked Schmeling about his fight with Louis. The dictator was upset that Schmeling was risking Germany's reputation in a fight against a black man when there was so little chance of victory. With his usual self-confidence, Schmeling assured his Fuehrer that he had a good chance to win, and Hitler presented the boxer with an autographed picture of himself. Schmeling hung the picture of Hitler in his study.

Louis went into training for his fight with Schmeling in early May 1936. Instead of setting up camp in familiar Pompton Lakes, Louis's managers decided to train in Lakewood, New Jersey. Lakewood was a resort town, a little warmer than New York City, and a popular off-season vacation spot for New Yorkers before traveling to Florida became easier and cheaper. Louis was so popular that thousands of spectators came to watch him train. Because Lakewood's hotels could accommodate more visitors than Pompton Lakes, Black and Roxborough thought they would make more money training there.

The resort atmosphere did not help Louis's training, but Louis was not in the mood, anyway. He had just turned twenty-two. He had faced the best boxers in the world and knocked them out, and neither he nor anyone else expected Max Schmeling to be different. Dangerously overconfident, Louis cut back on his roadwork and refused to skip rope or punch the bags. He was so eager to get his sparring over with that he refused to take the full minute's rest between rounds.

Louis did not get enough rest when he wasn't training. Lakewood had a good golf course, and Louis, who had been playing golf for over a year, had developed a real passion for the game. He often played with sportswriters, especially with Hype Igoe and Walter Stewart. Though golf may have helped Louis's relations with the press, it did not help his boxing. Jack Blackburn told Louis, "Chappie, that ain't good for you. The timing's different. And them muscles you use in golf, they ain't the same ones you use hitting a man. Besides, being out in the sun don't do you no good. You'll be dried out." For the first and last time in his career, Louis did not listen to his trainer.

Blackburn was just as unsuccessful trying to keep women away from Louis. Within boxing circles, there is a persistent belief that a fighter should not have sex in the weeks before a fight. Many trainers believe that sex tires a fighter and that the absence of sex makes a fighter meaner and more aggressive. A lack of medical corroboration has weakened those beliefs over the years, but in Louis's time "Thou shalt not make love before a fight" was one of boxing's commandments. Louis, who usually abstained while in training, broke that commandment often before the Schmeling fight. For a while his wife Marva stayed at the Stanley Hotel in Lakewood. Louis's managers asked her to leave because she was distracting Louis from training. She left, but Louis bedded down with a variety of camp followers.

As a result of all his extracurricular activity and indifferent training, Louis was not as sharp as usual in his sparring sessions. One of Louis's sparring partners was Jersey Joe Walcott, then a struggling black heavyweight from Camden, New Jersey, who later fought Louis twice for the world's championship. Walcott made Louis look bad in their first session. The next time Louis was out for revenge and managed to drop Walcott to the canvas, but not without great difficulty. Walcott left camp soon afterward.

A few reporters noted Louis's sluggishness in the ring, but they did not believe it would affect the outcome of the fight. Like the rest of the American public, sportswriters took Louis's dominance in the ring for granted. After watching Louis knock out Carnera, Levinsky, Baer, Uzcudun, and Retzlaff in a total of sixteen rounds, the writers all predicted that Louis would quickly dispose of Schmeling, too. After the Louis-Baer fight, when rumors of a Louis-Schmeling fight first cropped up, Paul Gallico had written, "Warning: To my friend Max Schmeling—stay in Germany. Have no truck with this man. He will do something to you from which you will never fully recover. You haven't a chance."

That sportswriters expected nothing less than a knockout may have added to Louis's overconfidence, but it eventually had a salutary effect on his press image. As reporters got used to Louis's remarkable talent, they were less threatened by it and less likely to ascribe it to savage instincts inherent in blacks. Louis, in turn, got used to reporters. He opened up more around the writers he knew and became more friendly and talkative. Ed Van Every of the *New York Sun* noted before the Baer fight, "Louis is learning how to talk to reporters without pulling into a shell; to meet the crowds that come to his camp to watch him and demand autographs; to laugh and smile once in a while." Walter Stewart of the *New York World-Telegram* wrote a perceptive article about Louis's changing image two months after the Baer fight:

> Time moved on . . . and the scribes began to note a slow change for the worse—Joe was smiling from time to time. The boys turned their assembled backs on this frightful

display with unanimous shudders, for this was hardly cricket. . . . It didn't fit in with the stark killer which had grown up between paragraphs. . . . Joe . . . has forced the press to shove "killer mask No. 54-Z" into the hell box and take up the uninspiring task of painting the Brown Butcher, &c., in the warm colors of a happy colored boy with murder in each hand and the deep laughter of Africa bubbling between perfect teeth.

As seams developed in the deadpan, "jungle killer" image of Louis, the image of Louis as a stereotypical "darkie" came to the fore. More and more, reporters concentrated on how much Louis slept and ate. The Associated Press quoted Monk Harris, one of Louis's black sparring partners, before the Uzcudun fight:

Joe is the eatingest and sleepingest man Ah ever saw. An' what's stranger, the more food he eats, the stronger and better he seems to get. Why it's nothing—nothing at all— for him to sit right down an' eat five chickens for one meal. How that man loves his chicken.

Harris went on to claim that Louis once devoured a twelve-pound turkey for a midnight snack.

White reporters frequently quoted blacks in that kind of Uncle Remus dialect. Joe Louis, who retained parts of a southern accent from his Alabama childhood, often got the Uncle Remus treatment, adding to his stereotypical image. A *New York Evening Journal* cartoonist wrote in a caption, "Use the word 'defeat' Joseph." A cartoon image of Louis said, "Sho. I pops 'em on de chin and dey drags 'em out by de feet." Cartoonists did more than quote Louis in dialect. They often lampooned his features by drawing him with huge lips and a big smile—the same man who had been portrayed a few months earlier as absolutely cruel and unsmiling. One cartoonist pictured Louis in training camp as unconcerned about his upcoming fight with Schmeling: "Worry? Sure I worry—How to crack a hundred in mah golf." Another scene in the cartoon showed Louis stealing food from the kitchen and his black cook, Bill Bottom, chiding him, "Joe—yo' spoil yo' dinnah." Louis replied, "Not my dinner! No deedy." A caption beneath said, "Joe can't go through the kitchen without grabbing a handful—an' eat!!! My-My." Another scene showed Louis sleeping in a hammock, with a caption that said, "Better not have any hammocks near the ring on fight night—or there just won't be any fight."

The jungle-killer image had not disappeared completely. Some writers still described Louis as a cruel, emotionless animal, especially those writers who did not cover Louis regularly and were not on familiar terms with him. A writer for *Time* magazine called Louis "surly and monosyllabic" several months before the Schmeling fight. A week before the fight, Meyer Berger wrote an article for the *New York Times Magazine* in which he rehashed some of the worst writing about Louis from the year before. Berger wrote:

> A physician who has observed the Louis routine compares the bomber to a primordial organism; says in temperament, he is like a one-celled beastie of the mire-and-steaming-ooze period. . . . Fighting, he displays boxing intelligence tantamount to the stalking instinct of the panther. . . . He becomes sheer animal.

The stereotypical treatment of Louis in the press indicated that Louis had not yet won full respect as a human being from white sportswriters and, by extension, the white public. By constantly identifying him as a Negro, by writing about him as a savage animal or a sleepy-eyed southern darkie, white writers defined Joe Louis as different from themselves. But whites did accept Louis as a celebrity and accepted his victories over white boxers. That was new and important ground, given the lack of other black celebrities and the memories of Jack Johnson.

The absence of a white reaction against Louis was a source of endless surprise to white sportswriters, who for years and years wrote columns about Louis's "popularity." The writers generally agreed that his modesty, good behavior, and sportsmanship in the ring had earned the tolerance of the white public.

Harry Stillwell Edwards of the *Atlanta Journal* wrote one of the more remarkable columns of this genre before the Schmeling fight:

> An interesting feature in the case of Joe Louis, the now famous prizefighter, is that he has the sympathy of the south. Not a loudly expressed sympathy, and none of it declared in the southern press. But just start a discussion of the chance for Schmeling in the bout next week, and note the reaction. You will hear the Louis saga in detail—how he was born in Alabama, the grandson of slaves belonging to the Barrows—yes, sir, a fine old family whose darkeys reflected the gentility of their owners—a quiet unassuming colored boy of correct habits; a boy who has never smoked, used alcoholic drinks or chewed tobacco; whose early environment held the bravest of the brave. . . . The significant point is that all "white hope" sentiment, which once went with any kind of white man who fought a black champion in the ring, is, at this time, altogether missing. The white south, that is the masculine element, especially readers of the sports pages of our press, is quietly pulling for the Alabama Twister—the name we have given Joe. . . .
>
> Entering into the south's good-will for this Alabama boy, is his record in the ring. He has fought fair and square in every instance, without ballahoo or bluster. Early in his career, his shrewd managers reminded him of his handicap of race and color, and impressed on him the value of modesty. Not to be ashamed of his race, but to help build it up in the eyes of the world, was, they urged, the best policy. The lesson stuck.

Even if Louis's black skin set him apart, his sudden rise to riches and fame struck a deep and universal chord in the American psyche. From Ben Franklin to Horatio Alger, rags to riches had been an article of faith in the new world, the American dream. The complexities of industrialization and the excesses of America's newly rich businessmen in the late nineteenth century had muddied the dream somewhat; in addition, large corporations came to dominate the American economy, and they were impersonal bureaucracies, often lacking an individual figurehead to capture the public imagination. Sport and entertainment figures thus became the embodiments of the Horatio Alger success story in the twentieth century. Recognizable individuals, operating free of bureaucracies, they also seemed to work outside the tangle of the regular economy. In the middle of the Great Depression, when the economy and the dream weren't working for many Americans, the success of individual sports figures and movie stars was important. That a black boy from the Detroit ghetto could earn several hundred thousand dollars in a single night was like a reaffirmation of faith.

Far from softpedaling Louis's wealth, Jacobs exploited the poor black boy's sudden affluence; it enhanced pubic fascination with Louis. For each fight, Jacobs publicized the percentage of the gross each fighter would get, the exact division of radio and movie fees, and other contractual details. After the fight he announced the attendance, the total gate, and each fighter's purse. The day after a fight Louis and Jacobs would perform a ritual for reporters and cameramen; Louis would come to Jacobs's office, and Jacobs would hand him a check, always in five or six figures, for his share of the gate.

And Louis was making fantastic amounts of money for those days. For the Carnera fight he received $60,000, for Levinsky, $53,000, for Baer, $240,000, for Uzcudun $39,000, for Retzlaff, $23,000. Louis had to take expenses off the top and split those purses with his managers and had to pay income tax on the rest, but the press rarely mentioned that; newspapers always reported Louis's gross purses. Reporters were fond of calculating how much Louis earned per minute. For knocking out Levinsky in the first round, for example, they figured Louis made about $25,000 a minute. The hours Louis spent training for the fight were conveniently forgotten.

Jacobs and Louis's managers told reporters that Louis was saving for the future, that as soon as he had enough salted away, he would retire. By late 1935 John Roxborough claimed that Louis would soon have over $100,000 in life insurance annuities. But this was a fabrication for the sake of image making. The Joe Louis of the newspaper clippings would have done Poor Richard proud; in reality, Louis spent money as fast as it came in.

Louis was making money because he was drawing big crowds. He was a knockout puncher, and fans liked sluggers better than clever, polished boxers who won by decisions. Louis was the most exciting boxer since Dempsey. He was a poor boy made good. And as a successful and celebrated black, he was an absolute phenomenon. Putting all that together, Louis was a sensation. Before the Schmeling fight Damon Runyon wrote:

> It is our guess that more has been written about Louis in the past two years than about any living man over a similar period of time, with the exception of Charles Lindbergh. The Louis record in this respect is utterly astounding in view of the fact that he isn't a champion.

Ed Van Every, a writer for the *New York Sun*, tried to cash in on the craze by quickly writing a book about Louis. Entitled *Joe Louis, Man and Super-Fighter*, the book came out just before the Schmeling fight. It was remarkable in several respects. For one thing, few twenty-two-year-olds are the subjects of full biographies. Even more remarkable, Van Every seemed to believe Louis was fulfilling a holy mission to increase racial tolerance in America. He wrote, "It is, and not extravagant to set down, as though the finger of God had singled this youth out for purposes of His own." Van Every titled his first chapter "Black Moses" and wrote:

> That the Negro race should find a Black Moses who was to prove of incalculable assistance to the great leaders of his people in lighting the way to a broader tolerance on the part of his white brother, and that this ambassador to the finer brotherhood should come up from the mayhap brutalizing paths and byways of pugilism, is as irreconcilable with plausibility as that a Negro could be acceptable in the role of heavyweight champion of the prize ring [again]. . . . For a Negro to become the champion heavyweight pugilist demands that he be something more than the superior human fighter with nature's weapons, since sheer prowess could not be crystallized into an acclaim where even those outside of his own race should insistently favor the Negro champion being recognized as the most worthy contender for the heavyweight boxing crown.

Van Every also believed that Louis and his managers were aware of Louis's role early on. He quoted John Roxborough talking to Louis:

"If you make good and should get to the top, we'll be no party to your letting your race down, for then you'd do your people a lot more harm than your success would be worth."

"I won't let my people down," promised Joe Louis Barrow solemnly.

Though Van Every and other writers continued to play up Joe Louis's popularity and his role as symbol of the black race, the press largely ignored the other symbolic implications of the first Louis-Schmeling fight. Schmeling came from Germany, where Adolf Hitler had been in power for three years. Hitler and the Nazis numbered blacks among the inferior races, and Americans were aware of the racist Nazi ideology.

Despite the isolationism of the United States throughout the 1930s, Americans were not blind to the evils and dangers abroad. The press reported on Europe arming, on German, Italian, Japanese, and Spanish troops on the march, and felt war coming. That sense of impending disaster was part of the fatalism with which many white Americans viewed their Depression-ridden world. On August 1, 1936, the day the Olympics opened in Berlin, the *New York Times* editorialized:

The Olympic Torch is more like a firebrand than a symbol of the welding flame of international sport. . . . All the light in Europe today is like that cast by the Olympic Torch. It is only a flare illuminating dark shapes and bewildering prospects.

By 1936 the establishment press took for granted a public awareness and condemnation of Nazi race policies. Nazi racism made some journalists think about American racism, though they didn't think too hard. The *New York Times* drew this distinction between prejudice in Germany and prejudice in the United States:

In Berlin they have a cheerful habit, whenever Americans criticize the peculiarities of Nazi race philosophy, of turning around and asking how about the way Negroes are treated in the United States. The answer is simple. The colored people in the United States labor under handicaps, discriminations, and in not too many cases, let us hope, injustice and cruelties. But very few decent Americans are proud about it and still fewer literate Americans have made a philosophy of the thing. When we deny certain opportunities and claims to the Negro in this country we do it in the good, old, thick-headed, prejudiced, irrational human fashion.

Perhaps subconsciously, writers did play on the undertone of the political and racial confrontation by constantly identifying Schmeling as a German or a Nazi, just as repetitiously and alliteratively as they identified Louis as a Negro. Writers called Schmeling "the terrific Teuton," "the Nazi nudger," and "the Heil Hitler hero." But the press made few overt references to the symbolic implications of the fight.

Neither did the Nazis, because they thought Schmeling would lose. Fearing a loss, Hitler expressed reservations about the fight to Schmeling, and Joseph Goebbels, the Nazi minister of propaganda, wrote an editorial against the match. But the Nazis could not suppress German interest. The Nazi paper *Volkischer Beobachter* sent a reporter, Arno Hellmis, to America for the fight and devoted several pages to coverage of the fighters in training.

American sportswriters were not inclined to cast Max Schmeling as the villainous representative of an evil Nazi regime. Schmeling had fought in America and made friends here before most Americans had even heard of the Nazis. One reporter wrote: "Almost every sports writer in this country likes Max, who is good natured, gentlemanly, sportsman-like, polite, thoughtful and almost every good thing imaginable." Reporters also admired Schmeling for his courage. By 1936 the sportswriters considered Louis unbeatable and openly pitied any fighter who had to get in a ring with him. Louis's previous opponents, especially Levinsky and Baer, had been unable to hide their fear of Louis from the writers, so the writers probed Schmeling for signs of apprehension. They asked him a thousand variations on the question "Are you afraid, Max?" The answer was always a convincing no.

Besides admiring Schmeling's character, the sportswriters had a natural sympathy for the underdog. Joe Louis had enjoyed that sympathy when he was young and untested. But now Louis was a prohibitive favorite; odds makers listed him at eight-to-one to beat Schmeling.

Arno Hellmis thought there was a racial element to American support for Schmeling. He told his German readers:

> America is in a boxing fever. . . . The racial factor is placed strongly in the foreground, and it is hoped that the representative of the white race will succeed in halting the unusual rise of the Negro. In fact there is no doubt that Max Schmeling, when he enters the ring on Thursday evening, will have the sympathy of all white spectators on his side, and the knowledge of this will be important moral support for him.

On July 18, 1936, Schmeling and Louis went into New York for the weigh-in, but the fight was postponed a day because of rain. Louis did not mind the wait, but the weather bothered him. Rain would keep the fans away, and he would make less money. July 19 was cloudy, and rain threatened until late in the afternoon. Only 40,000 fans showed up at Yankee Stadium, half the crowd Mike Jacobs had expected. Mrs. Lilly Barrow Brooks, Louis's mother, was in the crowd, watching her son fight for the first time.

Schmeling entered the ring first; Louis followed a few seconds later. The boxers and their handlers crowded around referee Arthur Donovan as he gave them prefight instructions. A microphone hanging over Donovan's head threw the referee's words out to the crowd. Louis looked at the floor as Donovan spoke; Schmeling stared at Louis. Schmeling's eyes seemed buried deep in their sockets, beneath his bushy, black, protruding eyebrows. Schmeling's black hair was greased straight back, forming a wave atop his head. The fighters shook hands, went back to their corners, opened their mouths for mouthpieces. At the bell Schmeling walked out slowly. As Louis approached, Schmeling leaned away, weight on his right foot, left arm up protecting his face, right hand cocked under his chin. Schmeling's legs looked thin.

Even while leaning away, Schmeling held his ground. He was a stationary fighter, rarely bobbing or weaving. Louis saw that Schmeling would be easy to jab—exactly what Schmeling hoped Louis would think. Louis jabbed, Schmeling's hair flew up, and Schmeling was just short with a right cross.

Throughout the first three rounds Louis continued to jab, occasionally following with a right hand. He closed Schmeling's left eye and piled up an impressive lead on points. The crowd cheered Louis, anticipating a knockout. But Schmeling was still unhurt, and he was beginning to get the timing of Louis's jabs. In the second round Schmeling landed a right hand counterpunch that momentarily dazed Louis. Between rounds Jack Blackburn warned Louis to watch out for Schmeling's right, to jab and keep his left hand high.

In the fourth round Louis hooked Schmeling with his left, and Schmeling landed a right to Louis's jaw. Louis jabbed, and Schmeling glanced a right-hand counter off Louis's chin. Schmeling was confident now, anticipating Louis's next jab. Louis came in again and threw a quick jab to Schmeling's face. Schmeling's neck rocked back under the impact, but he threw a compact right cross from the side and hit Louis square in the face. Louis staggered back several steps. He looked surprised. Louis crouched and covered up as Schmeling came in. Schmeling landed a right uppercut and a left cross, and Louis backed away from another right. Schmeling pawed at Louis with his left and threw a long right that dropped Louis on the seat of his pants. Yankee Stadium exploded. Joe Louis was down for the first time in his professional career.

Louis got up quickly, as if embarrassed, and hitched up his boxing shorts. When Schmeling came out of his neutral corner, Louis clinched and kept Schmeling away the rest of the round with left jabs.

In the fifth round Schmeling chased Louis. At the end of the round Schmeling was readying a right. The bell rang. Louis dropped his hands, and Schmeling landed the right on Louis's jaw. Louis's handlers jumped into the ring and dragged him back to his corner, but Louis had lost consciousness. He fought the rest of the way on instinct alone. During the sixth round Schmeling tired himself out throwing right hands against Louis's chin. The left side of Louis's face was swelling noticeably. Freddie Guinyard, Louis's boyhood friend, led Mrs. Brooks out of the stadium. "My God, my God, don't let him kill my child," she said. Marva Louis wanted to leave as well, but a friend told her to stay, that her husband would rally.

In the seventh round Schmeling rested, and to the crowd it looked like Louis was recovering. But in the eighth Schmeling took the offensive again. Out on his feet, Louis twice hit Schmeling below the belt. Through the ninth, tenth, and eleventh rounds Schmeling continued to land long, looping right hands to Louis's head. Louis threw punches, but his strength was gone. Louis was displaying incredible endurance. He had taken dozens of solid rights, but still he kept fighting. Schmeling had resigned himself to going for the decision instead of for a knockout, and the crowd thought Louis was still in the fight. So did radio announcers Clem McCarthy and Edwin C. Hill. Before the twelfth round Hill told a national audience:

> I want to tell you a word about the fairness of this crowd. . . . There isn't a trace of that which so many people have been afraid of, racial feeling or anti-Nazism, anything of that kind. These people here in this Yankee Stadium are realizing we've got two great athletes. One may be a little darker than the other, perhaps, that is, but there's no question of anything else. There's no booing of either fighter, neither of Louis or of Schmeling. They're giving each man the breaks. As I say, there's no hissing or booing.

Louis hit Schmeling low again early in the twelfth, and referee Donovan warned him again. By now Schmeling was afraid Louis was fouling intentionally. Under new rules adopted by the New York Boxing Commission, Donovan could not disqualify Louis for low blows; he could only award the round to Schmeling. And if Schmeling went down from a low blow and could not answer the count at ten, he would lose the fight even if the blow was a foul. Because Louis was losing on points, Schmeling believed his opponent had nothing to lose and was trying to win by a low-blow knockout. Schmeling decided to expend his energy and try to put Louis out before that could happen.

Schmeling drove Louis to the ropes with a left-right combination, followed Louis, and hit him with a left-right combination again. Louis clinched, and referee Donovan separated the fighters. Louis jabbed, but Schmeling ducked it, and Louis went back into a clinch. They broke. Schmeling ducked two jabs, hit Louis with a right, and followed with another left-right combination. Louis ducked a left jab and clinched again. He was barely hanging on. Schmeling heard people in the crowd yelling, "Kill him, kill him."

Schmeling hit Louis hard with a left, missed a right, and as Louis tried to start a left hook, Schmeling smashed another right to the jaw. Louis backed away, trying to push at Schmeling to keep the German at bay. A right uppercut from Schmeling brought Louis's hands down, his whole body sagging, and Schmeling threw a roundhouse right. An unmistakable look of fear and surprise came over Louis's face as he saw the punch coming. Louis turned with the force of the punch and fell to his knees, his arms hanging over the middle strand of the ropes. Louis cradled his head in his hands on the rope, then fell backward. He rolled over as if to get up, shook his head, rolled over again, almost on his stomach, and covered his head with his right glove. Donovan reached the count of ten and waved his hands over the invincible "Brown Bomber." Max Schmeling jumped into the air, both arms stretched straight over his head, his face lit with joy.

Far from treating Schmeling as a usurper, the white press and public toasted his victory. Hundreds of Americans sent him telegrams of congratulation, including civic officials like Mayor John Boyd Thatcher of Albany. "The bulk of the domestic congratulatory messages came from the South, where the feeling against Negroes runs high, and was expressed freely," reported the *New York Herald-Tribune*. The senior class of the high school in Lakewood, New Jersey, the town where Louis had trained for the bout, wrote Schmeling, "We couldn't stand him either." Schmeling himself commented sarcastically on the number of Americans jumping on his bandwagon, as writer Harry Markson remembered in an interview forty-six years later:

> The day after the fight, Max Schmeling and his manager, a man named Joe Jacobs, and some other newspapermen went down to a restaurant, a famous restaurant in those days called Dinty Moore's. We sat at a big round table. And everybody kept running over to Max and saying, "Congratulations, Max, you were great. I won a lot of money on you, Max. I won a lot of money on you." And this went on so long that finally Max turned to his manager, Joe Jacobs, and he said, "What's the matter," he said, "nobody bet on Louis?"
> Everybody bet on Louis.

The American press praised Schmeling for his intelligence and courage and for his victory against great odds. One writer said:

> Without exulting over the defeat of Joe Louis it is possible to rejoice at the victory of Max Schmeling because it was a victory against tremendous odds and a victory which revealed exceptional qualities of courage, poise, intelligence, and good, solid character. This has no reference to race or color but is a sizeup of the man as a fighter.

The white press, especially in the South, was quick to consign Louis to mediocrity. O. B. Keeler of the *Atlanta Journal*, never a Louis fan, wrote a column with the head "You Can Have the 'Brown Bomber.'" Keeler went on to say that Louis, "the Pet Pickaninny," was "just another good boxer who had been built-up." Ben Wahrman, a correspondent for the *Richmond Times-Dispatch*, asked what sportswriter would be the first "to change the Negro's name from 'Brown Bomber' to 'Brown Bummer.'" Newspapers all over the country quoted former champion Jack Dempsey, who had spent a great deal of his time in the preceding year sponsoring white hopes to oppose Louis:

Schmeling exposed the fact that Louis has a glass jaw and consequently cannot take a punch. All you have to do to beat him is to walk into him and bang him with a solid punch. I don't think he'll ever whip another good fighter.

Louis's defeat damaged his "jungle killer" image. Under the subhead " 'Dead-Pan' the Bunk," Bob Murphy wrote:

All of this stuff about Louis and the 'dead-pan-killer' business is so much bunk. This 22-year-old Negro is made of much the same stuff as any other boy of his age. He proved it in the dressing room when he wept unashamed.

Another headline proclaimed, "Schmeling Victory Proves to Ring World Every Man Is Human and Can Be Licked." No longer invincible, Louis was now "only" human. In defeat Louis aroused the sympathy of many writers and drew praise for his refusal to make excuses.

The German reaction to Schmeling's victory was predictably ecstatic. Adolf Hitler himself cabled Schmeling "Most cordial felicitations on your splendid victory," and sent flowers to Schmeling's wife, movie actress Annie Ondra. Minister of Propaganda Goebbels now perceived in the prizefight, which had been of no previous significance to the Reich, a splendid patriotic achievement and cabled Schmeling, "I know that you have fought for Germany. Your victory is a German victory. We are proud of you. Heil Hitler and hearty greetings." The press bureau of the Nazi regime enthusiastically embraced Schmeling as a great example of the "new youth" and declared that his victory was a triumph for Hitlerism.

Arno Hellmis, writing in the *Volkischer Beobachter*, inflated his crowd estimates to double the actual attendance and noted with satisfaction, "All America is enchanted by the great achievement of the German." Hellmis wrote that the American crowd had cheered Schmeling and said that the American press was calling Schmeling the greatest fighter ever. Obviously sensitive to American criticism of the Nazi regime, Hellmis wrote of Schmeling's victory, "How much this has accomplished for the German cause should not be underestimated."

In his account of the fight Hellmis constantly identified Louis as *"Der Neger"* and identified Schmeling as "white" several times. Hellmis wrote of Louis's low blows in the late rounds, "One cannot believe anymore that these were unintentional."

The captain of the German zeppelin *Hindenburg* gave Schmeling a special berth, and Schmeling returned to a triumphal welcome in Germany less than a week after the fight. When the *Hindenburg* landed in Frankfurt, Schmeling remembered in his autobiography, the landing area was "black with people." Schmeling went from Frankfurt to Berlin, where Hitler invited him to lunch. Schmeling brought along his wife and mother to meet the absolute ruler of the Third Reich. Hitler embarrassed Schmeling by making an exceedingly formal speech of congratulations, but the mood eventually relaxed. At one point Hitler said it was a shame he couldn't have seen the fight, and Schmeling told him that films of the bout were waiting at German customs. Mike Jacobs had given Schmeling full rights to overseas distribution of the films, because he didn't think the fight would last long enough to make the films salable. Hitler, a movie buff, immediately sent an aide to pick up the films and watched them with Schmeling later that day. In his memoirs Schmeling remembered Hitler slapping his thigh with satisfaction when Schmeling landed a punch.

The Nazis combined the fight films with film of Louis and Schmeling training and of Schmeling's reception at Frankfurt and made a full-length movie titled *Max Schmeling's Victory, A German Victory*. It played to full houses all over Germany.

American papers printed stories on the telegrams Schmeling received from Nazi leaders and ran pictures of Schmeling meeting with Hitler. All the hulabaloo began to tie Schmeling to the Nazis in the minds of some American reporters. Westbrook Pegler wrote:

> At no time during the months when Schmeling was preparing to fight Louis did the Nazi government accept any responsibility in the matter. Schmeling did not then enjoy the status of official patriot and representative of Nazi manhood. He was absolutely on his own, because there seemed an excellent chance that having already been knocked out

by a Jew [Max Baer] he would now be stretched in the resin at the feet of a cotton-field Negro. . . .

But before the night was over Schmeling had become a great German patriot, and his unexpected conquest of the colored boy had been taken over as a triumph for Adolf Hitler and his government.

While Max Schmeling was enjoying his hero's reception, Joe Louis holed up in a Harlem apartment, too embarrassed to go out. The left side of his jaw was swollen like a softball. For three days he ruminated over his loss. Louis was carrying a heavy load of shame and guilt for a twenty-two-year-old; he felt he had let down his family and his race. But as much as he hurt, Louis never suffered any doubts about his boxing ability. He blamed himself, his overconfidence, poor training, and womanizing for the loss and vowed never to make the same mistakes again. When the swelling went down, he slipped out of New York with Marva on a late train for Chicago.

Max Schmeling had temporarily knocked Louis out of the heavyweight picture and established himself as the number-one contender for the title. Looking forward to a championship fight between two white men, Schmeling and Jim Braddock, a white writer said, "May the best man win, but it doesn't make much difference now which one does."

6

"...AND NEW HEAVYWEIGHT CHAMPION OF THE WORLD"

Mike Jacobs, John Roxborough, and Julian Black didn't let Louis think too long about his loss. They scheduled Louis to fight Jack Sharkey in Yankee Stadium on August 18, just a month after the Schmeling fight. Sharkey was thirty-three. He had lost the heavyweight championship to Primo Carnera three years before and had retired several months and two more losses later. In 1935 he began a comeback, with indifferent results. Sharkey was no longer much of a fighter, but every fan knew his name. He was the perfect foil for Louis's comeback.

Before going into training, Joe and Marva Louis went to Detroit for a visit. Louis's stepfather, Pat Brooks, Sr., had suffered a stroke two days before the Schmeling fight. No one had told Louis for fear that it would upset him and throw off his performance. While Louis was in Detroit, Pat Brooks took a turn for the worse. He died in his bedroom with Louis and the whole family in attendance. Pat Brooks was the only father Louis had known, and Louis felt the loss deeply. Anxious to get his life back together, Louis left for Pompton Lakes right after the funeral.

While Louis trained for Sharkey, sports fans turned their attention to the upcoming Olympics. In track and field something that had been building since 1932 was becoming obvious: America's best sprinters and jumpers were black. In the 1932 Games Eddie Tolan, a black American, won the 100 and 200 meter sprints. Another black American, Ralph Metcalfe, finished second in the 100 and third in the 200. At the Big Ten Championships in May of 1935, Jesse Owens of Ohio State set world's records in the 100 and 220 yard dashes, the 220 yard low hurdles, and the broad jump—on the same day. Throughout 1935 and early 1936 Owens had only one real challenger to his title of world's fastest human, Eulace Peacock, who was also black. Peacock actually beat Owens twice in the 100, but he injured a leg early in 1936 and couldn't qualify for the American team in the final Olympic trials, held June 11 and 12 at Randalls Island in New York. When Peacock pulled up lame, other black sprinters won berths on the team.

At Randalls Island 11 blacks earned places on America's track and field team. Owens won the 100 and 200 meter dashes and the broad jump. Ralph Metcalfe and Mack Robinson, Jackie Robinson's older brother, also ran faster than any whites in 100 and 200. Archie Williams and Jimmy LuValle were one-two in the 400, and John Woodruff, freshman surprise from Pitt, won the 800. Cornelius Johnson and Dave Albritton tied for first in the high jump, setting a new world's record while they were at it. Johnny Brooks finished second to Owens in the broad jump. Their performances established American blacks as the favorites for six gold medals.

The Nazis were preparing the biggest Olympic show ever. In Berlin they had built an enormous Olympic complex, with a stadium seating 80,000 and an indoor pool seating 20,000 more. The Germans sold over 3,400,000 tickets, and were to host 6,000 athletes. As part of the pageantry, a series of runners carried an Olympic Torch lit in Greece all the way to Berlin.

The *New York Times* wrote an editorial detailing the German effort to show off, and predicted that the Nazis would softpedal their racial prejudice for the occasion. The *Times* was right. In his memoirs, Max Schmeling, who was in Berlin for the opening of the Olympic Games, remembered that *Der Sturmer*, an anti-Semitic hate sheet, disappeared from newsstands, and the "Juden unerwinsht" [Jews unwelcome] signs disappeared from the streets. Foreign papers and books by Herman Hesse and Thomas Mann, usually banned by the Nazis, were suddenly available again.

The Nazis apparently fooled Avery Brundage. In a ceremony welcoming the Americans to Germany, on July 24, 1936, Brundage said, "No nation since Ancient Greece has captured the true Olympic spirit as has Germany." The International Olympic Committee expelled American representative Ernest Jahnke, and replaced him with Brundage. Jahnke claimed the IOC dropped him for his opposition to Nazi hosting of the Games.

Actual competition began August 2, with Hitler looking on. During the second day of competition Cornelius Johnson won the high jump, with Dave Albritton second, and Jesse Owens qualified for the finals of the 100 meters in a world record 10.2 seconds. Hitler left the stadium five minutes before the presentation of medals to Johnson and Albritton. The next day Owens and Metcalfe finished one-two in the 100 meter finals, and again Hitler left before they received their medals. On August 4 John Woodruff won the 800 meters, and Jesse Owens beat Lutz Long of Germany in a close contest for the long jump. Owens and Long, who had become friends during the competition, were walking arm-in-arm after their last jumps when Hitler called Long over to his box to congratulate the silver medalist. Hitler did not congratulate Owens. Owens won his third gold medal the next day, setting a world's record of 20.7 seconds for the 200 meters around a turn. On August 7 Archie Williams completed a black American sweep of six individual gold medals by winning the 400 meters. Owens and Metcalfe were also picked over the only two Jews on America's track team for the gold medal-winning 400 meter relay squad.

For the first time, blacks as a group, not just as isolated individuals, had defeated whites in head-to-head athletic competition. Their success, like that of Joe Louis, posed questions and challenges to segregated America. The white press treated America's black track stars the same way it treated Louis, always identifying them as Negroes and sometimes quoting them in Uncle Remus dialect. As it had with Louis, the white press used race to explain black athletic prowess. White sportswriters believed that sprinting and jumping were natural skills. In the *Times* John Kieran wrote, "Apparently it takes time to work up endurance, but speed comes by nature." A writer for *News-*

week said, "Owens runs as easily as Bill (Bojangles) Robinson tap dances."

Once again, with little record of black athletic achievement from the past, white sportswriters quickly asserted that blacks were better natural athletes than whites. Braven Dyer of the *Los Angeles Times* wrote, "Chances are the Negro athletes of 500 years ago could run just as fast, jump just as high, and leap just as far as those of today. But they never got an opportunity to demonstrate their superiority over their white rivals."

Other writers not only related athletic prowess to race but used the opportunity to saddle blacks with pernicious racial stereotypes. Frederick Lewis Allen wrote, "Possibly Negroes are especially well fitted emotionally for the sort of brief, terrific effort which sprints and jumps require." Grantland Rice wrote of the black Olympic athletes: "Easily, almost lazily, and minus any show of extra effort, they have turned sport's greatest spectacle into the 'black parade of 1936.'"

More tolerant writers like Westbrook Pegler rejected "the freak theories and pseudo-scientific speculation that inevitably attend a Negro's rise." They branded as ignorant racism a theory that blacks had longer heels, which gave them greater speed. Pegler attacked other forms of racist explanations for the speed of black sprinters:

> It is a doubtful compliment to a Negro athlete who is qualified to attend college to attempt to account for his proficiency on the field by suggesting that he is still so close to the primitive that whenever he runs a foot-race in a formal meet between schools his civilization vanishes and he becomes again for the moment an African savage in breachcloth and nose ring legging it through the jungle.

More tolerant writers also stressed the training of blacks to prove that their speed was acquired, not inborn. *Newsweek* described the childhoods of Owens and Eulace Peacock: "Both grew up like other schoolboys in large cities. Their only abnormality consisted in running faster than their fellow students—but even to achieve this they submitted to rigorous coaching."

The context of the 1936 Games made the success of black

athletes even more remarkable and ironic. Hitler and the Nazis politicized and nationalized the Olympics as never before. They began the practice of adding up the medals each country's athletes had won, and Germany was the first country to claim it "won" the Olympics. All this generated a new interest in the Olympics and sharpened the paradox of black athletes representing the United States.

Some white papers tried to justify the spectacle of second-class citizens winning glory for America, and to assuage guilt feelings, by downplaying racism in America. Other whites obviously did not consider blacks their representatives. Grantland Rice referred to the black American athletes as "our Ethiopian phalanx" and "our Ethiopian troops." He apparently agreed with *Der Ansgriff*, the Nazi newspaper that claimed the United States had brought "black auxiliaries" to the Games. Rice observed that "the United States will be okay until it runs out of African entries," and suggested, "we may have to comb Africa again for sure winners." White reporters often wrote about Joe Louis the same way, describing him as an African, an Ethiopian, a Senegambian, or a Nubian.

The Berlin Olympics also cast athletic competitions between black Americans and Germans as symbolic tests of Nazi racism. Hitler started it by embracing Max Schmeling after his victory over Louis and by refusing to congratulate black Olympic medalists.

Preferring a single hero to a team, the media seized on Jesse Owens, the most spectacular performer in the Games. Like Louis, Owens was careful to present an inoffensive public image; he reinforced the positive impressions that Louis was making. But Owens did not stay in the spotlight long. He tried to cash in on his Olympic heroics, but he could not make a living out of his sport, and off the track Owens was just one more black man trying to make it in a white man's country. Back in New York, Owens learned that the Hotel New Yorker had refused to put up his parents, who had come from Cleveland to welcome him back to the States. To convert his fame and popularity into money, Owens had to sell more than his time and energy. He tap-danced on national tour with Eddie Cantor, and later raced exhibitions against horses and trains. Owens soon faded from the headlines, and Joe Louis was alone once again.

During the publicity buildup to the Louis-Sharkey fight, Jack Sharkey told reporters he had the "Indian sign" on black fighters. Earlier in his career Sharkey had beaten Harry Wills and George Godfrey, the leading black heavyweights of the late 1920s. Sharkey predicted he would have no trouble with Louis. After Louis's loss to Schmeling, many reporters believed Sharkey.

Jack Blackburn knew Sharkey would copy Schmeling's strategy and instructed sparring partners to throw right hands against Louis. The trainer worked over and over again with Louis on defenses against right-hand punches. But no amount of practice could substitute for a real fight. As Louis waited for the bell to start the fight on August 18, 1936, he was uncharacteristically nervous. It probably didn't help when the ring announcer introduced Max Schmeling, who was in America training for his title fight against Jim Braddock. The Yankee Stadium crowd loudly applauded Schmeling.

Louis started with a flurry, then boxed cautiously for the rest of the first round, quickly regaining any lost confidence by avoiding Sharkey's wild rights. Sharkey tried to keep Louis away by feinting at the beginning of the second round, but Louis nailed Sharkey with a short right that dropped him for a nine count. Sharkey went down again soon after, but managed to survive the round. In the third, Louis landed combinations at will. He knocked Sharkey down three times, and the third time Sharkey stayed down.

That same day champion James J. Braddock announced that he would ask the New York State Athletic Commission to postpone his fight with Max Schmeling. Braddock had developed arthritis in his right hand. The commission eventually granted Braddock's request. In the days before closed circuit television, when boxing promoters made most of their money from the gate, all big fights had to be held outside in stadiums; no indoor facilities, including Madison Square Garden, could accommodate a large enough crowd. That meant the most important fights took place in the summer, when the weather was dependable. The Madison Square Garden Corporation had to postpone the Braddock-Schmeling fight until the following summer.

The delay got Mike Jacobs thinking. It would give him time to rehabilitate Joe Louis's reputation as a contender, and it would give Jacobs time to lure Jimmy Braddock away from Jimmy Johnston and the Madison Square Garden Corporation. Jacobs set up a string of easy fights for Louis. After knocking out Sharkey, Louis took on Al Ettore September 22, 1936, in Philadelphia's Sesquicentennial Stadium. Ettore was a young fighter who had established himsef as the leading heavyweight contender in Pennsylvania and had ambitions to go further. He went no further than twenty-eight seconds into the fifth round against Louis, but Ettore was popular in Philadelphia, and the fight drew well. On October 9, Jacobs rented the Hippodrome in New York for a match between Louis and Jorge Brescia of Argentina. Louis knocked out Brescia in two rounds.

While Louis continued to fight and win, Jacobs worked to get Louis back in the championship picture. First he tried to arrange a Louis-Schmeling rematch that fall, because Schmeling had no one to fight until Braddock's hands healed. Jacobs offered Schmeling a $300,000 guarantee, but Schmeling correctly perceived that he would be better off waiting for a shot at the championship, especially because a fight with Braddock was a more comfortable prospect than another fight with Louis.

Next Jacobs negotiated with Braddock and Braddock's manager, Joe Gould. Gould and Jacobs understood each other. Like Jacobs, Gould was a New York Jew who had struggled up from poverty. He made a marginal living as a fight manager and had connections with the New York underworld. He was especially close to Owney Madden, the gangster who controlled Primo Carnera. Gould realized that he and Braddock controlled a valuable commodity in the heavyweight championship. Gould also had a realistic estimate of his fighter's capabilities. Jimmy Braddock's first defense of his title, whether against Schmeling or Louis, would probably be his last, and Gould was determined to strike a golden deal in return for offering up the championship.

Gould and Braddock were contractually committed to fight for Jimmy Johnston and the Madison Square Garden Corporation. The postponement of Braddock's fight with Schmeling didn't change that, but Mike Jacobs was not the kind of a man to let a contract stop him, and neither was Joe Gould. Jacobs and Herman Taylor, a Philadelphia promoter, offered Gould and Braddock a $500,000 guarantee for a twelve-round bout with Louis in Atlantic City. Jacobs set up the fight as an exhibition to get around Gould's contract with Madison Square Garden and to make the fight more attractive to Gould. Exhibitions were no-decision bouts; Braddock would lose his title only if Louis knocked him out. Jacobs and Louis's managers figured Louis would knock out Braddock easily. Even with a $500,000 guarantee, far more than Braddock stood to make from his 40 percent share of a fight with Schmeling, Gould hemmed and hawed. He wanted more.

In the meantime, the Louis entourage went to Cleveland for a fight with Eddie Simms on December 14, 1936. The fight was one of the shortest in boxing history. In less than twenty seconds Louis dropped Simms with a left hook. Simms managed to get up before referee Arthur Donovan counted ten, but when Donovan reached for Simms' gloves to wipe them off, the disoriented Simms said, "Let's go someplace. Let's get out of here. Let's go up on the roof or someplace," probably thinking that he was talking to some woman. Donovan stopped the fight.

While Louis went home for Christmas, John Roxborough traveled to New York to see Jacobs. He wanted to check on the negotiations with Gould. Jacobs reported that the negotiations were stuck, and the two men talked about arranging a fight for Louis in Miami.

When Roxborough left Jacobs's office, two men were waiting for him on the street. One was a gangster who worked for Owney Madden. "Got a man who wants to see you," he said. "Let's go for a ride." The pair drove Roxborough around the city for an hour while Roxborough got more and more frightened. His escorts were not speaking, a bad sign. Roxborough thought someone had put out a contract on him. Finally, the two thugs pulled into an alley and led Roxborough through the back entrance of a nightclub. To his relief, Roxborough found Joe Gould waiting for him.

Gould proposed a twelve-round exhibition between Braddock and Louis and assured Roxborough that Braddock was over the hill, so Louis was sure to win the title. There was a catch, though: Gould wanted 50 percent of Louis.

Gould's demand was outrageous. Roxborough spluttered, "No fifty percent, not fifty cents. Nothing. We don't need Braddock. If he had ten fights, he couldn't make as much as Joe can in one. He needs us. You need us. No deal and no exhibition." Gould lowered his demand to 25 percent, then 20 percent. Still Roxborough refused. Finally, Roxborough suggested that Gould talk to Jacobs about attaching a share of the promoter's future profits. Roxborough walked out, happy to be alive and to have resisted Gould. Roxborough went to a nearby bar and had a double scotch.

Joe Gould was under pressure himself. Rumors of the proposed Louis-Braddock exhibition were out, and Madison Square Garden was trying to stop it, saying an exhibition would demean the championship. Max Schmeling hopped aboard the S.S. *Bremen* and sailed into New York in mid-December. He went before the New York State Athletic Commission, complaining that he had been promised a title fight. The commission, which rightly recognized Schmeling as the leading heavyweight contender by virtue of his victory over Louis, forbade Braddock to fight an exhibition with Louis. The commission also made Braddock and Schmeling post $5,000 bonds that they would forfeit if they failed to show up for their scheduled bout on June 3, 1937. Chastened, Gould also signed another contract with the Garden, promising that Braddock would not fight Louis before the Schmeling fight.

Louis's prospects did not look good. He had beaten every prominent heavyweight except Schmeling and Braddock, and they were out of reach. Assuming Schmeling beat Braddock as expected, Louis could hope to meet him for the championship in August or September 1937. But Schmeling might refuse. He had shown no enthusiasm for a rematch with Louis. Having beaten Louis once, Schmeling might claim he had nothing to prove by meeting Louis again. Schmeling might return to Germany, where the Nazis would use the heavyweight championship as a propaganda tool. The Nazis might not let Schmeling meet Louis, or Schmeling might insist that Louis come to Germany for the fight, a truly frightening prospect for a black man in 1937. And Louis and his managers could never forget that white promoters and white fighters might seize any excuse to keep them from getting a chance at the title.

Louis and his managers could only keep the pressure on by continuing to fight and win. Louis went on tour during the first two weeks in January 1937. One of the fights, a two-round kayo of Steve Ketchell, somehow became part of Louis's official record, though it was just an exhibition. Louis returned to New York to fight Bob Pastor on January 29. Pastor, a former football star at New York University, had risen through the ranks of the Golden Gloves at the same time Louis had, though they had never met as amateurs. Jimmy Johnston, the boxing promoter for Madison Square Garden, managed Pastor, and for once he outsmarted Mike Jacobs. Johnston and Pastor's trainer, Freddie Brown, told Pastor to run away from Louis, to avoid any heavy exchange of punches. As a sellout Madison Square Garden crowd jeered, Louis halfheartedly chased Pastor around the ring. Pastor occasionally flipped out a jab before running off again. Jack Blackburn yelled at Louis to pin Pastor in a corner, but Louis couldn't do it. At the end of the ten-round fight Pastor was unhurt, and he ran back to his corner and jumped in the air, arms raised. Johnston had succeeded in making Louis look bad. Pastor thought he had won the fight, but the judges disagreed. Louis won a unanimous decision, with referee Arthur Donovan, always a Louis fan, scoring the fight eight rounds to two, Louis. The crowd showed its sympathy for the underdog and its anger at the boring exhibition by booing for thirty minutes.

In an interview forty-five years later, Bob Pastor was still convinced he beat Joe Louis that night. He claimed the judges knew that he had won, too. "They knew it, but they didn't know what to do, because Jacobs had Louis, and Johnston had

me, you understand? And so they had to make Louis the winner.
Oh yeah. . . . We didn't have any money, and Jacobs had all
the dough, and he had Louis, so he was paying 'em. I know what
happened."

Only a few writers criticized Pastor for running away, but
virtually all of them criticized Louis for failing to catch Pastor
and knock him out. They credited Pastor with a clever plan
and wrote that he had outsmarted Louis. After the Schmeling
fight the writers had said that Louis had difficulty adapting to
Schmeling's style, that he was a dumb boxer. To the writers, the
Pastor fight further proved Louis's lack of adaptability. This idea
of Louis being too slow and stupid to catch Pastor fit comfort-
abzly with Louis's darkie image.

Louis's next fight was more satisfying. On February 17, 1937,
he met Natie Brown, who had partially spoiled his debut in front
of the New York sportswriters two years before. This time
Louis caught Brown and knocked him out in the fourth round.

Two days after the Louis-Brown fight, Mike Jacobs and Joe
Gould turned the boxing world upside down. Joe Louis and
James J. Braddock signed contracts for a world's heavyweight
championship fight, to be held June 22, 1937, in Chicago.

Joe Gould had a noble explanation for the surprised reporters.
He was breaking his contract with Madison Square Garden because of public opposition to the Braddock-Schmeling fight. For
several months the Non-Sectarian Anti-Nazi League had bom-
barded the New York State Athletic Commission with telegrams.
League members feared that the Nazis would use Schmeling to
propaganda advantage should the German boxer win the title,
and they threatened to boycott the fight. The league had enough
political clout to get press coverage. Its leaders were Samuel
Untermeyer and Jeremiah T. Mahoney, the man who spear-
headed the unsuccessful opposition to the Berlin Olympics.
Fiorello LaGuardia, the mayor of New York, was one of the
league's vice-presidents. Though the league had an impressive
letterhead, it was hardly a grass-roots movement. Mike Jacobs
hadn't thought twice when the league and several other groups
boycotted the Louis-Schmeling fight. But now Joe Gould pre-

tended to be seriously concerned about a possible boycott. Gould also claimed to have polled sportswriters on the depth of anti-Nazi sentiment and said the writers had agreed a boycott would cut attendance. Under the circumstances, Gould said, the fight with Schmeling was too risky.

Gould's real reason was pecuniary. Gould had always preferred Louis over Schmeling as an opponent for Braddock, because Louis would draw a bigger crowd. In addition, Mike Jacobs, who was desperate to ensure his control over boxing by luring the heavyweight title away from Jimmy Johnston, had offered Gould better terms. Jacobs offered Gould and Braddock a $500,000 guarantee or half the gate and radio revenues, whichever was greater. Jacobs iced the deal by giving Gould and Braddock 10 percent of his net profits from heavyweight-title-fight promotions for the next decade should Braddock lose the fight.

Jacobs had paid a high price to get Louis a championship fight, but he stood to profit in the long run. Assuming Louis won, Jacobs would control the heavyweight championship, which was the key to control of boxing. Once again, Joe Louis was the lucky beneficiary of Mike Jacobs's self-interest. Two years before, Jacobs had needed a new star to challenge Madison Square Garden's monopoly on the heavyweight division and had been willing to gamble on a young black fighter. Now Jacobs needed a champion. Without the backing of a Mike Jacobs, a black heavyweight, even a Joe Louis, would have had little chance of fighting for the heavyweight title.

Jacobs set the fight in Chicago because he knew the New York State Athletic Commission would not allow it to take place in New York. But there was still the matter of Braddock's contract with Madison Square Garden. The Garden filed suit February 20, 1937, to enjoin Braddock from fighting Louis. But Jacobs's lawyer, Sol Strauss, had pored over the original contract Braddock had signed with the Garden before his fight with Max Baer. Strauss thought the contract was invalid because it obligated Braddock to make his first title defense for the Garden while imposing no corresponding conditions on the Garden itself.

While the Garden's suit worked its way through the courts, Blackburn, Roxborough, and Black decided to send Louis on a month-long tour to prepare for the Braddock fight. They rented a special railroad car for Louis and his sparring partners and scheduled twenty-one sparring exhibitions in thirty days throughout the Midwest and Southwest. At first Jack Blackburn acted as if the fight with Braddock would never occur. He had never believed that Louis could get a title fight, and now that the dream was so close, he was afraid to hope. But as Mike Jacobs continued to assure the Louis party that everything was working out, Blackburn began to work harder and more seriously with Louis than ever before. He even stopped drinking.

Blackburn worked on Louis's major weakness, a vulnerability to right-hand counterpunches. From the outset, Blackburn had taught Louis to be a counterpuncher. When his opponent was willing to lead, Louis never had any problems. But when Louis had to take the offensive against a retreating opponent, he became too predictable. He always jabbed with his left hand and looked for an opportunity to cross with his right. A smart opponent could anticipate Louis's jabs and counterpunch with a right, as Max Schmeling demonstrated. Blackburn wanted Louis to be less stationary on the offensive, to weave and duck more to prevent his opponent from getting a clear shot with a right. With a title fight in sight and the memory of the Schmeling defeat still lingering, Louis once again devoted himself to Blackburn's instruction, as he had before his first professional fight.

The tour ended in San Diego. Blackburn, Louis, and especially the sparring partners were exhausted, but the trip had accomplished its objective. Louis was in good shape, and his timing was sharp. He went to Julian Black's summer home in Stevensville, Michigan, to do light training before the opening of his training camp.

Louis and his managers had planned to set up camp in Lake Geneva, Wisconsin, seventy-five miles north of Chicago, but the Lake Geneva Homeowners Association didn't want any blacks in the neighborhood, so the Louis entourage chose Kenosha, Wisconsin, on Lake Michigan. Louis celebrated his twenty-third birthday in Kenosha on May 13 and began training the next day.

Max Schmeling arrived in America in early May and also began to train. Schmeling and Madison Square Garden still hoped that the courts would force Braddock to meet Schmeling on June 3, but Federal Judge Guy L. Fake refused to enjoin Braddock from fighting Louis. The Garden appealed the decision, and Schmeling continued to train, but the press soon realized that the Louis-Braddock fight was on. White sportswriters were generally sympathetic toward Schmeling and critical of Gould and Braddock. While a few worried that Schmeling might have taken the title back to Nazi Germany and refused to defend it in America, none could deny that Schmeling was the most deserving heavyweight contender. *Life* magazine summed up the general sentiment a day before the Braddock-Louis fight: "The man Braddock should really be fighting is Max Schmeling." Schmeling made himself look a little ridiculous by persisting in his training. The New York State Athletic Commission even conducted a farcical weighing-in ceremony on June 3 that Schmeling attended, sans Braddock, to the amusement of more than one sports columnist.

Surprisingly, throughout the months of contractual issues and legal confusion leading up to the Louis-Braddock bout, few reporters commented on the fight's social significance. Reporters occasionally noted that Louis was only the second black to fight for the world's heavyweight championship, the first black to get a shot since Jack Johnson, but they left it at that. Two years before, when Louis broke into the big time, white reporters had written at length about the issues raised by Louis's color. They had worried about the public's reaction to Louis and expressed fear that his fights might cause race riots. Later, when the white public seemed to accept Louis, many reporters commented on Louis's symbolic importance and wrote that he was bringing about an improvement in race relations. After his loss to Schmeling, however, the press coverage changed. The white public still seemed to accept Louis, and reporters now took that for granted. Louis lost his reputation for invincibility and the automatic respect that went with it. As a symbol, Joe Louis was difficult to read. No one was sure anymore how far Louis would go or what it would mean.

One reporter who did try to assess Louis's impact should he become champion was Shirley Povich of the *Washington Post*, who revealed the lack of enthusiasm for Louis on the eve of the championship fight:

> If, perchance, Joe Louis should come into the heavyweight championship of the world this evening at Chicago and Nordic Supremacy in the prize ring is ended for the time being, there is no reason to believe it would be a national calamity. . . . Joe Louis has been following [a] pattern of modesty, almost self-effacement. None of the blatancy that characterized the arrogant Jack Johnson has been noticed in Louis's conduct. He has proved himself just a big, playful brown boy who happens to be deadly serious when he's in that ring.

Never was there any serious talk in the white press about denying Louis a shot at the title. In April 1935, when Louis was just coming into national prominence, Arch Ward of the *Chicago Tribune* worried that boxing promoters might draw the color line against Louis. But by June 1935, after Louis had defeated Primo Carnera, white papers were writing in a self-congratulatory tone about the absence of a color line and the lack of any white-hope hysteria. White papers claimed that the racial tolerance of the white public had improved. It hadn't. After all, only a decade had passed since Dempsey and Tunney refused to fight Harry Wills. In fact, the happy coincidence of Mike Jacobs's self-interest and Louis's modest character and overwhelming skill had punctured segregation in boxing, and the lack of any public backlash had punctured a good many myths and fears. In Louis's case the color line was dead. The big story was Jimmy Braddock's backing out of his fight with Max Schmeling, not a black man finally getting a chance.

Braddock was the sentimental choice of the white press. Braddock had been an underdog all his life. He grew up in Hell's Kitchen and quit school at thirteen. After Joe Gould discovered him, Braddock fought well enough to meet Tommy Loughran for the light-heavyweight title in 1929. Loughran beat him in fifteen rounds, and Braddock hit the skids soon after. He broke a knuckle on his right hand, couldn't afford an operation to fix it, and it didn't heal properly. He kept fighting, anyway, and from 1930 to 1933 he lost more fights than he won against a succession of mediocre opponents. On September 25, 1933, the referee threw Braddock and his opponent, Abe Feldman, out of the ring and declared the fight no contest because both fighters were performing so badly. Braddock had to produce medical evidence of his injured hand to get paid for the fight, and after that he could not pass a physical to fight again.

Over the winter of 1933–34 Braddock took any job he could find. He tended bar and worked as a stevedore lifting railroad ties. With a wife and three children to support in the middle of the Depression, Braddock was fighting a losing battle with poverty. Only a loan from Joe Gould saved him from having his electricity cut off, and Braddock had to apply for welfare. He swung a pick for the Works Progress Administration, one of the New Deal relief agencies.

While his layoff from boxing did not help Braddock financially, it gave his right hand time to heal. He pestered Joe Gould to get him a fight. Luckily for Braddock, Jimmy Johnston was looking for a victim to feed Corn Griffin, an up-and-coming heavyweight, in a preliminary bout the night of the Carnera-Baer heavyweight championship fight, June 14, 1934. The Griffin-Braddock fight followed Johnston's script during the first round when Griffin knocked Braddock down, but Braddock picked himself up off the canvas and knocked out Griffin in the third round.

His prior failures conveniently forgotten, Braddock got fights against John Henry Lewis and Art Lasky, two leading contenders, and decisioned them both. As a result of the scarcity of talent in the heavyweight division, Braddock suddenly found himself the number-one contender for champion Max Baer's crown. Baer, who had fought nothing but exhibitions since winning the title from Carnera, finally agreed to fight Braddock. The sportswriters did not believe Braddock had a chance, and the oddsmakers listed him as a ten-to-one underdog. Max Baer didn't think Braddock had a chance, either, and as usual was in terrible shape for the fight. Braddock boxed circles around Baer to win a unanimous decision and a new nickname from the sportswriters—they called him the "Cinderella man."

While no one thought Braddock was a great boxer, everybody liked him. Braddock was an honest, congenial, and courageous man. He was also without prejudice. George Nicholson, a black boxer who worked as a sparring partner for Braddock and later for Louis, said of Braddock, "He was a wonderful guy. Always treated everybody the same. When we put rocks in the beds of the guys in training camp, we would put them in his, too. We ate together, showered together, all equals." Braddock deserves credit for giving Louis a title fight. He never threatened to draw the color line.

Many of Braddock's friends among the working press hoped he would win. Bud Shaver of the *Detroit Times* wrote, "Sentiment, I suspect, is all on the side of the Irishman, because he is a Cinderella man with a wife and a brood of kids and short of dough as a family man always is." Besides being so likable, Braddock was white. Bill Corum identified him as "the white man" and said Braddock would be fighting on "pride of race and courage." Ed Hughes of the *Brooklyn Daily Eagle* wrote, "Plainly there is a strong racial itch to see the white man conquer the Negro." Whites were rooting for Braddock, even if they thought he would lose.

In contrast, the white press painted an unflattering portrait of Louis. After his loss to Schmeling and his fight with Bob Pastor, Louis's public image hit its lowest point. White reporters still constantly identified Louis as a Negro, and their descriptions of him conformed more and more to the stereotype of a lazy darkie. *Life* magazine printed the following photo captions: "The challenger rarely smiles. Here Louis grins because a workout is over. He hates workouts and getting up out of bed." "In the ring, Louis is lithe, shuffling and stolid. Outside he is lethargic, uncommunicative, unimaginative."

R. G. Lynch of the *Milwaukee Journal* wrote a column with the headline "Fight? Joe Louis Sits and Plays Jazz Records."

The hulking, lazy brown boy might have been lolling in a cabin doorway down in Alabama, listening to somebody inside making mouth music. Instead, he lounged in a huge easy chair just off the two-story living room of a yellow stone palace on the lakeshore south of Kenosha and played jazz records on a squeaky portable phonograph. It was Joe Louis, and an uninformed visitor would never have thought that anybody had ever called this smooth-faced, placid, slightly sullen negro youth a jungle killer or that he expected to take the world heavyweight boxing championship away from Jimmy Braddock next month.

A few weeks before the fight Bill Corum of the *New York Journal* wrote of Louis:

> There isn't an ounce of killer in him. Not the slightest zest for fighting. He's a big, superbly built Negro youth who was born to listen to jazz music, eat a lot of fried chicken, play ball with the gang on the corner, and never do a lick of heavy work he could escape. The chances are he came by all those inclinations quite naturally.

Though Jimmy Braddock had no more education than Louis, showed no more native intelligence, and certainly had nothing in his ring record to indicate any special ring savvy, reporters claimed that Braddock was the smarter fighter. Some reporters even thought that Braddock's superior intelligence might figure in the fight's outcome. McCormick of the *Post* picked Braddock to win after Braddock claimed that he had a revolutionary strategy that he would employ against Louis. McCormick wrote, "Louis' lack of adaptability and inability to change his set ways probably will make him run into the same trap time after time."

Mike Jacobs aided and abetted the stereotyping of Louis. Jacobs knew that Braddock had little chance and was afraid that if the public saw the fight in its true light, as a mismatch, few would pay to see it. So Jacobs did his best to build up Braddock and tear Louis down. From Grand Beach, Michigan, where Braddock was training, Jacobs's press agent wrote glowing reports about the champion's workouts. Jersey Jones, Jacobs's publicist for the Louis camp, did just the opposite. Jones suggested again and again that Louis was fat and lazy, that success had gone to his head, and that Louis was not training properly. Jones quoted a fictitious expert, "Success may have come to him [Louis] too quickly, too easily. Soft living may have taken its toll." Jones's suggestions caught on. The *Literary Digest*, a major magazine later absorbed by *Time*, wrote that some boxing experts were worried that wealth and easy living had increased Louis's "inherent laziness." Murray Goodman of the Universal News Service quoted another expert, once again probably a Jersey Jones creation:

> Louis is still living on velvet. It's too bad a guy with such natural talents for fighting should be hit by new-found wealth. He is fatter and he is slower. His slowness may be partly due to his lackadaisical attitude for things, but he is no longer the fighter with ice in his veins.

Jack Miley of the *New York Daily News* wrote:

> Joe was never used to easy living and he loves it. Not that he dissipates or goes to extremes, so far as I know. But any young fellow, accustomed to earning his bread by the sweat of his brow, who now sleeps ten or twelve hours a day and stuffs himself with food like a gourmand isn't the kind of guy I wish to bet my dough on. . . . Joe was a natural fighter. He will never be any better than he was the day he first pulled on a glove. He performs by instinct and no-body will ever be able to pound anything through his kinky skull.

Reporters not only projected a negative personal image of Louis; they also criticized his boxing skills. Once again, Mike Jacobs's publicity agent, Jersey Jones, led the way. In his press releases Jones asked the question, "Just how good is the Brown Bomber?" and wrote, "Louis is not the fighter he was two years ago." Remembering Louis's loss to Schmeling and his fight with Bob Pastor, Grantland Rice pointed out, "Within the last ten months Louis has lost considerable prestige." Over and over again reporters questioned Louis's ability to take a punch, mentioned his vulnerability to right-hand punches, and doubted his intelligence in the ring. Frank Graham of the *New York Sun* probably set the record for absurd criticism of Louis when he suggested, "[Louis] doesn't even know how to jab." Louis had a great jab, strong and quick, certainly the best jab of any heavyweight fighter up to his time and perhaps the greatest jab in heavyweight history.

Louis's training schedule did nothing to quell the writers' doubts. Louis was sharp from his month-long exhibition tour, so Blackburn told him to go easy in his sparring sessions. On the verge of a title fight, Blackburn did not want to risk a hand injury. So Louis concentrated on roadwork, running ten miles a day, and boxed cautiously. Reporters who watched Louis spar were unaware of the strategy and wrote that Louis looked terrible. Jack Miley's impressions were typical:

> I don't know what has happened to Louis. Nobody does, including himself. But, judged by his training camp workouts, the boy just isn't there. He is slow and lazy. He has lost his sock. He acts as if he doesn't care. He seems to be just going through the motions of preparing himself for his shot at the title.

To a certain extent, Joe Louis was the victim of his own greatness. After his sensational knockouts of Carnera, Levinsky, Baer, and Uzcudun, reporters expected him to win every fight by a knockout. Not even Louis could fulfill such expectations. Writers magnified Louis's loss to Schmeling and his failure to catch Bob Pastor. And just as Louis's color had evoked deep-seated cultural fears when he was winning, Louis's blackness no doubt accounted for the nature and depth of some reporters' criticisms when he failed. Surely the white press wouldn't have turned so strongly against Louis if he had been white; after all, he had lost only one fight. Indeed, the same writers who were finding so much at fault in Louis were discovering admirable skills in Braddock, who had lost twenty-nine fights in his career.

More than 45,000 people jammed Chicago's Comiskey Park the night of June 22, 1937. Most of Louis's black fans, numbering some 20,000, filled the bleachers overlooking the field where the ring was pitched.

Inside the White Sox dressing room, James J. Braddock and Joe Louis sat on either side of a wooden partition and awaited the call. As challenger, Louis was supposed to enter the ring first, but Braddock got tired of waiting. The champion left his dressing room and made his way to the ring as the crowd began to cheer. Braddock was wearing a green robe with a big white shamrock on the back. Louis climbed into the ring soon after, wearing his lucky blue and red-trimmed robe. The fighters waited impatiently through the prefight rituals—introductions of Jack Dempsey, Gene Tunney, John Henry Lewis, Sixto Escobar, and Barney Ross, and referee Tommy Thomas's instructions. Louis stripped down to purple trunks, with the initials JL. Braddock wore dark trunks. The champion looked fit and slim but not as muscular as Louis.

As Louis waited in his corner Jack Blackburn said, "This is it, Chappie. You come home a champ tonight." Jimmy Braddock crossed himself as the bell rang and walked out quickly to meet Louis. Braddock swung a wild right to begin the fight, and Louis backed away.

Coming out of a twisting, fighting clinch late in the first round, Louis jabbed and followed with an overhand right. Braddock held on to the top of Louis's shoulders. Louis broke away and swung an overhand right that Braddock blocked. Now backed against the ropes, Braddock landed a right to Louis's body. Louis missed a left hook, and Braddock held the top of Louis's head with his left glove.

Louis again got free. He hit Braddock with a right to the body, a solid left hook to the jaw, and a right to the jaw. Braddock's head snapped from side to side, but he covered up, blocked a Louis right, and swung a short right uppercut that knocked Louis off his feet.

Louis got up immediately and jogged toward the opposite corner of the ring. Braddock brought his gloves up to shoulder level, in a compact and determined stance, and followed. Louis was hurt, but his head was clear, and he turned to fight. Braddock came in swinging a wild right, and Louis ducked. In tight, Braddock threw a left-right combination to Louis's body. Louis blocked a Braddock right as he ducked and weaved, putting

Blackburn's teaching into practice. Louis blocked a left, missed his own left, and landed a right cross and a left uppercut that made Braddock fall into him. The referee broke the clinch, and both fighters missed with jabs and rights. Louis missed a left and hitched up his trunks. Louis missed a left-right combination. Braddock landed a right to the body, but Louis blocked a shot at his head. The bell rang. Both fighters looked at each other to make sure the other had heard it, then dropped their arms. Louis stared at Braddock briefly as Braddock walked back to his corner, rubbing his nose.

When Louis reached his corner, Jack Blackburn screamed, "Why didn't you take a nine count? You can't get up so fast that nobody in the place didn't see you was down. And keep jabbing."

During the second round Louis scored consistently with jabs as Braddock tried to crowd him. Toward the end of the round Louis started a left-right combination, and the second punch, an overhand right, landed solidly. Louis chopped Braddock again with a right, landed a left hook to Braddock's face, then drew his left back and whipped it into Braddock's jaw again. Badly hurt, Braddock tried to wrestle with Louis, then tried to push him away with an outstretched left glove. Louis tried another left but missed, missed a right uppercut, and the bell rang, saving Braddock.

Louis knew he had Braddock, but Jack Blackburn advised caution: "Wait, wait . . . take it easy. He's game, and he knows a lot. Keep sticking and countering. Don't get in too close. Let him do the crowding. He'll come apart in five or six rounds. I'll tell you when to shoot."

Louis boxed Braddock through the third round, landing a few good shots to the body. By the fourth round Braddock's punches were beginning to lose their steam, though he looked fine. In the middle of the fourth Braddock tried a big left hook that Louis blocked. Braddock blocked two jabs and landed a left hook. The punch didn't seem to hurt Louis, who shot back a short left that spun Braddock's head and shoulders. Louis backed away from Braddock's left hand, which was waving weakly. Braddock tried to jab, Louis jabbed, and they clinched. Referee

Thomas broke them, and Louis opened his mouth in a circle, showing his mouthpiece. Louis advanced on Braddock, and— lightning fast—jabbed, threw a right hook to the body and a left hook to the jaw. Braddock's left foot came off the floor, but he recovered his balance and tried an ineffectual right and left. Braddock tried a right uppercut; Louis blocked it and barely missed with a whistling right. Louis jabbed and missed a right; Braddock missed a right. Louis hitched up his trunks and landed a good left jab, but Braddock blocked the right that followed. They clinched, broke, and threw tentative jabs. Braddock landed a left hook. Louis backed away, then came back in, jabbing and ducking an overhand right from Braddock. Both fighters landed jabs, Louis landed two more jabs, and Braddock missed a right uppercut at the bell.

By the seventh round Braddock was visibly tired. He had a bad cut over his left eye and a split lip, but he was still punching. Louis blocked a left hook, dodged a right, ducked another right. Braddock looked sluggish. Louis dodged a wild left and another left. Braddock threw another left that tickled Louis's chin, and they clinched. Braddock spent himself with that flurry, and Louis took the offensive. Louis missed a left-right combination, and Braddock clinched. Louis jabbed. Braddock threw a long right to the side of Louis's body and clinched again. Braddock's feet dragged on the canvas as he came out of the clinch. Louis jabbed, jabbed, jabbed, jabbed again. Braddock missed another wild right. Louis missed a jab, Braddock missed a right and clinched, but Louis stepped away and landed an overhand right to Braddock's chin. Braddock covered up. Louis jabbed again. Braddock missed another right, then tried a left that Louis blocked. Louis missed a left-right combination, and Braddock missed as he tried to counterpunch. Braddock clinched again and backed Louis toward the ropes. The referee broke them, and they pawed at each other with lefts. Louis felt Braddock was set up for a knockout and was about to throw a right when the bell rang. Louis walked lightly back to his corner, looking back at Braddock. Before Louis got to his stool, the weary champ was already sitting down and being worked on by his seconds.

In Braddock's corner, Joe Gould suggested they throw in the towel. Braddock looked at Gould and said through bloody lips, "If you do, I'll never speak to you again as long as I live."

Opening the eighth round, Braddock was holding his hands too high. When Louis was just getting started as a professional, Blackburn had told him to watch an opponent's hands. When a boxer was fresh he would hold them at normal height. When he got tired he would have to make an effort to keep his hands up and would raise them too high. When his hands dropped, he was finished.

As Braddock walked toward him, Louis jabbed, then backed up and circled Braddock. Louis landed a good jab, blocked a left hook and a right hook, and landed a right hook of his own. Jimmy Braddock backed up. He jabbed, threw a weak uppercut, and clinched. Braddock had nothing left. Louis jabbed twice, and Braddock's hands started to come down. Joe Gould yelled, "Keep your hands up, keep your hands up." Braddock jabbed, missed a right cross, and Louis jabbed and backed away from a Braddock uppercut. Braddock jabbed and Louis jabbed, and Louis brought his left hand back for a quick left hook that Braddock dodged. Back on his heels, Braddock waved his left and right in pathetic punches that never got close to Louis. Louis blocked a left hook, missed with his own left, and threw a left hook that landed. Braddock jabbed weakly. Louis jabbed Braddock to the body and landed a good jab on Braddock's face. Braddock missed a weak right, and Louis feinted with his left, knocking Braddock's left glove away, and landed a vicious overhand right. As if in slow motion, Braddock bent over at the waist, started to come up, and fell sideways over his right leg. He hit the canvas face down.

The Comiskey Park crowd broke into a long scream of anticipation. Referee Thomas pointed Louis to a neutral corner, and slowly Louis turned his back on Braddock and walked away. When he reached the neutral corner, Louis still did not look at Braddock; he looked out over the crowd instead.

Tommy Thomas knelt over Braddock and began to count, the excitement showing on his face, his right hand moving up and down with the palm open. Thomas rose to his feet when he reached ten and waved his right hand over Braddock. Joe Louis came out of the neutral corner and raised his right hand, and Thomas touched his arm and held it aloft briefly as they walked past each other. Without looking at Braddock, who was still unconscious on the canvas, Louis put his arm and head down and walked to his corner. Louis's handlers were getting into the ring. Jack Blackburn, his bald head shining, towel around his neck, gave Louis a light embrace, talking to his fighter and nodding, then reached up and took out Louis's mouthpiece. Julian Black hugged Louis, and a crowd of policemen surrounded them. The winner, and new heavyweight champion of the world, was a black man.

Joe Louis was the youngest champion in history and only the second black titleholder. Yet he was not the central figure in the postfight press coverage. White reporters revealed the depth of public sentiment for Braddock by portraying the fallen champion as a hero. To be sure, reporters credited Louis for outclassing Braddock, but Braddock's guts impressed the writers more. For eight rounds Braddock had absorbed terrific punishment—he needed twenty-three stitches after the fight—but refused to quit. Braddock was a very human character in defeat. Reporters portrayed him as an old man who had never been a great boxer, who had refused to accept the certainty of his impending defeat, and who had faced defeat when it came with courage and dignity.

Dan Parker of the *New York Daily Mirror* wrote:

> The exhibition of courage the gallant Anglo-Irishman gave before that final bolt of lightning struck him on the side of the jaw awakened admiration and compassion for him in the heart of everyone in that vast crowd. The old champ withstood punches that would have felled ten ordinary heavyweights, without bowing. Not till that superright cross came out of nowhere in the eighth to numb his brain did gallant Jimmy go to the canvas. And then he went in a heap—a heap that didn't twitch a muscle. Little Joe Gould, his faithful pal and manager, averted his head and sobbed. Jim was all through. But, in defeat, he had

achieved the high spot of his career as the heavyweight champion of the world.

Bill McCormick of the *Washington Post* carried his sympathy for Braddock beyond reason, praising Braddock and criticizing Louis to such extremes that it was hard to believe after his account that Louis actually won the fight. McCormick wrote that Louis was in full retreat, afraid and almost sniveling, after Braddock knocked him down in the first round. McCormick described the second round as even, said Louis was reeling, and wrote, "Joe seemed a badly frightened boy." McCormick said Louis was groggy at the bell in round three and out on his feet in round six.

In contrast to the human picture they presented of Braddock, white reporters portrayed Louis as dominant, cruel, impersonal. For example, Henry McLemore of the United Press wrote:

> In Germany executioners wear silk toppers and knock off the victim's head with an axe of burnished steel.
> In France, they go in for white ties, tails, and a guillotine.
> But over here we are simple folk, without frills. Our head executioner, Joe Louis, just slips on a pair of purple tights, shuffles his feet a few times, and lashes out with nut-brown fists, bundled into cement hardness.

Time magazine wrote of Louis's "cool, poised cruelty." One Associated Press reporter described the knockout:

> Then, in the next instant, Louis drove a cruel right-hand smash to the jaw and Braddock sank to the floor, rolling over on his right side, with his head resting on his arm. He remained motionless as the referee counted over him.
> This was the moment Louis had been waiting for. He was standing in a neutral corner with a vicious scowl on his face. Instead of looking at the fallen Braddock, he stared with a sneer at Braddock's handlers. No doubt he was thinking to himself, "Well, I told you I'd lick your guy and there he is."

Louis's victory inspired renewed jungle-killer imagery from some writers. United Press writer Jack Cuddy began his story on the fight: "Jostling Joe Louis rose from the floor like a jungle man tonight to wrest the world heavyweight championship from James J. Braddock." However unfair and racist this commentary, the Braddock fight largely restored Louis's reputation as a fighter. Grantland Rice wrote: "Louis was a far different fighter from the man that lost to Schmeling. He was cool and crafty. He took his time. . . . He proved that he had come a long way in defense from his Schmeling debacle."

Shirley Povich of the *Washington Post* dismissed critics who claimed that Louis's title was tainted by his loss to Schmeling. Povich pointed out that Dempsey, Tunney, Sharkey, Schmeling, Baer, and Braddock had all lost fights before winning their titles. Louis had won the title fairly and impressively from the champ, and that was what counted. Povich concluded prophetically, "Methinks Louis is in for a long reign as champion—the longest perhaps in the history of the heavyweight division."

Dan Parker of the *New York Daily Mirror*, always one of Louis's stoutest fans, wrote:

> Louis fooled not only the experts but Jim Braddock himself. Deliberately, his camp set out to create the impression that Joe was through as a top line fighter; that he had lost his punch and his keenness for combat. The experts fell for it as only fight experts can. . . .
>
> How wrong almost everyone has been about Louis. They called him dumb. They said he was a sucker for a right. They questioned his courage—all after a lucky combination of circumstances, that perhaps could never happen again, enabled Max Schmeling to score a knockout over him a year ago. I think it was lucky for Mr. Schmeling he wasn't in there Tuesday night instead of Braddock.

But the press would not fully accept Louis as a great fighter until he met Schmeling again. Louis himself was anxious to erase the only blemish on his record. In his dressing room after the fight, Louis said, "Bring on Schmeling," and said he would not feel like a real champion until he had beaten the German.

Schmeling was in London, trying to arrange a fight with Tommy Farr, the heavyweight champion of the British Isles. Angry at being passed over for a chance at the title, Schmeling claimed the championship for himself by default. He told an International News Service reporter:

> The Chicago result simplifies the situation. It makes my forthcoming fight with Farr the logical world title contest. I have no intention of putting myself in the position of challenger. Louis has got to come to me if he wants to fight. I have already beaten Louis and there is no reason why my fight with Farr should not be for the world's championship.

That was wishful thinking, however. Schmeling may indeed have been gypped out of a championship bout, but Louis nevertheless was the champ. The same white sportswriters who harbored doubts about his ability and prejudice about his race nevertheless accepted Louis as heavyweight champion.

7

"IN A FOOTNOTE AT LEAST"

Now that he was heavyweight champion, Louis spent the first few weeks of July 1937 touring the Midwest with his Brown Bomber Softball Team, the group of Detroit schoolboy friends he had been financing since 1935. By the established traditions of boxing, Louis was entitled to a vacation. The heavyweight title carried tremendous prestige, and the champion could earn a good living fighting exhibitions and making peronal appearances. Previous champions had been reluctant to risk such a prize. After defeating Jack Johnson in 1915, Jess Willard defended his title only once before losing to Jack Dempsey in 1919. Dempsey defended his title five times in seven years. Gene Tunney took his title from Dempsey in 1926 and defended it twice before retiring in 1928. Between August 1928 and June 1937 there had been a grand total of seven heavyweight championship fights, with a shifting cast of undistinguished characters. Jimmy Braddock, Louis's predecessor, had held the championship two years without fighting.

But those champions had been white. Julian Black and John Roxborough felt the American public would not accept an inactive black champion. Mike Jacobs also wanted Louis to fight frequently. No title fights meant no big profits for the promoter. And Louis's spending habits ate up even his largest purses, leaving him in constant need of additional income. Louis and his managers signed a new five-year contract with Jacobs, committing themselves to four fights a year.

Everyone knew who Louis's next opponent should be. The new champion wanted Max Schmeling, and Schmeling wanted a shot at the championship. But Jacobs was unable to strike an agreement with Schmeling for a title fight against Louis in 1937. Schmeling demanded 30 percent of the gate; Jacobs insisted he take the challenger's normal share of 20 percent.

Schmeling turned Jacobs down and went ahead with his plans to fight Tommy Farr, the Welsh coal miner who was champion of the British Isles. Schmeling was still smarting from having gone through the motions of training and weighing in in New York, hoping to fight Braddock, while Braddock was training to fight Louis instead. Though the American press had been critical of Braddock for switching opponents, Schmeling felt humiliated and suspected an American conspiracy to keep the championship away from him. Schmeling had visions of beating Farr and declaring himself the European champion. He hoped the European title would put him in a better bargaining position with Jacobs.

Once again, Mike Jacobs and his money outmaneuvered Schmeling. Jacobs offered Farr a $60,000 guarantee, plus 25 percent of the radio and movie rights, to fight Louis in New York on August 26, 1937. The offer nearly doubled what Farr stood to make in a fight with Schmeling, and Farr agreed to fight Louis instead.

Schmeling, forced to play the role of spectator once more, visited Pompton Lakes as Louis wound up his training for the Farr fight. While Louis sparred, he saw Schmeling and the German's trainer, Max Machon, whispering together. After the workout Schmeling and Louis talked and posed for photographers. As usual, Louis said little. Although he went along with Jacobs's choice of Farr, Louis would have preferred to fight Schmeling. With the utter self-confidence that marks a great athlete, Louis never doubted that his own failure to train properly and his carelessness in the ring had been the only reasons for Schmeling's earlier victory. A year after that defeat, after trying on three different occasions to arrange a rematch, Louis still found himself posing for pictures with Schmeling and talking to reporters who believed that Schmeling was the better fighter. And Louis could see that Schmeling himself believed it. Louis resented Schmeling's status and self-confidence. He knew he could beat Schmeling.

When ring announcer Harry Balogh introduced Max Schmeling before the Louis-Farr fight in August, the Yankee Stadium crowd cheered. The cheers must have had a hollow ring in Schmeling's ears. The German boxer had learned that Mike Jacobs, not the boxing public, controlled his sport. Louis won a tough fifteen-round decision over Farr, and several days later Schmeling signed to fight Louis the following summer. Schmeling settled for 20 percent of the gate, plus a percentage of the radio and movie rights.

The delay was to prove disastrous for Schmeling. He would be almost thirty-three years old when he stepped into the ring against Louis in June 1938, an age when most boxers are past their prime. Louis, who would turn twenty-four in May 1938, was still approaching his physical peak.

Even worse for Schmeling, Adolf Hitler increased the pace of German rearmament and territorial expansion over the winter and spring of 1937–38. Up to that time, Hitler had contented himself with the gradual and systematic violation of the limits imposed on Germany's military establishment by the Versailles Treaty. Now Hitler embarked on a more radical course. At a secret meeting on November 5, 1937, Hitler told his military leaders, "The aim of German policy [is] to make secure and preserve the racial community and enlarge it. It [is] therefore a question of space." Hitler wanted new territory to the east. He would take advantage of any opportunity to overrun Austria and Czechoslovakia.

Hitler used an escalating series of demands and threats to demoralize the Austrian government and annexed Austria in March 1938. Soon thereafter he stepped up the German propaganda campaign against Czechoslovakia, ostensibly on behalf of the three million Sudeten Germans within Czech borders. German and Czech troops mobilized.

America joined in the general alarm about Hitler's ambitions. In addition, Americans were repelled by news of increased persecution of Jews and suppression of civil liberties in Germany.

World events made it increasingly difficult for Americans to disassociate Max Schmeling from his fascist homeland.

The aftermath of the first Louis-Schmeling fight wedded Schmeling to the Nazis in the American press. American reporters were unanimous in the perception that the Nazis had disapproved of the first Louis-Schmeling fight because they believed Schmeling would lose, then had claimed Schmeling's victory as a national and racial triumph.

The 1936 Olympics in Berlin added to the impression that the Nazis viewed sports as a test of their racist and nationalistic ideology. The performances of Jesse Owens and a host of other black track-and-field athletes highlighted the symbolic aspects of contests between American blacks and Germans. Now a German boxer was sailing to America for a fight with the black heavyweight champion of the world. The swastika hugged Schmeling like flypaper.

The Non-Sectarian Anti-Nazi League and the American Jewish Committee threatened to boycott the fight. Mike Jacobs, a Jew himself, tried to defuse the protests by announcing that he would donate a percentage of the proceeds to aid Jewish refugees from Germany. Jacobs also told the anti-Nazi groups that Louis would win and embarrass Hitler.

The boycott never materialized, and the political and racial angles fueled interest in the bout. In the *New York World-Telegram* Joe Williams wrote:

> Certainly Mike [Jacobs] needn't worry about racial antipathies affecting the turnout. As a matter of fact, there is an ancient pugilistic device known as the steam-up, which in past years was utilized to stimulate sentiment against fighters. But here's a hate motif ready made.
>
> Those who view in Schmeling a political symbol will be desperately hopeful for his downfall. If they have the cash they'll come, because you can do your wishful thinking a lot better when you're on the scene.

Pres. Franklin Roosevelt helped politicize the fight even more. In the spring of 1938 the Colored Elks invited Louis to Washington for their national convention as guest of honor.

FDR took advantage of Louis's visit and invited him to the White House. During the course of a brief conversation, Roosevelt said, "Lean over, Joe, so I can feel your muscles." The New York aristocrat told the son of an Alabama sharecropper, "Joe, we need muscles like yours to beat Germany."

When Schmeling sailed into New York aboard the S.S. *Bremen* in early May, he sensed a change in the American atmosphere. As usual, Mike Jacobs hired a tugboat for reporters who wanted to interview Schmeling on board the *Bremen*. In 1936 the reporters had been solely concerned with boxing; they had wanted to know if Schmeling was afraid of Louis. Now they asked Schmeling about Hitler and Nazi race policies. Do you consider yourself a member of the super race? What would happen to you in Germany, Max, if you lost? Schmeling reminded the reporters, many of whom he had known for years, "I am a fighter, not a politician. . . . I am no superman in any way."

When Schmeling got off the boat, a crowd of picketers was waiting for him. Signs called him a "Parade Aryan" and sarcastically referred to him as a member of the "master race." Jacobs hustled Schmeling into a car and took a roundabout route to Schmeling's hotel, but demonstrators were waiting there, too. When Schmeling walked out on the streets, people raised their right arms in contemptuous Nazi salutes. In his memoirs, published in 1980, Schmeling recalled:

> I was desperate. It was only two years since the same city had congratulated me so enthusiastically. . . . Now for the first time I began to realize it was no longer a matter of business. The goal that united all of them, promoters, editors, and boxing functionaries, was of a political nature: they had accepted a German champion in 1931, but a world champion that came from Hitler-Germany was unacceptable to all.
>
> Perhaps this reaction was understandable. As I had come back to Germany after the first fight with Joe Louis, I saw my fight depicted in the headlines and cartoons as a racial battle. My victory had been a "German victory." On the other hand [the American] people blamed me for the con-

gratulatory telegrams of the Nazi leaders and the occasional contact with them. Roosevelt had also invited Joe Louis into the White House before the fight. And the politicization of sport which was pushed so hard by the Third Reich found a sort of echo on the other side of the Atlantic. The one group came to emulate the other one, and this was bad for sport.

These are all thoughts decades later. At the time I was a young man with only the thought of a title fight in my head. I had tried in all honesty to persuade Hitler of the virtues of my Jewish manager, Joe Jacobs [no relation to Mike Jacobs]. Now I wanted to make clear to the Americans my good right to a title fight.

The one attempt was as naive as the other.

Nat Fleischer, editor of *Ring* magazine, prepared a radio script for Schmeling to read, appealing to the sportsmanship of the American public. No radio station would air it. Badly shaken by his reception, Schmeling left New York city earlier than planned. He could not get to the solitude of his Speculator, New York, training camp quickly enough.

The American press emphasized the symbolic confrontation between Schmeling and Louis by portraying both fighters in terms of ethnic stereotypes. Showing their usual preoccupation with elegant variation and racial and national identity, sportswriters constantly identified Schmeling as "the German," "the Teuton," *"Der Schlager,"* "Moxie," "Herr Schmeling," and "the Black Uhlan." The black press often referred to him as "the Nazi-man." In 1936 American journalists had described Schmeling as a courageous, hardworking underdog with a sense of humor. Now they made him into a grim, stiff businessman. The early stories that set the tone for the fight buildup talked about what great shape Schmeling was in. Schmeling told repoters he never let himself get more than five pounds over his fighting weight. Reporters often quoted him as saying, "Fighting is my business."

Hugh Bradley of the *New York Post*, in a column entitled "Grim Perseverance Marks Schmeling's Training Camp Life," wrote:

Schmeling is a "loner." Even Max Machon, Schmeling's trainer . . . is not really close to him. He talks pleasantly enough over a wide range of topics when the mood, or the necessity, is on him. But no interviewer has yet brought out the real Schmeling through conversation. . . . You go away from him with the impression of an aloof, cold, grim, even bitter Schmeling lurking in the background of a suave interior. When he talks politics he speaks pieces that might well have come out of a handbook of party discipline. When inquiry interferes with his logic at such times he resorts to the diplomat's subterfuge of parrying question with question until the matter is sidetracked. . . .

Where purely physical matters are concerned he never attempts to duck. When he skips rope he does not merely go through the appointed motions for the prescribed time. If he makes a misstep he starts the routine all over again.

In contrast to the image of Schmeling working earnestly, writers continued to write about Louis as a lazy, stereotypical darkie. Arthur Sampson of the *Boston Herald* wrote: "Louis is naturally lazy by nature and has to be forced or driven into condition." Hugh Bradley wrote:

He has no skill at skipping rope, dislikes shadow boxing and road work. Even the drills with sparring partners have palled on him because so often repeated. His idea is that championships are won and defended inside the ring by the simple process of boffing the other fellow on the button. Arduous weeks of preparation . . . have no appeal to him.

In truth, Louis was a hard worker who fought so often that he was rarely out of condition. And for the Schmeling rematch Louis was training harder and more enthusiastically than ever. John Roxborough told any reporters who would listen that the Schmeling defeat had transformed Louis. Roxborough remembered that Louis had been overconfident before the first Schmeling fight and hadn't trained properly. "The Joe Louis . . . who made feeble feints at training for the first Max Schmeling fight, was an uncontrollable, willfully stubborn, spoiled boy." This time, Roxborough said, "he couldn't get into Pompton Lakes fast enough. His present mental attitude is the best I've ever known him to attain. . . . His eagerness has captivated the whole camp."

The real tip-off to Louis's determination was an empty space in his closet. Louis took his golf clubs to all of his training camps, even to Kenosha, Wisconsin, when he was training to fight Jimmy Braddock for the world's championship. But this time he did not bring his clubs to Pompton Lakes.

In their attempts to predict the fight's outcome, white sportswriters used stereotypes to analyze the strengths and weaknesses of the two fighters. The writers described Louis as a natural athlete who could not think in the ring. Schmeling emerged from newspaper columns as a smart and methodical boxer with limited physical assets.

Bill Corum of the *New York Journal and American* wrote:

> I don't believe anybody is going to TEACH Joe Louis how to fight. I do believe that he was born knowing and that he is the best and most exciting heavyweight of modern times when he is fighting by instinct, instead of trying to fight by the numbers.
>
> How does anybody propose to make Joe a better methodical fighter than the Teutonic Schmeling, who is old Herr Methodical himself?
>
> There are certain gifts that the Negro race, as a race, and Louis, as an individual, have as a heritage. The ability carefully to work out a methodical plan and adhere to it, is not among them. That's for Schmeling.

Though the reporters unanimously labeled Louis a natural athlete, they did not rate him a great fighter. His loss to Schmeling and his failure to knock out Bob Pastor and Tommy Farr created doubts. A majority of boxing writers picked Louis to win, not because they thought he was a great fighter but only because they were even less enthusiastic about Schmeling's ability. Dan Parker was one of only a handful of writers willing to praise Louis's ability before the fight. Parker pointed out, "[Louis] has accomplished more in the four years he has been fighting as a professional than any heavyweight in history." The *Omaha World-Herald* expressed the prevailing opinion: "Neither is a great fighter; neither is a great boxer. One

[Schmeling] was not a great champion. The other has not been a great champion."

Harking back to Louis's old jungle-killer image, many reporters still felt that somewhere beneath Louis's black skin lurked a savage animal. If Louis could tap that spirit in the ring, Bill Corum wrote, he could overwhelm Schmeling:

> It may be possible to make a tiger into an easy going, well trained house pet. Still, he was a better tiger when he was in the jungle. And Joe Louis was at his best as a fighter when he was a tiger of the ring. Which is what he was. And can be again, I think, if they'll just shove him out there under those floodlights and say:
> "Now go on!"

Louis had, in fact, decided to attack from the beginning. Watching films of the first bout with Schmeling, Louis and Blackburn saw that Schmeling needed to set himself before throwing his right hand. When Louis had been on the offensive in the early rounds, he had been able to back Schmeling up. It was only when Louis relinquished the offensive, when he failed to follow his jab with other punches, that Schmeling had time to set and counter his right hand over Louis's left. This time Louis would keep the pressure on Schmeling, backing him up and giving him no chance to retaliate. It was an aggressive strategy, and a smart one.

This strategy corresponded with Louis's mood. He had waited two years to avenge his loss to Schmeling. Only a decisive victory would erase that defeat from his own mind. And apart from professional pride, Louis also felt great personal hostility toward Schmeling. Schmeling had accused Louis of deliberately fouling late in their first fight and had said that Louis was the kind of man who remembered a beating, that the memory would make him afraid.

Louis did not hide his anger from reporters. Harvey Boyle of the *Pittsburgh Post-Gazette* wrote:

> Usually Louis, on the side of diplomacy, and handled expertly in his public relations, has been pleasant with all

foemen, stressing the virtues of his opponent, playing down his own part. Because of this attitude, whether sincere or posed, he has, in spite of his color, risen to eminence with a modicum of prejudice against him.

He has, for the moment, however, dropped the old college spirit toward a fraternity brother, and he has been quoted several times as saying he would rather beat Schmeling than any fellow he has met. This is natural in view of the knockout he suffered and Schmeling's fouling charge.

Murray Lewin of the *New York Daily Mirror* quoted an uncharacteristically angry Louis:

I am out for revenge. All I ask of Schmeling is that he stand up and fight without quitting. I'll give him enough to remember me for life and make him hang up his gloves for all time. I've waited for two years for this chance and now my time has come.

John Roxborough told John Kieran of the *New York Times*:

Ordinarily, you know, Joe doesn't care who the other fellow is. It's just another fight for Joe. But this Schmeling— on account of that other fight and what everybody has been saying—well, it's sorta got under Joe's skin. This time it isn't just another fight; it's a chance to catch up with Schmeling and square an account.

The symbolic aspects of the fight added to Louis's resolve. As the fight approached, rumors began to fly. Adolf Hitler would make Schmeling minister of sport if he recaptured the title. Max Machon, Schmeling's trainer, had a Nazi uniform in his closet. Schmeling said that no black man could beat a member of the master race. None of this was true, but the people around Louis, trying to motivate him, had every reason to repeat the rumors to Louis and encourage him to believe them. Shirley Povich, who covered the fight for the *Washington Post*, recalled years later, "I think [Louis] was led to hate Schmeling and what the Nazis stood for. You can understand that. It's a common thing, that if you hate the Jews, other people, you hate Negroes."

Press coverage of the fight also highlighted its symbolic aspects. American newspapers emphasized the international character of the fight by running wire stories on the buildup in Germany. The Associated Press reported from Berlin:

> German fans leave only one choice for Maxie—a comeback. His German admirers—and there are millions, from Reichsfuehrer Hitler down—hate the thought of defeat.
>
> Newspapers do not say it, but it is tacitly understood that a Louis victory would be taken here as a disgrace from the Nazi racial viewpoint. Some sports followers predict oblivion would be Schmeling's punishment.

American reporters worried about the possible consequences of a Schmeling victory. They often expressed fear that Schmeling would take his title back to Germany if he won and refuse to defend it in America. Again and again Schmeling promised he would return to New York to fight, because New York was the only place for a boxer to make real money. But reporters kept asking him about it, and many suspected that Schmeling was lying or that the Nazis would forbid him to return to America.

Geoffrey Simpson of the *London Daily Mail* wrote:

> It is the title [Schmeling] wants on behalf of himself and the German nation. If successful he promises to defend the championship in the United States next September, but my guess is that he will take the next boat back to Germany. That's what the Americans are scared of.

The American perception that the Nazis considered Schmeling their representative caused a natural counterreaction. The press often wrote of Louis as the American representative and sometimes openly rooted for him to win. An editorial writer for the *Beckley (W. Va.) Post-Herald* said:

> Since the future of boxing is involved, most persons are now hoping that Louis will win.
>
> Everybody fears that Max will take his title back to Germany—in case he wins it. Nobody with a sense of fairness wants to see the next heavyweight championship fight staged in the land bossed by Hitler. . . .

About 75 percent of the fight fans in New York are Jewish. Schmeling represents one of the worst enemies in the world, so far as these sportsmen are concerned. They are definitely right. . . .

Race prejudice should have NO place in sports. But Hitler has created a situation which the civilized world cannot and will not overlook. In trying to prove that the Germans are supreme in all things he has made an 18-karat jackass of himself and caused the Nazis to be despised almost throughout the world.

Using sentiment—and judgment too—I choose Joe Louis, an American Negro, to beat the ears off Max.

Bill Henry of the *Los Angeles Times* described the fight as a "pugilistic drama starring Joe Louis as the hero and Max Schmeling as villain," Even those writers who thought Schmeling would win often described the fight in symbolic terms and hoped they were wrong. Hugh Bradley of the *New York Post* wrote a column picking Schmeling, entitled, "Logic, Hope Clash As Max Schmeling Gets Nod Over Joe." The story began, "Tonight two men swing fists for the heavyweight championship of the world. I do not like one of these men and greatly detest the system he represents."

American hostility toward Germany and Schmeling increased when the U.S. government indicted eighteen American citizens four days before the fight, accusing them of spying on America for the Nazis. A British observer, writing for the *Manchester Guardian*, summed up American sentiments on the eve of the fight:

> There is no question that the anti-Jewish drive in Germany and the sensational American spy indictment in which several Germans are involved have caused many Americans to hope fervently that Joe Louis will beat Max Schmeling in their world championship fight here to-night.
>
> As an individual Schmeling is obviously popular with most people, but as a German he will have to bear the brunt of Americans' dislike of many of Germany's recent actions. To them he is a symbol of Nazism.

The German press also noted the American press's symbolic approach to the fight. The *Volkischer Beobachter*, a Nazi organ, said the day before the fight:

But that which the American newspapers publish exceeds all swindles that have existed up to now. Under a cloud of lies they try to make clear to their readers that Germany just wants to prove racial superiority through a victory by Schmeling. Yes, they even state that it would go badly for our man in Germany in case of a defeat. . . . This time, [Schmeling] has been made, not by us, but in the yellow press of America, a representative of Nazi Germany, who is supposed to be an important agent of German propaganda.

Der Ansgriff, another Nazi paper, accused the United States of "baiting of the worst sort and stupid attacks" on Schmeling and said the Americans were making "a racial question and political affair" out of the fight.

There was no question that the American public attached a strong symbolic importance to the second Louis-Schmeling fight and accepted Louis—a black man—as the representative of American strength and virtue. That was revolutionary—so much so that some writers felt obliged to downplay the significance of Louis's role. Bill Corum wrote, "The fight will decide the supremacy between Joe Louis and Max Schmeling. Just that. Nothing more." He went on: "I cannot believe that Schmeling will be completely discredited in Germany if he loses, any more than I believe Louis will be in Harlem if he is beaten." Grantland Rice wrote, "In the general scheme of things, both men are completely unimportant."

Some journalists tried to write Schmeling out of the part that circumstances had created for him. Burris Jenkins, Jr., a cartoonist for the *New York Journal and American*, depicted Louis and Schmeling fighting each other, illuminated by a searchlight labeled "politics." A shadowy figure and a scroll that read "Nordic Supremacy" rose above Schmeling. Abraham Lincoln and a scroll that read "That All Men Are Created Equal" rose above Louis. In a caption, Jenkins wrote, "You can't blame

Schmeling—a likeable, courageous, honest fighter—for whatever political propaganda his nation's leaders try to attach to his victory or defeat."

Four days before the fight, the *New York Times* printed this letter from a reader in Chicago:

> To Sports Editor of the *New York Times*:
> On listening to the [Barney] Ross-[Henry] Armstrong fight a short time ago, an announcement was made of the upcoming Joe Louis-Max Schmeling bout. Upon the announcing of the name of Schmeling, a "boo" proceeded from the crowd and great cheers resounded for Joe Louis, who will represent our country in this particular event. . . . Being a firm upholder and believer of all-American standards and principles, it is my opinion that if we receive Max Schmeling as a guest and likewise treat him as such, with the good old-fashioned sportsmanship we have been known to express, surely we cannot lose a thing but rather gain more respect from all of our foreign cousins. . . .
> Are we to be biased and bigoted toward one individual? Schmeling has nothing to do with the government of his country.
> We have always boasted about being such good sports, now why not prove it since we have the opportunity? Come on, let's be Americans all the way through—show them that we know how to be gentlemen and gentlewomen.
> With sincere wishes that America retains the title.
> Myrtle S. Weigand

Schmeling himself understood what was happening. Certainly he neither wanted nor deserved the role as representative of Nazism. He refused to comment on Nazi race ideology or on persecutions against the Jews, but he defended the German people against charges of racism. He told Jack Mahon of the *New York Daily News*: "Germans are the fairest people in the world. They mobbed that little fellow Jesse Owens when he was there with the Olympic team in '36 and he beat Germans, didn't they?"

On the other hand, Schmeling was a patriotic German, and he was not yet a public critic of Hitler's regime—to be fair, he

could not afford to be. Hitler and the Nazis had helped make
Schmeling a national hero. An autographed picture of Hitler
hung in the study of Schmeling's home in Germany. Schmeling
denied that Hitler viewed the fight as a test of his racist ideology.
"This is just another heavyweight fight," Schmeling told Mahon:

> Of course, Hitler and all Germany is interested in my at-
> tempt to win back the championship. I have had so much
> trouble getting my chance they are all rooting for me. But
> sport is sport in Germany—nothing more. Hitler is very
> interested in boxing. He devoted a whole page to it in his
> book called "My Struggle." That does not mean, however,
> he would put me in prison or even be seriously concerned
> if I was beaten.

As so many Germans did during the 1930s, Schmeling saw a
good side of the Nazi government. He told Gene Kessler, who
was as willing to use exaggerated dialect for a German as for a
black, "Ve haff no strikes in Germany. Most everybody has a
job. Times are goot. Ve have only one union. Ve have only one
party. Everyone agreeable. Everybody happy."

Schmeling had already experienced the hostility of American
crowds in New York. In the supercharged prefight atmosphere,
he had good reason to fear his reception when he went back
into the city and Yankee Stadium. He and his trainer, Max
Machon, also had reason to suspect that the boxing commission,
the referee, judges, and even the promoter would all favor Louis.

Rumors also reached Schmeling's camp that Louis was working himself into a vengeful rage. This was perhaps the most
fearsome prospect of all and the surest sign that the fight had
gotten out of hand. Watching Louis perform six months before
their first fight, Schmeling had been impressed with Louis's
coolness and professionalism. Schmeling considered Louis and
himself part of the same brotherhood, men who fought because
they were good at it. Professional boxers did not pay much
attention to prefight publicity; they didn't get mad at each
other. After World War II Schmeling took great pains to bring
about a reconciliation with Louis. The way the press played the
two boxers off against each other clearly bothered Schmeling.

Even after beating Louis once, Schmeling knew Louis was a dangerous and talented fighter. Schmeling expected Louis to fight cautiously, to be defensive against a man who had already knocked him out once. But an angry and inspired Louis would be an unknown quantity. And Schmeling knew where that anger and inspiration would come from. He got it just right in his memoirs:

> Joe Louis, who yesterday had been celebrated by the colored population of Harlem as the exponent of an underprivileged class, was suddenly the symbol of freedom and equal rights of all men and races against the Nazi threat. Soon it also trickled through that someone had also said to Louis himself that I wanted to demonstrate in the coming fight the superiority of whites over Negroes. Joe, the Negro, found himself unwittingly in the role of a national hero, of all Americans.

It was a role that America had never before accorded to a black, and Louis accepted it without making too much of this surprising turn of events. In a ghosted article syndicated nationwide on the day of the fight, he said:

> Tonight I not only fight the battle of my life to revenge the lone blot on my record, but I fight for America against the challenge of a foreign invader, Max Schmeling. This isn't just one man against another or Joe Louis boxing Max Schmeling; it is the good old U.S.A. versus Germany.

It is important to note, however, that even on the eve of a fight in which most Americans were rooting for him to defeat the symbol of Nazi Germany, Americans honored Joe Louis more as a symbol than as a man. As a boxer, his quality was still in question; many American sportswriters thought Schmeling would win. Some southern reporters, like O. B. Keeler of the *Atlanta Journal* and Bob Jones of the *Richmond Times-Dispatch*, were rooting for Schmeling.

June 22, 1938, was a Wednesday. Carl Nelson, Louis's bodyguard, woke the heavyweight champion of the world at nine A.M. Louis left for New York City at ten, in a car with Jack

Blackburn, Julian Black, John Roxborough, and Nelson, escorted by three state troopers. The car pulled up in front of the New York Boxing Commission's office at eleven. A crowd of people and newsreel cameras were waiting. Louis wore a light suit without a tie, a polka-dot scarf, a white hat with a black band around the base of the crown, and dark sunglasses with two small, perfect circles for lenses. This invisible man walked between two walls of spectators into the commission's office with slow, easy strides.

Inside, Louis stripped down to boxing shorts for the weigh-in. Schmeling was there, also in shorts. Reporters and photographers wearing suits surrounded the two athletes, staring, snapping pictures, taking notes, occasionally calling out something to Louis or Schmeling. The two fighters nodded to each other, not speaking. Schmeling weighed in at 193, Louis at 198½.

Louis spent the afternoon at a friend's apartment. At three he ate a salad and a steak, then went for a walk along the Harlem River with Blackburn and his friend Freddie Wilson. "How you feel, Joe?" Wilson asked Louis.

"I'm scared."

"Scared?" Wilson asked.

"Yeah, I'm scared I might kill Schmeling tonight," Louis said.

Louis and his party drove to Yankee Stadium at seven. "There were cops wherever you looked," Louis recalled. "When we got to the stadium, you could hardly get in. . . . Going up, we didn't laugh much. Nobody made jokes. It was an important fight."

In his dressing room at Yankee Stadium, less than three hours before the most important fight of his life, Joe Louis went to sleep. Blackburn, Roxborough, Black, and the rest of Louis's entourage waited, talking softly so as not to wake their fighter. Night fell. Outside, members of the Non-Sectarian Anti-Nazi League distributed leaflets calling for a boycott of German goods. Communists handed out leaflets asking the fans to give three cheers for Louis and to boo Schmeling. Over 70,000 people walked into Yankee Stadium, filling the grandstand and bleachers that overlooked the baseball field, milling around on the infield before taking their seats in the neat rows of folding chairs that stretched away from the ring on all sides. Cigarette smoke hung in the muggy air.

At nine P.M., Blackburn woke Louis. Mike Jacobs stepped into the dressing room and said, "Joe, I told these folks you're gonna knock that German out. Don't make a sucker out of me, and make it a quick knockout." Blackburn taped Louis's hands, a familiar, soothing ritual for both of them. Blackburn stretched the tape diagonally across Louis's palms and then straight across the knuckles, curling Louis's fingers into a half fist. Blackburn said, "Keep cool. It's going to be all right." Louis watched Blackburn work, occasionally flexing his fingers to test the bandages and to feel the tape against his hands. He told Blackburn, "In three rounds, Chappie. If I don't have Schmeling knocked out, you better come in and get me, because after that, I'm through."

Blackburn said, "No, it's all right. You can go fifteen rounds." But Louis had no intention of letting the fight go the limit. He would either knock Schmeling out early or exhaust himself trying.

Usually Louis shadowboxed for ten minutes before a fight. This night he shadowboxed for half an hour, until it was time to go into the ring. His arms cut the air, with no opponent there to measure their speed and power, with no fans there to watch save his friends, the men who had invested in him, and the trainer who had taught him to throw those punches better than any man in the world.

When he was through, Louis put on a flannel robe and a blue silk robe over it. The champion and his handlers walked to the door of the dressing room. An escort of uniformed policemen surrounded them and led them to the ring.

In the other dressing room Max Schmeling was nervous, unusually so. He heard the cheers from the crowd as the fans caught sight of Louis, a noise that built as Louis entered the ring. Schmeling left his dressing room and walked to the ring in the middle of a police escort. The crowd applauded, but fans on the infield threw banana peels, cigarette packs, and paper cups at Schmeling as he passed. Schmeling covered his head with a towel to protect himself. Once he reached the ring policemen formed a square inside the ropes to block any more thrown objects.

Max Machon left Schmeling to go over to Louis's corner and watch as Louis put on his gloves. Doc Casey, an American who had worked Schmeling's corner for years as a second, had been so shocked by the prefight hysteria that he did not go into the ring with Schmeling. The New York Boxing Commission had banned Schmeling's manager, Joe Jacobs, from the ring because of his connection with Tony Galento, a boxer temporarily out of favor with the commission. In the middle of a sea of people, Schmeling felt lonely.

Over the radio Clem McCarthy told seventy million listeners this was "the greatest fight of our generation." Ring announcer Harry Balogh introduced Jim Braddock, Jack Sharkey, and Max Baer, all former heavyweight champions, all Louis knockout victims. The crowd booed. Balogh introduced the fighters. The crowd cheered both men but cheered louder for Louis.

Referee Arthur Donovan called the two fighters to the center of the ring for instructions. With a sixth sense, Donovan said, "I don't want anybody from your corners sticking his head through the ropes during this fight. It may cause serious trouble." The fighters went back to their corners, and the ring emptied. Louis danced and punched the air. As he waited for the bell, Louis moved up and down on his toes and hitched up his trunks. He looked anxious. Sweat shone on his brown skin.

In the other corner Max Schmeling stood still, arms hanging at his sides, and stared at Louis. Schmeling hadn't shaved. His black, shaggy eyebrows stood out on his face. Max Machon stood outside the ropes on the ring apron, his left hand patting Schmeling's arm, talking to his fighter. Machon was four or five inches shorter than Schmeling. He wore baggy gray trousers and a white long-sleeved shirt. A white towel hung around his neck. Just before the fight began, Machon dropped his arm from Schmeling's shoulder and looked across the ring at Louis. Machon looked back at Schmeling, then turned away as the bell rang.

Schmeling walked out quickly to meet Louis and wiped his brow with his right hand. The two fighters circled each other, heads and shoulders bobbing in quick jerks. Schmeling used the same stance he had in their first fight, leaning backward with his left hand up and his right cocked near his chin. Schmeling backed two steps away, and Louis followed. Louis jabbed, popping Schmeling's greased hair up, jabbed again, and dropped his shoulder for a left hook that landed to Schmeling's face. Schmeling leaned in, Louis pushed him back and threw a short left uppercut that Schmeling ducked, and they broke. Schmeling brushed his forehead with his right glove, leaned back, and waved his left out at Louis. Schmeling backed toward the ropes. Louis suddenly flew at Schmeling, feinting with his right hand, jump stepping with his left foot and throwing a left hook from the waist that went around Schmeling's right hand and landed on the side of Schmeling's head.

Schmeling leaned forward into Louis, gloves covering both sides of his head, and Louis bent down to meet him head to head in a clinch. Louis rose up with a right uppercut that Schmeling partially blocked, then rocked Schmeling back with a left and drove the German into the ropes with a right cross. Louis followed with a straight left that caught Schmeling in the eye and a right to the head, Schmeling ducking with the punch and leaning into Louis.

Louis leaned back and threw a left hook that Schmeling ducked. Schmeling put out his left arm fully extended, as if to push Louis away. Louis ducked under it and leaned forward, backing Schmeling into the ropes, and threw a left just as Schmeling threw his first punch of the night, a weak right. Louis followed with an overhand right. Schmeling ducked, covered up, and leaned down, still trapped against the ropes.

The fighters clinched. Louis tried to work Schmeling's body in tight with a right that Schmeling blocked. Schmeling leaned into Louis with his head and shoulders and brought his right around Louis's arms but could not reach Louis's side with it. Louis tried another right in tight, leaned away and missed with a left hook, and they broke.

Louis immediately jabbed, then pulled his left hand back very high and ducked away, anticipating a right from Schmeling. Schmeling just jabbed weakly with his left, tickling Louis's chest. Louis jabbed, jabbed again, and crossed with a right to Schmeling's face. Schmeling clinched again. Louis pushed him away with both hands, and as Schmeling went backward, his mouth opened, and his eyebrows arched in reflexive fear. Schmeling raised his right hand in front of his face, glove open, with the thumb sticking out, but quickly backed away and resumed his stance.

Louis moved in on Schmeling again, jabbed to Schmeling's face, pulled back for a left hook that Schmeling blocked, but followed with a quick overhand right that landed solidly, driving Schmeling's head down. Schmeling clinched again. Max Machon was yelling, "Move, Max, move!" Louis pushed Schmeling away, and again Schmeling's right hand came up reflexively before he settled back into his stance.

Schmeling leaned away from Louis with an anxious look on his face. Schmeling pawed the air twice with his left. Louis pushed Schmeling's left hand away with his right and dropped down for a big left hook that Schmeling ducked, but now Schmeling was against the ropes. Louis leaned forward with the momentum of his blow, and the two fighters bent over at the waist, their heads and shoulders locked together, gloves up around their chins. Louis tried a right uppercut that Schmeling blocked, landed a weak left to Schmeling's face, drove his left solidly into Schmeling's face again, and threw an overhand right from the shoulder that won the fight. Schmeling blacked out, staggering backward, arms flailing out to catch his balance. Schmeling caught the top strand of the ropes with his right hand and held on, acting only on instinct now.

With Schmeling turned sideways to him and leaning on the ropes, Louis tried to hold Schmeling's chin in place with his left but was unable to reach Schmeling's face with a right hand, Schmeling somehow warding him off with his left arm. Louis drove a left into the middle of Schmeling's stomach. Schmeling bent over and stumbled but hung onto the rope with his right hand. Louis swung a left hook for the head, but Schmeling ducked back against the ropes, turning his body away from Louis, exposing his left side. Louis stuck out his left for Schmeling's chin, as if to hold it in place or get the range for his next punch, and threw a roundhouse right that went under Schmeling's left arm and landed on the side of Schmeling's back. The punch was so powerful that it broke two vertebrae. Schmeling screamed in pain, his mouth opening in a circle, but Louis closed Schmeling's mouth quickly with a left to the body and a left to the head, then an overhand right to the head, a left hook, and an overhand right. Schmeling leaned into the ropes and held on to them with both hands. Another left hook and overhand right made Schmeling's knees buckle; he would have gone down, but his chin caught on the top rope.

Referee Donovan stepped in and pushed Louis away, giving Schmeling a standing count. Schmeling turned, his right hand still on the top strand of the ropes, his left arm and elbow pressing against his side where Louis had hit him. Schmeling moved forward and tried to resume his stance but could not raise his left arm. Donovan hesitated and stopped counting at two. Schmeling was out on his feet and could not take advantage of the full count. The pause in the action was so brief that few spectators understood what was happening.

Louis rushed at Schmeling and threw a left-right combination that snapped Schmeling's head sideways. Schmeling fell forward and rolled over on his back, then rolled on his side. Referee Donovan nearly ran Louis to a neutral corner, but when he turned back to Schmeling, the German was already on his feet. Donovan forgot to wipe the resin from Schmeling's gloves.

Louis approached Schmeling again, and Schmeling ducked on rubbery legs. Louis stood him up with a left hook to the head and dropped Schmeling to his hands and knees with a right cross. Schmeling got up immediately, just as Donovan was beginning to lead Louis to a neutral corner. This time Donovan remembered to wipe Schmeling's gloves on his shirtfront. Schmeling looked over Donovan's shoulder at Louis, who was bouncing up and down, waiting for the referee to get out of the way. Donovan dropped Schmeling's gloves, and once more Schmeling tried to get into his stance. Louis jabbed to get the range, pushed away Schmeling's outstretched left with his right, and threw a left jab to the face, a right to Schmeling's damaged left side, a left hook and a right cross, and Schmeling fell.

Max Machon threw a white towel into the ring. Arthur Donovan led Louis to a neutral corner, where Louis waited in his usual pose, hands on top of the ropes on either side of the corner post. Donovan picked up the towel and threw it on the ropes; there it hung perfectly folded on the middle strand. New York boxing rules did not allow a fighter's corner to surrender. Only the referee could stop the fight.

In the center of the ring, Max Schmeling pushed himself up with his arms, his legs curled under him. Schmeling got to his hands and knees, tried to stand up on his right foot, failed, and went back to his knees. Donovan stood over Schmeling and picked up the count from the official timekeeper. Clem McCarthy growled to the radio audience, "The count is five. Five . . . six . . . seven . . . eight."

Max Machon ran into the ring, afraid the Americans would maim his friend. The crowd had been yelling at full volume for over a minute. Donovan pushed Machon away. Donovan knew Schmeling could not continue. Confused and hurried, with Louis's handlers rushing him from the other side of the ring, as surprised by what had happened as the crowd, Donovan quickly waved his arms over Schmeling. Donovan had stopped the fight before the count reached ten. Official result: technical knockout, at 2:04 of the first round. Donovan lifted Schmeling under the armpits and got Schmeling up on his feet. Donovan's left arm cradled Schmeling's head until Max Machon led the beaten fighter away.

After the fight Schmeling's dressing room was quiet. Schmeling told the NBC radio audience: "Ladies and gentlemen I have not much to say. I very sorry, but, I won't make any excuse, but I get such a terrible hit, the first hit I get in the left kidneys, I was so paralyzed I couldn't even move. And then after it was all over, you know." Schmeling's trainer, Max Machon, and his American manager, Joe Jacobs, claimed that Louis had hit Schmeling with an illegal kidney punch—a foul. Under the pressure of reporters' questions, Schmeling, still befuddled from the beating he had taken, also said he had been fouled. Schmeling got dressed, and an ambulance took him to Polyclinic Hospital.

Louis, as always, remained calm, and his joy was understated. One of the many reporters who crowded around the champion in his dressing room described him as shy. Still quiet and a little uneasy around writers, Louis announced, "I'm sure enough champion now." *Life* magazine quoted Louis's recollections of the body punch that had hurt Schmeling so badly: "I just hit him, tha's all. I hit him right in the ribs and I guess maybe it was a lucky punch but man, did he scream! I thought it was a lady in the ringside cryin'. He just screamed, tha's all." Louis tried to describe his feelings after his greatest victory. "Something of a relief, I guess, I don't know. But I feel better about being champion." A reporter asked Louis if he would fight Schmeling again. "What for?" Louis replied. "Didn't I just beat him?"

In a two-minute capsule, the second Louis-Schmeling fight epitomized the qualities that made Joe Louis a great boxer. When he climbed into the ring against Schmeling, Louis faced all the pressures of an athletic championship and more. Having lost to Schmeling before, the fight would decide whether Louis would be rated a success or an also-ran; it was the crucible of his career. Moreover, he carried all the hopes of his race into a fight against the symbol of militant racism. If Louis had lost, he would have been criticized as a boxer and derided as another losing Negro. Few human beings face tests like that the Schmeling fight posed for Louis, a single event that will decide whether a life's work will be a success or a failure, with no second chances and the whole world watching. Louis was only twenty-four, and he was not the sort of man who lay awake nights thinking of all these things. It was an accident that his personal test was fraught with historic significance. Nevertheless, vibrating with the moment like some sublime tuning fork, Joe Louis tapped his sense of self, his courage, self-control, and his physical talent and performed heroically.

Louis's victory was sudden and complete. It shocked most of the sportswriters who saw it and erased all doubt about Louis's ability as a boxer. White sportswriters were unrestrained in their praise. Dave Walsh of the *Philadelphia Record* wrote, "Louis is unquestionably a great fighter. He got nailed and came back. It was the finest boxing and hitting that I and Schmeling ever saw." James P. Dawson of the *New York Times*: "Louis at last is undisputed champion. He's a great fighter, and there's no one around to beat him. Schmeling never had a chance." Richards Vidmer of the *New York Herald-Tribune*: "Louis is the best in the world today and I don't know how many yesterdays." Buck O'Neill, *Washington Times*: "Louis established himself one of the greatest fighters of all time. No fighter ever lived, including Dempsey, who could throw shorter or faster punches with such terrific power." Dan Parker of the *New York Daily Mirror*: "Louis has finally come into his full estate as a great world's champion. If any one doubts his greatness after his masterful job last night, he's plain plumb prejudiced."

Reporters thought Louis had returned to the form he had shown earlier in his career, when his destructiveness had inspired jungle-killer imagery. Lewis F. Atchison of the *Washington Post* began his account of the fight, "Joe Louis, the lethargic, chicken-eating young colored boy, reverted to his dreaded role of the 'brown bomber' tonight. . . ." Henry McLemore of the United Press used some of the most blatant jungle-killer language:

> The slow-motion picture of the 124 seconds of the Joe Louis-Max Schmeling fight is probably the most faithful recording ever made of human savagery.
>
> The picture is much more terrifying to watch than the fight was. In the Yankee Stadium the rapidity with which the butchering occurred, against the background of noise and excitement, prevented anyone from getting a cold and objective view of it. In the quiet darkness of the small theatre where I saw the fight pictures yesterday afternoon I was appalled by the knowledge that this ruthless, unmerciful killer there on the screen was one and the same man as the Joe Louis who I had just left a few minutes before— a Joe Louis who talked of ice cream, and trips to Europe, and his new pin-striped suit.
>
> I saw Joe again after I had seen the pictures, and although he was sitting in the same chair and talking in the same low voice, I didn't feel fully comfortable around him. It was as if I had seen a savage tiger behind the bar of a cage suddenly loosed to walk free among the people who had been watching him.

The Louis of the slow-motion pictures has no connection with ice cream and pin-stripe suits and discussions of the weather. He is a jungle man, as completely primitive as any savage, out to destroy the thing he hates. Even the style of fighting he had been patiently taught was abandoned. He fought instinctively and not by any man-made pattern.

Louis had given the reporters the impression that he was mad at Schmeling before the fight, and the reporters thought his performance all the more vicious because they assumed Louis had fought out of hatred. UP writer Jack Cuddy described Louis's attack on Schmeling as "panther-like," and wrote: ". . . the Detroit Negro's mask-like face showed its hatred only through the eyes that gleamed at the former champion like those of an irate cobra."
Bill Corum wrote:

He's the greatest fighter I ever saw, or ever expect to see. Somebody'll beat him. But nobody will ever beat the Joe Louis you saw last night.
Not a Joe Louis who is young, well trained—and mad.
Mark that last. When the animal in this placid, quiet Negro boy surges into his fists, then it's river, stay away from that door. When he's a tan tiger cat, he's the killer supreme.

American reporters had no sympathy with Schmeling's claim that he had been fouled. One reporter likened Schmeling's cries of "foul" in his locker room to a "song on a broken phonograph." Schmeling's foul claim seemed like a weak excuse. Louis had made no excuses two years before when he lost to Schmeling. More than one reporter compared Louis's sportsmanship on that occasion with Schmeling's lack of it. Mike Jacobs invited reporters to watch slow-motion films of the fight, which revealed that Schmeling was already on his way to defeat when Louis hit him in the side. The film also showed that Schmeling had turned his side toward Louis.

Newspaper coverage on June 23, the day after the fight, concentrated on Louis's physical dominance and ferocity and on Schmeling's foul claims. The next day, June 24, newspaper stories on the fight changed their emphasis. Looking for a feature angle on what was already old news, American newspapers seized on the international implications of the fight. The *New York Times'* Amsterdam correspondent wired home this report on reaction to the fight in the Netherlands:

> Interest was general since the fight was considered not only a sporting event but political—those who are not sympathetic to national socialism hoping for a Louis victory to disprove German racial doctrines while the pro-Nazis hoped a Schmeling victory would prove the superiority of pure Aryan blood.
>
> It can generally be said, however, that the majority favored Louis. . . .

In reporting Germany's reaction, the *Times* noted that Hitler sent a message of sympathy to Annie Ondra, Schmeling's blond movie-star wife, and that Propaganda Minister Joseph Goebbels sent her a bouquet of flowers. The AP and UP Berlin correspondents reported that Germans were shocked by the suddenness of the fight's outcome but were determined to prove to the world that Schmeling would not suffer any loss of affection or status. Both wire services said that Germans were already making excuses for Schmeling's defeat. The AP report from Berlin read:

> The newspaper *Zwoelf Uhr-Blatt* charged "certain American businessmen" should be blamed for Schmeling's defeat. It said they "hindered the fight to the point where . . . only a miracle would enable Schmeling to win. . . . The title had to remain in America. That was the purpose of all the maneuvers against the German. . . .
>
> "And, therefore, Schmeling was not allowed to climb into the ring until the time when there was a chance that Schmeling, two years older, no longer was too great a danger."

The United Press reported, "There were many explanations for the speed of Louis's victory, but it was said generally that a kidney blow delivered in the first few seconds was responsible."

The Nazis did, in fact, blame Schmeling's defeat on a foul. They edited films of the fight, leaving out the sequence of Louis's blows that preceded his punch to Schmeling's side. The day after the fight German Ambassador Hans Heinrich Dieckhoff visited Schmeling in the hospital. Dieckhoff asked Schmeling to file a protest. Schmeling assumed Dieckhoff was on an official mission for the Nazi government. By that time, however, Schmeling's head had cleared, and he had retracted his foul charge. He told Dieckhoff there had been no foul. Dieckhoff, doubtless none too enthusiastic about his forced errand, looked relieved.

Nazi newspapers also downplayed the significance of Schmeling's loss. Two years before, when Schmeling defeated Louis, the Nazis had been quick to say that Schmeling's victory had been a German victory. This time Arno Hellmis of the *Volkischer Beobachter* wrote: "One thing has to be said quite clearly. The defeat of a boxer does not mean any loss of national prestige." *Der Ansgriff* said, "It is bitter, but it is not a national disaster. There is just as little ground today as yesterday for Germany to make of a fight a race or political question, as the other side did."

In contrast, the American press exulted, and claimed Louis's victory as an American victory. The *New York Daily News* said, "As long as [Louis] is around, the United States need have no fear of relinquishing . . . the crown." *Ring* magazine reported:

> The World's heavyweight boxing title stayed American and non-Aryan when, in 2 min. 4 sec. on the muggy night of June 22, Joe Louis, Negro champion, knocked out Max Schmeling, the white hope of Germany. . . . The German press fulminated, blaming their hero's defeat on American machinations. But anti-Nazis gloated.

Even blatant racists had to accept Louis as America's representative. O. B. Keeler of the *Atlanta Journal*, who always rooted against Louis and had picked Schmeling to win, wrote:

> Joe Louis now is heavyweight boxing champion of the world, and so far as this correspondent can see there is

nothing to be done about it. Our fastest runners are colored boys, and our longest jumpers, and highest leapers. And now our champion fighting man with the fists is Joseph Louis Barrow.

Syndicated columnist Hugh S. Johnson wrote:

The piteous flash I got of Schmeling, wrecked and out on his feet, was vivid pictorial disproof of this nonsense about Aryan physical supremacy.

The average of white intelligence is above the average of black intelligence probably because the white race is several thousand years further away from jungle savagery. But, for the same reason, the average of white physical equipment is lower.

If the black men had an equal opportunity to compete in athletics there might not be any white champions at all. Certainly there would be fewer on a percentage basis. . . .

It is nothing for us to weep about and seek white hopes. These black boys are Americans—a whole lot more distinctly so than more recently arrived citizens of, say, the Schmeling type. There should be just as much pride in their progress and prowess under our system as in the triumph of any other American. For all their misfortunes and shortcomings they are our people—Negroes, yes, but our Negroes.

Cartoonists played up the racial symbolism of the fight and ridiculed Adolf Hitler. A *Chicago Daily News* editorial cartoon pictured a plane labeled "Brown Bomber" flying off as a bomb exploded behind a dismayed caricature of Hitler. Many papers also printed editorials commenting on the symbolic significance of the Louis-Schmeling fight. The *Boston Globe* commented on the irony that "brown Joe was accepted by multitudes as the representative of world democracy . . . [which] is strange when the undemocratic treatment of Negroes by many who boast of their own attitude toward freedom and equality is recalled." The *New York Post* was pleased that "the fact that a Negro happens to be the heavyweight titleholder stirs no resentment, rouses no racial feeling. . . . Grandfather wouldn't have believed that possible. . . . But Grandfather may have been wrong about a number of things, including the rate at which America was progressing toward tolerance."

The *New York Times*, dependably stolid, dissented:

> In a world and at a time when almost all the news we get is fraught with significance, the prizefight doesn't mean anything. It doesn't mean that . . . the Negro race is or is not rising in the economic scale, or anything else. . . . Tomorrow will be exactly what it would otherwise have been. Nothing has happened.

That the *Times* felt the necessity to tell its readers nothing had happened meant its readers knew better. In the eyes of most Americans, Joe Louis had exploded the myth of white supremacy. In the process he had won a measure of acceptance as America's national representative, something no black had ever enjoyed before. Louis was a revolutionary by coincidence.

Heywood Broun, writing in the *New York World-Telegram*, had some appreciation of the historic role Louis was playing out:

> One hundred years from now some historian may theorize, in a footnote at least, that the decline of Nazi prestige began with a left hook delivered by a former unskilled automotive worker who had never studied the policies of Neville Chamberlain and had no opinion whatever in regard to the situation in Czechoslovakia. . . .
>
> And possibly there could be a further footnote. It was known that Schmeling regarded himself as a Nazi symbol. It is not known whether Joe Louis consciously regards himself as a representative of his race and as one under dedication to advance its prestige. I can't remember that he has ever said anything about it. But that may have been in his heart when he exploded the Nordic myth with a bombing glove.

8

BUMS OF THE MONTH

Mike Jacobs had moved quickly to assure himself of a virtual monopoly over big-time boxing. Jacobs's control of Louis was the key. Louis had the title, and he was the number-one draw in boxing. Every competent heavyweight wanted to fight Louis, and only by fighting for Jacobs could any contender get that privilege—and the big money that went with it. Nor was Jacobs's dominance limited to the heavyweight division. Jacobs was making lots of money promoting Louis's fights, and Louis had revived a general interest in boxing. Jacobs could afford to offer bigger guarantees to fighters in the lighter weight classes. Most of the best boxers in the United States signed with Jacobs. On September 23, 1937, Jacobs staged a "Carnival of Champions" at the Polo Grounds, offering boxing fans four title fights on the same night—in the lightweight, welterweight, middleweight, and bantamweight divisions. Jacobs lost money that night because he overpaid the fighters, but he didn't mind. He had sewn up four more champions.

Finally, Col. John Reed Kilpatrick, president of the Madison Square Garden Corporation, bowed to the inevitable and put Jacobs in charge of promoting fights for the Garden. Jacobs now controlled all the major arenas in New York and most of the best boxers in America. His monopoly was complete, and his position earned him money, fame, and prestige. Jacobs still chose not to eat lunch with Kilpatrick and the other WASPs

UNCROWNED

CHAMPION

©

In an early publicity photograph the young but promising Joe Louis
strikes a classic pose. (Library of Congress)

Louis poses with the "Italian Giant," Primo Carnera, at the weigh-in before their fight, June 25, 1935. White reporters mistook Louis's expression of shyness and discomfort for sullenness. (National Archives)

Head characteristically down, Louis walks to a neutral corner after flooring ex-champ Max Baer in the third round of their fight, September 24, 1935. Baer took a ten-count on one knee in the next round, later telling reporters, "When I get executed, people are going to have to pay more than $25 a seat to watch it." The referee is Arthur Donovan. (National Archives)

Referee Arthur Donovan reaches the count of ten and waves his arms over a groggy Louis in the twelfth round of the first Louis-Schmeling fight, June 19, 1936, Louis's only loss before his 1949 retirement. (National Archives)

On June 24, 1937, two days after winning the heavyweight title, Louis posed for a photographer in his mother's home. His wife Marva is at the left, while Louis's mother serves the new champ a plate of fried chicken. Such pictures were typical of Louis's public image at the time. (National Archives)

His greatest victory suddenly and securely in hand, Louis stares down at Max Schmeling while referee Arthur Donovan points Louis to a neutral corner. (National Archives)

Pvt. Joe Louis says...

"We're going to do our part ...and we'll win because we're on God's side"

Army publicists used Joe Louis to sell the war and national unity. (Library of Congress)

Louis visits wounded GIs at Lovell General Hospital on one of his many morale-building tours for the army during World War II. (National Archives)

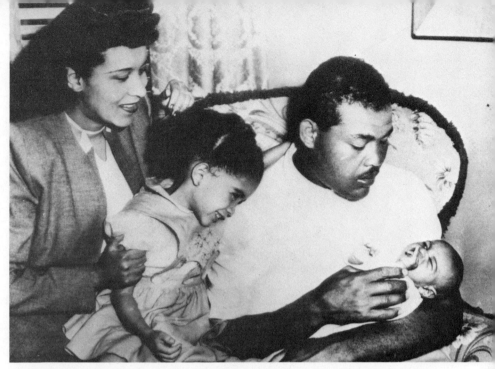

Louis holds his baby son, Joe Louis Barrow, Jr., as his daughter, Jaqueline, and wife, Marva, look on, July 3, 1947. (National Archives)

Louis trades his gloves, symbolizing his impending retirement, to promoter Mike Jacobs in exchange for his share of the purse from the second fight with Jersey Joe Walcott, June 26, 1948. Louis's left eye is evidence of his declining skills. (National Archives)

Louis at ease with a crowd of reporters at Toots Shor's restaurant in New York, March 8, 1949, five days after he officially relinquished the heavyweight title and retired for the first time. (National Archives)

The retired champion posed with new heavyweight champ, Ezzard Charles, on June 8, 1949, while Charles was in training to fight Gus Lesnevich. A year later Louis came out of retirement and lost a fifteen-round decision to Charles. (National Archives)

in the Garden's exclusive dining club, but he now had a degree of social acceptance he had never enjoyed as a Jewish kid on the make.

Although a wealthy man, Jacobs continued his restless pursuit of the dollar. Now that the 20th Century Sporting Club had made it to the top, Jacobs saw no reason to share his profits with Ed Frayne, Bill Farnsworth, or Damon Runyon, the three Hearst newspapermen who were his secret partners. The week that Joe Louis beat Jimmy Braddock for the heavyweight championship, in June 1937, the Hearst organization combined its two New York papers, the *Journal* and the *American*. Ed Frayne, sports editor of the old *American*, got the job as sports editor of the new paper, and Bill Farnsworth, former sports editor of the old *Journal*, lost his job with Hearst. In need of work, Farnsworth went to Jacobs. Jacobs hired him but treated him like a lackey rather than a partner. He made the former sports editor show up early to open the mail and order coffee. Finally, Farnsworth quit, and Jacobs bought out his share in the 20th Century Sporting Club.

Jacobs took care of his remaining two secret partners after Louis's second fight with Schmeling. Jacobs knew that newspapers competing with the Hearst organization would love to print allegations of conflict of interest involving Hearst sportswriters. So in August 1938, while in Saratoga, New York, for the races, Jacobs told Joe Williams of the *New York World-Telegram* that Runyon, Frayne, and Farnsworth had been in on the 20th Century Sporting Club from the start and that Frayne and Runyon were still sharing in its profits. Williams gave the story to Harry Grayson, who worked for the Newspaper Enterprise Alliance, a Scripps-Howard service. The next day, August 13, 1938, the *World-Telegram* ran a story with the headline "Mike Jacobs Admits Hearst Writers Share in Boxing Swag," and other Scripps-Howard newspapers all over the country gleefully carried another version of the same story. Since Frayne and Runyon regularly wrote stories about the 20th Century Sporting Club and the fights it promoted, their involvement with Jacobs called into question their objectivity as reporters. The

Hearst organization could not allow such a blatant conflict of interest, and Jacobs bought out Runyon and Frayne cheap, at $25,000 each.

Jacobs even complained about the 10 percent of his profits that were going to Joe Gould and Jimmy Braddock, the price he had paid to get Louis a title fight. Gould had a contract with Jacobs's signature on it, and Jacobs could not get rid of him as easily as he shed Frayne, Farnsworth, and Runyon, so he came up with another solution: he simply didn't pay Gould. Eventually, Gould sued Jacobs for his share of the promoter's profits. Wielding the threat of protracted legal difficulties, Jacobs got Gould to accept a cash settlement in place of their agreement of 10 percent for ten years.

Meanwhile, Jacobs's main attraction was enjoying a six-month vacation. Joe Louis had eliminated the last of the major pretenders to his heavyweight throne when he defeated Max Schmeling. John Henry Lewis, a black fighter who had held the light-heavyweight championship for three years, was campaigning for a heavyweight title fight. John Henry had won a number of fights from second-line heavyweights, and he was a quick and polished boxer. Mike Jacobs hesitated to make the match. He had won his gamble on the gate appeal of one black boxer, but the old prejudices were still strong, and two blacks had never squared off for the heavyweight title. Joe Louis hesitated, too. He considered John Henry Lewis a friend and didn't want to hurt him.

But pressure built for the match. A few white reporters wrote some nonsense about Louis being afraid of John Henry and about the black champion drawing the color line. The most effective pressure came from John Henry himself. John Henry Lewis and Joe Louis were friends, and they had a sympathy for each other that came from sharing the position of black champion in a white man's profession. Gus Greenlee, John Henry's manager, also had a passing friendship and a shared status with Julian Black and John Roxborough. Like Black and Roxborough, Greenlee was a black numbers operator. He also owned the Pittsburgh Crawfords, a Negro League baseball team. John Henry Lewis had already lost lateral vision in one eye. He wanted to get out of boxing before he lost sight in the eye altogether, but first he wanted a big purse. At 180 pounds and with a bad eye, John Henry was not an even match for Louis. He was asking a favor, and the Louis camp was willing to go along. Black, Roxborough, and Louis told Jacobs to sign the match up.

Jacobs scheduled the match for January 25, 1939, in Madison Square Garden. He kept ticket prices low, fearing a lack of demand from white customers. The Garden sold out. Louis still felt bad about the fight. Jack Blackburn suggested he would be more merciful if he went for an early knockout instead of trying to carry his friend, and Louis agreed. He knocked John Henry down three times in the first round, and referee Arthur Donovan stopped the fight. John Henry Lewis announced his retirement soon after.

On April 17, 1939, Louis met Jack Roper in Los Angeles. Roper was a rangy, competent heavyweight, and during the first half of round one he looked good, trading flurries of punches with the champion. Roper would lead first with his right, then with his left. Louis was confused. Roper staggered Louis with a left hook. But the champion also landed a few solid punches of his own.

Midway through the first round Roper and Louis stood only a few feet apart for ten or fifteen seconds without throwing any punches. Each was trying to get the other to lead. Louis finally moved in, missing with a left and a right and falling into a clinch. Roper backed Louis toward the ropes, and as they broke, Roper hit Louis with a left. Louis backed closer to the ropes. As Roper followed, Louis landed a left hook to Roper's head, and as Roper turned with the force of the punch, Louis came out to get him. The champion slid by Roper's side to maneuver Roper toward the ropes, then threw a right to the head. Roper missed a hard left hook, Louis backing away and crossing with a right. Roper ducked another right and tried to clinch, but Louis straightened him up with a left uppercut, missed with a right, then scored right-left-right to Roper's body. He dodged a Roper left and attacked: left hook, right to the face, left hook, right hook. Roper fell flat on his stomach.

Louis's momentum carried him into the ropes. He immediately headed for a neutral corner, looking back just once at his fallen opponent. Roper rose to his knees and put his right arm on the top rope. He dragged himself toward the corner on his knees so he could get his left hand on the rope at the other side of the corner post. He got both hands on the top strands but then fell backward, his left arm catching the middle strand. Roper put his right hand back on the top strand and pulled himself back up to his knees. He put his right hand down to wipe the side of his trunks, then reached up and grabbed the top of the corner post. He moved his left hand from the middle to the top strand of the ropes. His right hand slid along the rope until his hands came together, and Roper leaned forward, his head between the ropes, as the referee counted 10. Roper turned toward the ref and even then—although counted out—tried to get up again before he fell on his elbows, his body flat out on the canvas.

Roper did better in the postfight interviews. When a radio announcer asked him what happened, Roper replied, "I zigged when I shoulda zagged."

Louis's victories over Roper and John Henry Lewis were impressive, but they were not overwhelming financial successes. The Louis camp made only $34,000 from the John Henry Lewis fight, before expenses and taxes. The Roper fight did little better. With summer approaching, Mike Jacobs cast about for an opponent who could draw a big crowd for an outdoor fight with Louis. No heavyweight had better than an outside chance of beating Louis, so Jacobs settled for personality instead. He signed Dominick Anthony Galento, better known as "Two-Ton Tony," to fight Louis June 28 in Yankee Stadium. Galento was burly and strong and fat; he stood five feet nine inches tall and weighed 225 pounds. Galento didn't worry about the considerable swelling around his waist. He had been fighting professionally for ten years and had never heeded traditional boxing wisdom concerning training and conditioning. He did no roadwork and let his considerable appetite run free. Galento had bought a saloon with his ring earnings and claimed to do his training behind the bar, where he opened beer bottles with his teeth for the entertainment of sportswriters and denigrated Louis's talent. In his New Jersey accent Galento announced, "I'll moida da bum."

Galento was a press agent's dream. For all his bluster and bad-boy behavior, he struck a sympathetic chord. This improbable fat man was the average guy going up against a great champion, who, in contrast, seemed an unbeatable, untouchable figure. The fight shaped up as great theater.

Boxing experts did not expect much of a fight. Galento's record was spotty. He had lost several fights early in his career and had temporarily given up the sport to work as a bouncer. When Joe Jacobs had agreed to manage him, however, his career had taken off. Jacobs, who was Max Schmeling's American manager, had built Galento into a contender with a series of wins over mediocre opponents. Before the Louis fight Galento had knocked out Nathan Mann and Harry Thomas. Mann was a mob-controlled fighter; the Pennsylvania Boxing Commission suspended him for his performance against Galento. Years later, Thomas said he had been paid to lose to Galento. Galento was a slow and undisciplined fighter, he had a short reach, and he was so obviously out of shape that he could not last in a long fight against the always superbly conditioned Louis.

Galento did have several ring assets, however. He fought out of a crouch and was a threat to leap out with a left hook at any time. Galento was surprisingly strong, and he could take a punch. Most important, he was fearless.

Only a brave man would have said the things Galento said about Louis before their fight. Other fighters had questioned Louis's abilities before their fights with him; that was part of any fight's publicity buildup. Galento and his manager, Joe Jacobs, went further. Jacobs claimed that Louis had held a metal bar inside his right glove the night he knocked out Max Schmeling. Jacobs insisted that Louis's gloves be checked carefully before the fight. Properly outraged, the Louis camp made Jacobs retract his accusation under the threat of legal action, but Jacobs had accomplished his purpose. He had aroused further interest in the Louis-Galento fight, and he was getting under Louis's skin. Galento was also trying to psych Louis. He would call the champion on the phone, insult him, and predict a knockout victory.

Galento and Mike Jacobs's hype attracted nearly 40,000 spectators to Yankee Stadium the night of June 28, 1939. Louis was already on the edge of anger when he entered the ring, and Galento quickly pushed him over the edge. Barney Nagler remembered, "Galento said some terrible things to Louis during the introductions. 'I'm going to fuck your wife'—he said terrible things like that." For perhaps the only time in his career, Louis let himself get caught up in a good, old-fashioned brawl. In the first round Galento leaped out of his crouch, landed a left hook on Louis's jaw, and quickly followed with a right and another left. Louis was visibly shaken, but Galento did not have the skill to follow up his advantage, and Louis pulled himself together. In his corner between rounds, Jack Blackburn reminded Louis to box, and the champion came out of his corner for the second round and began to hammer away at Galento. The saloonkeeper cut easily, and Louis had him bleeding from his eyes, nose, and mouth. Louis hit Galento so hard that he almost lifted him off the canvas. Galento dropped, but he somehow got to his feet and survived the round.

In the third round Louis was overconfident and intent on finishing Galento. Galento surprised him with a powerful left hook, and Louis went down on his rear end. Louis was dazed, but he got up at the count of two. By the time Louis's head cleared, he was madder than ever before in his career. Galento had insulted him and now had embarrassed him. In the fourth round Louis cut Galento to ribbons, and the referee stopped the fight. Barney Nagler remembered, "The hardest punches I ever saw Louis throw were against Tony Galento. Every time he hit him it made little breaks in the skin as though [Galento] cut himself shaving." Years later Galento and Louis became friends, but Louis admitted he was mad at Galento that night. Louis's share of the Galento purse was $114,000 before expenses, his managers' shares, and taxes.

In September, Louis fought in Detroit, his hometown, for the first time as champion. His opponent was Bob Pastor, a leading heavyweight contender and the man who had survived ten rounds against Louis in early 1937 by running away. In their first fight Pastor had merely been following the instructions of his manager, Jimmy Johnston, and this time Pastor was determined to prove he could mix it with Louis. Louis dropped him to the canvas three times in the first round, and Pastor was out on his feet. Fighting purely on instinct, he survived the round and went on fighting. At the end of the sixth round, Pastor's head suddenly cleared. He remembered:

> When I come back to the corner after the sixth round was finished, I said, "Well, what round is it? Second?" And he [trainer Freddie Brown] said, "Yeah, it's the seventh, you're going good." Oooooh.
> I was out on my feet for the first six rounds. And I come back and won the seventh, eighth, ninth, and tenth, and I was five-four-one going into the eleventh round. And then that punch came again, boy. I went down. I got up, moved around trying to hold, but he hit me again, down I went again. I got up, and the referee stopped it. Which was nice, cause he saved my life, probably saved my life. I couldn't see out of one eye, and he was hitting me pretty well. He was a terrific puncher.

Twenty days before the Pastor fight Nazi Germany invaded Poland, and World War II began. The United States was little affected at first, and most Americans still hoped to avoid becoming entangled in the war. For Joe Louis life went on as usual. He fought often, so he was in training for most of the year. Between fights he spent his money freely and went through the usual rounds of nightclubs and girl friends and fights and reconciliations with his wife and the usual search for a worthy opponent. There were none to be found in the United States, so Mike Jacobs resorted to the old boxing promoter's trick: he imported an unknown from abroad. Jacobs signed Arturo Godoy of Chile to meet Louis on February 9, 1940, in Madison Square Garden.

Godoy was only an inch shorter than Louis, and he weighed 202 pounds to Louis's 203. Godoy had a craggy face with a pug nose, a jutting forehead, and short, curly dark hair. He fought Louis with a confused, anguished look on his face, as if he were trying to force himself to be ferocious. He fought from a ridiculous crouch, bent over at the knees and waist. His strategy against Louis was to crowd the champion and clinch whenever possible. For some reason Louis was not in the mood to fight, and for obvious reasons he had trouble taking Godoy seriously. Louis could not get any punching room against Godoy, and as Godoy repeatedly bear hugged him, Louis looked more and more disgusted.

Referee Arthur Donovan also quickly became disgusted with the challenger's tactics and kept up a steady stream of chatter at Godoy, telling him, "C'mon, get away. C'mon, get away. C'mon, break 'em." Donovan had to drag Godoy away from Louis several times after the bell rang to end a round. The fifteenth round ended appropriately, with Donovan trying to break a clinch. Godoy was unmarked and very happy. He hugged Louis and kissed him, then danced around the ring. Louis just stared at Godoy as the challenger jumped up and down in the air.

Eventually, Godoy settled down, and the two fighters waited for the decision, standing in the center of the ring with towels around their necks. Godoy's American trainer, Al Weill, a fat and bespectacled white man with a round face and a receding hairline, held Godoy's left arm expectantly.

Ring announcer Harry Balogh spoke into a microphone. "The decision. Winner and still heavyweight champion . . . Joe Louis." There were a few scattered boos from the crowd of 16,000. Al Weill grimaced and slapped his left hand through the air in a tantrum, and Godoy raised his right hand in the air and waved, also grimacing. It was a unanimous and obvious decision— Godoy had hardly thrown a punch all night.

Mike Jacobs followed the Godoy fiasco with another disaster, matching Louis with an Iowa fighter named Johnny Paycheck on March 29 in the Garden. Former champion Jack Dempsey was touting Paycheck as a white hope, and Paycheck had knocked out a lot of fighters in the Midwest. Against Louis, though, Paycheck was out of his league, and he knew it. Paycheck had an unmistakable look of fear on his face as he walked down the aisle to the ring, and once the fight started, he could

not muster the courage to throw punches. When Louis bored
in, the balding Paycheck circled away. After a few minutes of
this circling, Louis maneuvered Paycheck against the ropes.
Backed into a corner, Paycheck finally started a punch, a right
hand, just as Louis started a right hand. Both punches missed,
but Louis followed with a left hook to the jaw. Louis ducked
after he threw the left to avoid retaliation, but Paycheck wasn't
a good enough boxer to counter. He dropped to his knees, his
right hand holding onto the middle strand of the ropes, waited
for the referee to count nine, got up, and stayed out of Louis's
way the rest of the round.

In round two Louis pursued Paycheck until Paycheck made
the mistake of standing still long enough to throw an ineffectual
left. Louis countered with an overhand right that landed flush
on Paycheck's jaw. Paycheck's head snapped back, and he fell
flat on his back, body straight, arms in the air. Referee Donovan
didn't even bother to count. He pulled the mouthpiece out of
Paycheck's mouth, and one of Paycheck's handlers poured a
bucket of water over the downed fighter's head. Louis told
reporters his fight with Paycheck had been a vacation.

The best Mike Jacobs could come up with for Louis's big
fight of the summer of 1940 was a rematch with Arturo Godoy
on June 20. Only 26,000 spectators showed up at Yankee Stadium. This time Louis knew what to expect from Godoy, and
he was determined to make up for his bad showing against the
Chilean in their first fight. Godoy was promising he would
knock Louis out. Clem McCarthy asked Louis what he thought
about the challenger's threats. "Any dog can wag his tail," Louis
said.

By the end of the seventh round Godoy was in trouble. His
face was bloody and puffed. He was bending at the waist and
at the knees, dodging from side to side, his head as close to the
floor as he could get it. But when his head bobbed up, Louis hit
him with a right cross and missed with a left as Godoy clinched.
Louis pushed him off with his outstretched left and landed a
weak left-right combination. Godoy tried to go back into his
crouch, and Louis hit him with a wicked right to the head.
Louis missed with a left jab, then landed a left hook and a right

hook in quick succession, jerking Godoy's head back and forth. Godoy fell.

Godoy got up in a hurry and rushed toward Louis, but referee Billy Cavanaugh stopped Godoy long enough to wipe off his gloves, and the bell rang.

In the eighth round Godoy bored in again, moving the champion toward the ropes. Louis landed a left hook, a right cross, and another left hook as Godoy leaned in. Godoy still moved in, trying to clinch, and Louis, bouncing off the ropes and going sideways, nailed Godoy with a right cross. Godoy fell again. The South American waited for the count on both knees, then charged up, referee Cavanaugh slowing Godoy's suicidal rush toward Louis long enough to wipe his gloves. Louis backed toward the ropes as Godoy charged him, missed a right uppercut, but landed a left uppercut before Godoy could clinch. The referee broke them, and Louis again backed against the ropes, throwing punches to Godoy's head. Louis came off the ropes, jabbed, and crossed with his right as Godoy tried to duck. Godoy tried to hang on to Louis, but Louis backed away and Godoy fell to his knees. Referee Cavanaugh waved his hands over Godoy to end the fight; the challenger was now helpless. Godoy got up and tried to charge Louis again. By then his handlers were in the ring, and they joined the referee as he tried to hold Godoy back.

Louis had turned his back on Godoy and walked back to his corner. One of Louis's handlers was toweling off the champion's head. Hearing the commotion, Louis turned around, casually held his gloves up in case Godoy reached him, and watched as Godoy's handlers, Cavanaugh, and a cop pulled poor Godoy away.

In Europe at this time the Germans were consolidating their hold on France after a shockingly successful two-week blitzkrieg. Hitler now effectively controlled most of Western Europe, and England was in danger of invasion. The United States geared up for the first peacetime draft in its history. Before the second Godoy fight, Louis registered at Local Draft Board 8 in Chicago.

Mike Jacobs feared the United States would enter the war and he was determined to make as much money out of Louis as possible before his meal-ticket champion got drafted. Jacobs waited several months for a capable challenger to emerge. None did, so Jacobs planned a series of fights for Louis all over the country. In early 1940, when Jacobs had announced that Louis would fight Arturo Godoy and Johnny Paycheck in successive months, Jack Miley of the *New York Post* referred to Louis's schedule as the "Bum-of-the-Month Club." Every sportswriter in the country picked up the phrase and repeated it as Louis knocked out Al McCoy on December 16, 1940, Red Burman on January 31, 1941, Gus Dorazio on February 17, Abe Simon on March 21, and Tony Musto on April 8. Calling Louis's opponents bums was unfair; they were the best heavyweights available. Louis himself said in his autobiography:

> Those guys I fought were not bums. They were hard-working professionals trying to make a dollar, too. I knew the training they went through, and I knew the dreams they had. No different from me. I respected every man I fought. It's no easy job getting up in that ring; you got to have a special kind of balls.

Red Burman was typical of Louis's opponents during that period, and he put up the best fight, constantly attacking until Louis knocked him out in the fifth round. In the third round of their fight Louis fell to the canvas briefly. Louis claimed Burman hit him a glancing blow and that he had slipped, but Burman is sure he knocked Louis down. Between his rounds as a security guard in a shopping mall outside Baltimore, Burman said he wasn't afraid when he got in the ring with Louis. "It was a big opportunity. When I was in the ring, I wasn't scared of nobody. I mean, he's got two hands; he ain't got more hands than I got. I always had the feeling I could beat anyone else in the world. He changed my mind that night." Louis knocked Burman out with body punches, a rarity in boxing and a sign of the severe pounding Burman took. After the fight, Burman passed blood in his urine.

For fighters like Red Burman, a match with Louis was the biggest moneymaking event in their lives. But for Louis, the financial returns of his fight-a-month campaign were disappointing. Louis and his managers received less than $80,000 total for the McCoy, Dorazio, Simon, and Musto fights. The day of May 23, it did not look like Louis's financial luck was improving. That night Louis was scheduled to fight Buddy Baer, Max's younger brother, in Washington, D.C.'s Griffith Stadium. It rained all day. Arthur Donovan, who had come down to referee the fight, assumed it was off, so he went to a bar and got drunk. Ordinarily, Donovan would have been right—Mike Jacobs would have announced a postponement early in the morning. But the Washington Senators baseball team was coming back to town, and Griffith Stadium wouldn't be available for the next few days. Luckily for Jacobs, the weather cleared up early that evening, and more than 20,000 fans showed up, including thousands of southern blacks who had come up to Washington for the fight.

Buddy Baer was the tallest opponent Louis ever faced—he was 6 feet 6½ inches tall. He never became as good a fighter as his older brother, and few sportswriters felt that Buddy had a chance to beat Louis. But Baer surprised the sportswriters and Louis by nailing the champion with a combination of three punches in the first round, culminating with a left hook that knocked Louis through the ropes. Louis landed on the ring apron but made it back to the ring by the count of four. When his professional pride was stung, Louis became a truly dangerous fighter. He quickly began to punish Baer, but the challenger absorbed a lot of punishment and kept throwing punches of his own. He bruised Louis's right eye and opened a cut under Louis's left eye in the fifth round.

In the sixth round Louis dropped Baer with a right. Baer rose at the count of seven, only to be knocked down again. With the crowd roaring, Baer staggered to his feet at the count of nine, and the bell rang to end the sixth round. Louis didn't hear the bell, and he rushed across the ring and coldcocked Baer with a right. Ancil Hoffman, Baer's manager, and Ray Arcel, his trainer, had to carry Baer to his corner. When the bell rang for the seventh round, Baer was still out. Hoffman and Arcel refused to leave the ring. They claimed that referee Donovan should disqualify Louis for hitting Baer after the bell. Donovan, who had desperately tried to sober up before the fight, faced the most difficult decision of his career. Donovan was a Louis fan, and he worked for Mike Jacobs. He decided to disqualify Baer for failing to answer the bell for the seventh round. Clearly, Louis had not fouled intentionally, and just as clearly, he was winning the fight. But Donovan should at least have given Baer extra time to recover from Louis's blow struck after the bell.

Louis had fought six times in six months. He was tired and jaded by constant training. But Mike Jacobs had signed Louis for another fight in June, and it was against Billy Conn, the most capable opponent Louis had faced in years. Conn grew up in the East Liberty section of Pittsburgh, an area especially hard hit by the Depression. Conn began to box professionally as a skinny sixteen-year-old. Like Louis, Conn was lucky enough to find a good trainer, Johnny Ray. "He was drunk all the time, see," Conn told me. "He was a Jewish guy. He's the only Jewish guy I know that was drunk all the time. But he knew more drunk than the other guys knew sober. In the corner he was always drunk." Conn learned quickly, and after four years of boxing almost exclusively in western Pennsylvania and West Virginia, Mike Jacobs sent for Conn to fight Fred Apostoli, then the middleweight titleholder. An unknown, and a $2\frac{1}{2}$-to-1 underdog, Conn boxed the ears off Apostoli on January 6, 1939, and won a ten-round decision. Apostoli wanted a rematch, and the two men fought again a month later, with Conn winning another decision in fifteen rounds. In July, Conn won the New York State light-heavyweight championship from Melio Bettina, a title he vacated a year later to compete against the heavyweights. Conn knocked out Bob Pastor and decisioned Al McCoy to establish his credentials as a challenger. Conn never gained enough weight to be a full-fledged heavyweight, but he didn't have to. He was a remarkably quick and clever boxer, and his hands were too fast for most of his opponents. Conn was also good box office. He was a handsome Irishman with a boyish grin and just the right mixture of cockiness and youth. Mike

Jacobs admitted that he would not mind if Conn beat Louis, since Conn was popular and might inject new interest into the heavyweight division Joe Louis had dominated for three years.

Jacobs and his publicists injected some hostility into the buildup, trying to arouse further public interest in the fight. Conn made appropriately brash predictions of victory. When reporters asked Louis whether he would be able to catch up with Conn's quick feet, Louis supposedly said, "He can run, but he can't hide." Shirley Povich insists Louis first used that line before his second fight with Bob Pastor, but the quote became part of the Louis-Conn buildup.

The Louis camp also let word out that Louis was mad at Conn for some things Conn supposedly had said while rooting for fellow Pittsburgher Fritzie Zivic over Henry Armstrong, a black fighter. The Louis entourage supposedly sat behind Conn at the fight and claimed to have heard Conn drop some racist remarks. Forty years later Billy Conn remembered all the publicity and laughed. "I liked Joe Louis. It's all bullshit to build it up. . . . We didn't call each other names. That's for kids, kids' stuff." On June 17, the day before the fight, newspapers picked up the story that Conn and his sweetheart, Mary Louise Smith, had applied for a marriage license, but Miss Smith's father, a former major league baseball player, objected. The story further endeared the underdog Conn to the public.

Louis was aware of the public sentiment for Conn. He worried that if he weighed in over 200 pounds, while Conn weighed in at around 170, he would seem like a bully beating up a smaller man. So Louis, who usually took it easy on his last day of training, worked hard the day before the fight, running and going through his full routine of exercises in the gym. He also dried out, not eating, and drinking as little as possible. Louis weighed in at 199½ the morning of the fight. He felt tired and weak.

Watching Louis and Conn weigh in was Don Dunphy, who would announce the fight over the Mutual Radio Network that night. For years the NBC network and one sponsor, Adams Hats, had broadcast Mike Jacobs's fights. In the spring of 1941, however, Mutual and its sponsor, Gillette, outbid NBC for the broadcasting contract with Jacobs. Mutual held an audition to

pick an announcer during the light-heavyweight title fight between Anton Christofordis and Gus Lesnevich on May 22.
Dunphy and his competitors took turns calling the rounds.
Dunphy said of the audition, "I tell people later that the other
announcers were tripping over those names, and I just called
them Tony and Gus." Dunphy won the audition, and his calm,
piercing delivery became the voice of boxing during the sport's
golden years.

The Louis-Conn fight was Dunphy's first big match, and as
he said forty years later:

> My whole career kind of turned on this one event. . . . I
> went up to Louis after the weigh-in, and I said, "I want to
> wish you good luck tonight." He kind of surprised me; he
> said, "Well, I want to wish you good luck, too." He real-
> ized how important this was to me. To him it was another
> fight. And I thought that was very gracious of him.

Unlike sportswriters, Dunphy and the major radio announcers
of the era—Clem McCarthy, Edwin C. Hill, Ted Husing, Sam
Taub, and Bill Stern—rarely identified Louis as a "Negro" or
referred to his race at all. The difference was probably due
largely to the difference in the two media. Announcers usually
called fighters by their first or last names and stuck with those
names throughout. They didn't have the time or the need to
think up variations on Louis's name. They had enough trouble
trying to keep up with the action. Print journalists, with more
time to think about what they were writing and with Louis's
name staring at them from the previous sentence, were more
likely to vary their references to Louis, and those variations
often included references to his color.

With Dunphy, a kindly man whose voice is as distinctive
over the phone today as it was over the radio forty years ago
and who is still working as a fight announcer, not identifying
Louis as a Negro was also a conscious policy:

> I never referred to color . . . and now people treat it differ-
> ently. And yet I still find it hard to do that after not having
> done it so many years. Now occasionally I will say, "He's
> the black fellow," or, "He's the white fellow," but in those

days you didn't do it. As a matter of fact, our sports announcers' fraternity got some kind of an award from B'nai
B'rith for that particular fact. . . . I wanted to be color
blind.

Close to 55,000 people filled the Polo Grounds in New York
to see Conn and Louis fight. Conn, a slow starter throughout
his career, was careful to stay away from Louis during the first
round. He appeared nervous as he danced away, and once he
slipped as he tried to jab and run at the same time. In the second
round Conn began to warm up and engaged in a few exchanges
with the champion. At one point Louis pinned Conn against the
ropes, landed a few punches, and seemed to be in control. But
in the third and fourth rounds Conn stood up to some of Louis's
shots and began to beat the champion to the punch. Sensing
that his fighter was letting Conn get his rhythm, Jack Blackburn
told Louis to pick up the pace. Louis clearly won the fifth and
sixth rounds, opening a cut on Conn's nose. But Conn used his
speed to weather the storm and was unhurt when he came out
for the seventh round. Louis was tired. The fight began to slip
away from the champion.

Conn was making Louis walk around the ring after him, and
he easily avoided Louis's long leads. When he danced into range,
Conn could throw three punches in succession before Louis had
a chance to retaliate. Conn's hands were too quick for Louis, and
even though the smaller Conn was not hurting Louis badly, he
was taking the lead on points. During the fighting, Conn said.
"You've got a fight on your hands tonight, Joe," and Louis replied, "I know it."

During the tenth round, with his title at risk, Joe Louis did
a rather remarkable thing. He was walking after Conn, and the
challenger was backing toward the ropes. Suddenly, Conn's
right leg slipped out from under him, and Conn had to grab
the ropes to avoid falling. Conn was momentarily helpless, and
by the rules of boxing Louis was entitled to take advantage of
the situation and hit Conn. Instead, he backed away and waited
for Conn to regain his balance. Louis reacted from habit; he
never hit his opponents when they slipped, and he didn't hit on
the break or use other underhanded tactics. Louis's gesture to-

ward Conn revealed his ingrained sportsmanship, but it was also a measure of his deep confidence. Even while he was losing control of the fight, Louis never lost his calm and did not feel desperate enough to take advantage of Conn's slip.

In the eleventh round Conn continued his dominance, landing good flurries in close as the champion covered up. After the round ended, one of Conn's handlers rushed out to meet Conn, almost hugging him. Conn put his right hand in the air, exultant. By the end of the twelfth round Conn was in complete control. Coming out of a clinch, he threw a left hook to Louis's body. Louis covered up, and Conn followed with a lightning quick hook to the head and a right-cross–left-hook combination to the face that staggered Louis. Another left made Louis step sideways and fall back into the ropes.

Conn went in to get Louis. He threw a left to the body, then drew the left back and barely missed a hook to Louis's head. Louis grabbed Conn with both hands, smothering a Conn right. Conn tried to throw Louis around his left side and hit him with a left at the same time, but Louis held on and dragged Conn with him, and for a moment the fight looked like a comical wrestling match. The referee broke the two fighters, and Conn came in throwing a left hook. Louis ducked and held again, and again the referee had to break them. Conn hurt Louis with a left, but Louis backed away from another left just in time. Conn tried another left that missed. Louis smothered a left-right combination and clinched again. Conn wrapped his left around Louis's head, and they broke. Louis jabbed, then backed away from a big left hook and countered with a left to the face and hit Conn with a short right as the challenger came in, and the bell rang.

Conn had had Louis in trouble and was well ahead on points. His handlers and his trainer, Johnny Ray, told Conn to box cautiously the rest of the way, because he would surely win the decision and the title that way. But Conn thought he could knock Louis out, and a knockout would bring greater glory.

Three rounds to go. In the champion's corner Jack Blackburn and assistant trainer Mannie Seamon told Louis that to win, he would have to knock Conn out. When the bell rang for the thirteenth round, the two fighters came out of their corners and circled each other. Conn threw a left-right combination. Louis covered up and clinched, and the referee broke them. Louis landed a solid jab and blocked a Conn left. Conn feinted, and Louis jabbed again. Conn landed a right to the body, and the fighters clinched. Conn was no longer thinking about dancing away from Louis. He wanted to stay on the offensive, hoping for a knockout. In tight, Conn threw a left to the body and missed a left aimed at Louis's face, and Louis jabbed and threw a right cross that Conn slipped. Louis missed a jab and missed another as Conn ducked and moved in, but Louis landed a right cross in tight that knocked Conn off balance, and Louis put his left out and held Conn's right glove and threw a right uppercut that snapped Conn's head back and followed with a left hook, Conn clinching and leaning in. Louis backed away and landed a right uppercut and left hook. Tired as he was, Joe Louis could still punch. Conn's head was bouncing like a yo-yo. Louis missed a right, and both fighters threw lefts and got their arms hooked together. Conn landed a left hook on the top of Louis's head, but Louis crossed with a right and grazed Conn's face with a left hook. Conn tried a left and a right to Louis's body, but Louis smothered the punches in close. Conn wrapped his left around Louis's head, landed a right hook to the side of Louis's face, tried a left hook that Louis blocked, then landed a solid right to the head and left to the body, and once again Louis covered up. Conn missed a left around Louis's head that pushed Louis's shoulders down, landed a right uppercut, and missed a left and landed a right cross and a solid left hook to Louis's head. Conn missed a right uppercut but landed another left to the head, and Louis put both arms around Conn and held on. The referee broke them.

Louis came out of the clinch unhurt, even after all the punches Conn had landed, and Billy Conn stayed in range. Louis jabbed, blocked a Conn left hook, and clinched again. Conn came out of the clinch with a left to the body, a solid right cross, and missed a left as Louis jumped at him with his own wild left. The fighters clinched, and the referee broke them. Louis ducked a Conn left hook, and as Conn came in to clinch, Louis missed a right to the head. Louis pushed Conn away into the ropes and jabbed, and Billy Conn dodged and leaned in to avoid a Louis right. The referee broke the clinch.

Conn backed away, then started a left-jab–overhand-right combination, but Joe Louis stepped aside to slip the jab and beat Conn to the punch with his own overhand right. It was the one solid punch Louis needed, and it slowed Conn just enough. Conn bent at the waist with the effects of the punch, and Louis backed away and circled for punching room. Conn tried to lean in, but Louis swung a right hook that Conn had to dodge by backing toward the ropes. Louis jabbed, Conn covered up, and Louis landed a right to the body and left to the body. Conn tried to lean in again, but Louis stepped to the side, and Conn came out of his crouch with a left that landed on Louis's face but had no sting. Louis threw an overhand right that hurt Conn. As Conn tried to clinch, Louis stepped back and hit him with a solid right uppercut. Conn's hair flew up. Conn fell into Louis, and Louis tried another uppercut, but he was backed into the ropes and didn't have room. Louis pushed Conn around so that Conn's back was to the ropes and threw another right. Conn, still hanging on, managed to smother the punch and even tried a weak left of his own, but Louis countered with a short, sharp right that gave him punching room. Louis put his left out to the side of Conn's face, measuring, and took it back and threw a right to the top of Conn's head and pushed Conn out toward the center of the ring as Conn tried to clinch. Louis held the dazed Conn at arm's length and threw a right uppercut that jarred Conn, and Conn fell into Louis again.

Louis backed away, and then so did Conn, but Conn suddenly lunged into another clinch, trying to hold on to Louis. Louis hit him with a right uppercut, and Conn blocked another one as Louis backed away from Conn. Conn landed a left hook and tried to clinch, but Louis hardly noticed the punch and easily pushed Conn away. Conn backed away, his hands low. Louis followed and threw a jab, then a murderous overhand right, getting his full weight into the punch. Conn, now completely unconscious though somehow still standing, leaned into Louis, but Louis stepped back and landed a left hook and a right to the body that spun Conn around him. As Conn went by on Louis's left side, Louis followed him with a right that cuffed Conn on the back of the head and then a right hook and left jab and right uppercut, and still Conn leaned in. Louis landed a left hook and a right cross with everything on it, and Conn spun slightly around and still clinched.

Louis threw a left to the body, stepped back and threw a right uppercut, a left hook, and a right cross, and readied another right as Conn took a small step with his left foot, leaning forward. Conn just fell that way, his body bent at the waist. Conn fell onto his right side, and his head hit the canvas and bounced up before coming to rest.

Louis looked at Conn and then turned and walked away, his shoulders rising as he took one deep breath. Louis turned around in his neutral corner in his usual pose, one arm draped on either side of the corner post. Conn sat up and looked at Louis, and Louis stepped forward with his left foot and kind of leaned forward, arms still holding the ropes and supporting his weight as they spread-eagled behind him. Conn got one knee up at the count of ten, and as he started to get to his feet, the referee waved his hands. Two seconds remained in the round.

Louis came off the ropes with his arms at his sides, his hips swinging. Louis walked toward Conn, and Conn was looking at Louis, but the referee turned Conn's head and patted Conn on the back. Louis walked by as if to pat Conn on the back, as well, but the referee got in his way, so Louis just walked past with his head down.

Conn's handlers came into the ring, took out Conn's mouthpiece, and splashed him with water from a sponge before wiping his face with it. Forty years later Billy Conn, who lives in a beautiful home in Pittsburgh and still has an easy smile and the restless energy of an athlete, remembered the punishment he took before falling that night and just laughed. "I had a strong neck."

Ethnic-conscious sportswriters found an easy explanation for Conn's defeat. They wrote that Conn's Irish blood got him caught up in the fighting and made him go for the knockout instead of boxing cautiously and going for the decision. Conn's manager, Johnny Ray, agreed. Ray said of his fighter, "If he hadda Jewish head instead of an Irish one, he'd be the champ."

Mike Jacobs was delighted with the Conn-Louis fight. It had revived interest in the heavyweight division, drawn $451,743 in gate receipts, and ensured that a rematch between the two fighters would draw much more. But Jacobs faced a dilemma. To give Bill Conn a title shot, Jacobs had passed over Lou Nova, a good-sized, tough fighter who had clearly established himself as the number-one contender by twice knocking out Max Baer. Nova was ahead of his time, or maybe it was just that he came from California. He claimed to have studied Yoga and to possess a "cosmic punch." Nova and his cosmic punch had received a lot of publicity, and there was considerable pressure from the press to give Nova a title shot. A Louis-Nova fight would draw a big crowd, and doubtless Jacobs reasoned that a Conn-Louis rematch would be even more popular if boxing fans had a while to think about it. Jacobs signed Louis and Nova to fight September 29, 1941, in the Polo Grounds and planned to match Louis and Conn the following year. Some 56,000 fans watched Louis spar cautiously with Nova for five rounds, then demolish the Californian in the sixth. The number-one heavyweight contender was just one more easy knockout victim for the champion. The "cosmic punch" turned out to be an ordinary right cross that Nova could not land to any great effect against Louis.

From June of 1938, when he knocked out Max Schmeling, to September of 1941, when he knocked out Lou Nova, Joe Louis's public image became slightly more favorable. By then Louis was a universally familiar figure, and during that period reporters and the American public acquired a fixed idea of what Joe Louis was like.

The central part of Louis's image was his reputation as a fighter. His convincing victory over Schmeling had erased all doubts as to his ability, and in the next three years Louis defended his title fifteen times, winning thirteen of those fights by knockouts. (The Buddy Baer fight was officially recorded as a "disqualification.") No champion had ever fought so often or so completely dominated the heavyweight division. By January 1939 Ed Van Every of the *New York Sun* wrote that Louis was generally believed to be the best fighter of all time. Richards Vidmer and Bill Corum expressed the same conclusion in colums they wrote in 1939, and Grantland Rice wrote that Louis was holding up as an athlete after becoming rich and famous better than anyone he had ever seen. Lester Scott of the *New York World-Telegram* wrote a column in early 1939 with the headline "There Should Be a Law Against Putting Men in Ring with Louis." Journalistic respect for Louis's ability probably reached its height on the day Louis fought Gus Dorazio, February 17, 1941. A *Washington Post* headline read "15,000 to See Champ 'Risk' Heavy Title."

Louis was so good that no one took his opponents seriously. This depressed attendance at Louis's fights and also made his opponents the butt of jokes, "Bum-of-the-Month Club" being just one example. On a National Urban League Program aired over the ABC radio network on March 30, 1941, two actors did a skit, a dialogue between Louis's fictional next opponent, Eddie One-Round Green, and Green's manager. The manager asked his fighter to imagine his fight with Louis—he began the skit as follows:

> "It's the first round. Joe Louis climbs into the ring like a tiger. What do you do?"
> "I climbs out of the ring like another tiger."
> "Any other man would run. But you don't."
> "What's the matter? Am I glued to the floor?"
> "It's the fifteenth round, and you're crawling around the ring on your hands and knees. What are you doing on your hands and knees?"
> "Looking for a trap door."
> "Joe Louis is covered with blood. Your nose is broken. Both your eyes are black, and your jaw is cracked. Now is the time to see what you're made of."
> "What's he gonna do? Turn me inside out?"
> "The crowd is yelling to the referee, 'Stop it. Stop it.' And what do you say?"

"Okay with me."

"I can't stand to see you take any more punishment, so what do I do?"

"You close your eyes?"

"No, I throw in the towel, and they give the fight to Louis."

"Let him have it; I don't want it."

"But you fought so well that they give you a reward."

"Oh yeah? What do they give me?"

"They give you a return fight with Joe Louis."

"Oh no they don't."

"Oh yes they do."

"Oh no they don't."

While Louis's dominance brought him attention and respect from the American public, it often made him seem impersonal and distant. Boxing crowds always applauded him, but they tended to root for his underdog opponents. The white press often noted and shared the public's sentiment for Louis's opponents, though white reporters were careful to say the sentiment was not racially motivated. In December of 1938 *Newsweek* magazine said:

Another White Hope search—less hysterical but the same sort of movement that bestirred fight fans when Jack Johnson, Negro, held the championship (1910–1915)—is on to unearth a replacement for Joe Louis. In the current quest race plays but a minor role, however, for the second Negro ever to hold the heavyweight title is a respected and popular fighter. Rather, the hunt is prompted by the realization that none of the present-day well-known heavyweights has a good chance to beat the Brown Bomber, and a longing on the part of boxing experts to be the first to discover the unsung hero who must inevitably come from obscurity to knock Louis' block off.

Tom Meany of *PM*, a New York afternoon paper, wrote before the Conn fight that most boxing fans were rooting for Conn. "This isn't because the public dislikes the Bomber, who has been an exemplary champion; it's merely because the public likes a change." After the fight John Kieran of the *New York Times* noted:

> Most of the onlookers wanted to see Conn win. It had to be that way. Not because of any difference in color in the warriors. If there were any present who felt that way, they were an insignificant minority. But the shuffler was the champion. He had been the champion for four years. The crowd usually goes for the newcomer, the challenger, the younger man trying to scale the heights against known odds and heavy odds.

White reporters not only praised Louis's boxing skills; they praised him as a man. From the beginning of Louis's career John Roxborough, Julian Black, and Mike Jacobs had sold Joe Louis as a well-behaved, modest, sportsmanlike "colored boy" with a mission to make a good impression on whites, and Louis continued to act according to the official script. He worked hard in training, he didn't brag or insult his opponents before a fight, he kept his composure in the ring, fought cleanly, didn't gloat over his victories, still didn't drink or smoke, and avoided public scandal. He did all those things as a twenty-seven-year-old champion just as naturally as he had done them as a shy, twenty-one-year-old challenger. Reporters who watched the Louis routine continue unchanged for years developed a real affection for Louis. Barney Nagler remembered, "Everybody [in the press] had this feeling about Louis, and so everything that was reported about Louis was mostly positive." Louis's public image had come full circle. Once again, the dominant picture of Joe Louis in the minds of the white public was of a quiet, modest, sportsmanlike, and well-behaved black man. This image of Louis was so strong by the spring of 1941 that Buddy Baer, who had a legitimate gripe against Louis, did not dare to contradict it. Louis had knocked Baer down with a blow that clearly landed after the bell in the sixth round, and Baer had been unable to come out for the seventh round. In his dressing room Baer said, "Joe's a great fighter and a credit to his race, but he hit me after the bell."

Louis added to the favorable impressions he was making on the nation's sportswriters by opening up to them more and more. Louis had gradually improved his communication with reporters during the first several years of his career, and after the second Schmeling fight Louis's confidence grew markedly, just as the press, at long last, fully accepted him as champion. In an article for the *Saturday Evening Post* entitled "Introducing—the New Joe Louis," Caswell Adams wrote that the second Schmeling fight had changed Louis's

> whole attitude toward the world. . . . He used to clam up when talking to white men, but ever since that Schmeling smashing he's been just as chatty with them as with Negroes. He used to think that sports writers were there merely to find comic copy, and to kid him before other white men. But now he trusts the writers he's grown to know, and his memory for them and for the faces and the names of everyone he's met is remarkable.

Because Louis remained far and away the most famous and salient black personality in America, many sportswriters again suggested that Louis had a symbolic importance beyond the prize ring. After Louis almost lost his title to Billy Conn, Ed Sullivan wrote in his "Little Old New York" column:

> The fists of Joe Louis are the megaphones and microphones of his race on the nights that he defends his championship. . . . He is, to all intents and purposes, never an individual—he is all the sorrows and joys, and fears and hopes and the melody of an entire race. . . . He is a compound of every little cabin in the Southland, every tenement or apartment in the Harlems of the North; he is the memory of every injustice practiced upon his people and the memory of every triumph. . . .
>
> In eighteen victories, Louis has done more to influence better relations between two races than any single individual. . . .
>
> So, when Louis is dethroned, he can step down and out in the full knowledge that he has brought the two races

closer together than ever they were before; and that accomplishment, in these days, is fraught with important
significance.

Even the redundant tributes to Louis contained evidence of
white preoccupation with, and prejudice against, the color of
the champion's skin. White reporters reflected the unselfcon-
scious racism of American society by continuing to stereotype
Joe Louis. The jungle killer and southern darkie images had
faded, but the attitudes that had inspired them still popped up.
After each Louis knockout, some writer would drag out jungle
killer imagery to describe the action. White reporters still commented on how much Louis ate and slept and still quoted him
in dialect. The AP advance for Louis's fight with Gus Dorazio
in February 1941 said that the champion was thinking more of
the chicken and pork chops he would eat after the fight than
about his opponent. As late as 1941, Willard Mullin, the superb
sports cartoonist for the *New York World-Telegram*, drew
small caricatures of Louis with huge lips. John Kieran of the
New York Times still called Louis "shufflin' Joe." And Joe
Williams voiced a widely held opinion when he described Louis
as "a fellow who isn't supposed to have too much between the
ears at best."

To be fair, these descriptions did not come only from white
writers. Earl Brown, a black reporter, did a close-up on Louis
for *Life* magazine in 1940 that typified the negative aspects of
Louis's southern darkie image. Brown wrote that Louis slept
twelve hours a day, that he didn't like to read or wear shoes:

> One of his luxuries is having his corns trimmed by his wife,
> Marva, with whom his relations are otherwise not flawless.
> . . . Friends say that she has more common sense than her
> husband. . . . Louis's managers have taught him, as best they
> could, proper methods for washing his ears, combing his
> hair and holding a fork. . . .

Louis did conform in some ways to black stereotypes, but
Brown and a host of other writers exaggerated those character-
istics. And even if such descriptions had been wholly accurate,
by today's standards no reporter would have written them and

no editor would have published them. Louis had moved things along in his six years of prominence, but he was still alone; it was uphill work. The white press and white society remained insensitive to their own racism.

So although Joe Louis's public image had improved by the outbreak of World War II, he had hardly caused a revolution—yet. The white press respected him as an athlete, praised him for his character—and continued to identify him as a Negro and stereotype him. Louis had not yet won full acceptance on human terms; neither he nor any other black had fully awakened the conscience of white America. But Louis had started the process.

9

"SOME BLACK MOTHER'S SON"

Barred from the mainstream of American society, black Americans developed their own distinct culture, a mix of African traditions and a sense of race identity maintained in the face of unrelenting hostility from whites. Black culture is tough to penetrate; thus many white scholars have assumed that blacks have no cultural identity. Blacks did not leave behind much in the way of the written sources on which historians depend and in many ways kept their culture hidden from whites.

> Got one mind for white folks to see,
> 'Nother for what I know is me;
> He don't know, he don't know my mind.

Since white papers ignored them, blacks formed their own press. Black papers like the *Pittsburgh Courier*, the *Baltimore Afro-American*, the *Chicago Defender*, and the *New York Amsterdam News* appeared weekly, with Harlem society pages, pictures of black brides, and news from the Negro baseball leagues. Following the journalistic style of their day, black reporters identified a person as "white."

Black papers were essentially middle class and conservative in character. They had a strong integrationist and assimilationist emphasis, evident in their ads for skin whiteners and hair straighteners, in their editorials, and in cartoons like the one the *Chicago Defender* ran in June 1935. Entitled "Looking into the Future," the cartoon pictured scenes of blacks and whites eating together in a hotel restaurant, a black movie cameraman, a black airline pilot, a black police captain, a civil engineer, a symphony conductor, a black army officer commanding integrated troops, a black major league baseball player, and a black train engineer. To black readers, the cartoon must have looked like science fiction.

The black press actively worked to promote recognition of black leaders, artists, and heroes so absent from the white press. Honor students got prominent coverage, as did blacks entering, or graduating from, the service academies. Black papers covered black baseball stars, who played in segregated obscurity until Jackie Robinson broke baseball's color line in 1947. The *Pittsburgh Courier* ran a cartoon-illustrated series on black history that looked just like a Ripley's "Believe It or Not" rebuke to establishment history.

Black papers covered Louis well before any white papers did. The *Chicago Defender* published a full-page cartoon tribute to him when he won the AAU light-heavyweight title in St. Louis as an amateur. In December 1934 the *Defender* warned then-champion Max Baer, "Look out Maxie—Louis is threatening." Other black papers printed accounts of Louis's life story six months before white papers paid any attention to Louis and quoted Max Baer saying he wouldn't draw the color line.

Thanks to the black press, by late 1934 Louis was becoming a familiar figure in black America. Louis remembered in his autobiography:

> I started noticing some things I thought were strange. A lot of black people would come to me and want to kiss me, pump my hand. I thought they were congratulating me for my fighting skills. Now they started saying things like, "Joe, you're our savior," and "Show them whites!" and sometimes they'd just shout, "Brown Bomber, Brown Bomber!" I didn't understand, then.

As a leading heavyweight contender, Louis had already made more progress in the white world than any but a handful of blacks. And when Louis got his big break and went to New York for his fight with Primo Carnera, he immediately became the most prominent black in America. Louis took Harlem by storm. Before he went into training for Carnera, Roxborough and Black booked him into the Harlem Opera House. Louis filled the place four times a day for a brief show; he climaxed his performance by punching a speed bag into the audience while a band played *Anchors Aweigh*. Louis soon left Harlem for Pompton Lakes, and the crowds followed him. Thousands of blacks flocked to Louis's training camp on weekends. Roxborough and Black charged admission and profited from a thriving concessions business.

Louis stepped into the ring against Carnera on June 25, 1935, as the new but unproved hero of blacks all over America. There was no live broadcast of the fight; Mike Jacobs thought radio would hurt the gate. When Louis's victory was finally announced on the radio, blacks in every major northern city joined in an astounding spontaneous celebration. Thousands of blacks poured into the streets to dance, form impromptu parades, and commandeer streetcars. They brought traffic to a standstill, weaving in front of and around cars, and made fun of any whites they saw.

In Harlem 20,000 blacks, at seventy-five cents a head, jammed the Savoy ballroom for the celebration and the promise of an appearance by Louis himself. The crowd cheered Louis's victory but soon grew impatient waiting for Louis to show up. Understandably tired after the fight, Louis wanted to go to bed, and even Bill Robinson, the famous black tap dancer, could not convince him to make an appearance. Finally, someone told Louis that he had to show up to prevent a riot. Louis reluctantly arrived at the Savoy at 2:30 A.M. and spoke a few words into a dead microphone. The crowd was making so much noise that the words would have been lost anyway, but Louis's appearance mollified his fans, and the crowd broke up.

In Detroit a crowd gathered around the house Louis had bought for his mother and called for her to come out, cheering when she finally opened the door and waved.

Similar demonstrations followed every Louis victory for over a decade. Louis's fights became major social events for most blacks. The black press printed the names of upper-class blacks in the ringside seats at Louis's fights; it was a sort of social register. Most blacks could not afford to see Louis fight in person, so they listened to the fights on the radio and looked forward to celebrating in the streets afterward. In the midst of the Great Depression, with no other signs of improvement in race relations, blacks had precious little to celebrate, and Louis assumed a special significance. He became a symbol of success for all blacks, just as his success earned him symbolic status among whites.

In the South celebrations had to be more restrained, but blacks there felt the symbolism of Louis's fights just as strongly. Maya Angelou, in her account of life in the southern black belt, *I Know Why the Caged Bird Sings*, described rural blacks crowding into her uncle's village store to listen to the radio broadcast of a Louis fight:

> The last inch of space was filled, yet people continued to wedge themselves along the walls of the Store. Uncle Willie had turned the radio up to its last notch so that youngsters on the porch wouldn't miss a word. . . .
> "They're in a clinch, Louis is trying to fight his way out."
> Some bitter comedian on the porch said, "That white man don't mind hugging that niggah now, I betcha." . . .
> "He's got Louis against the ropes and now it's a left to the body and a right to the ribs. . . . It's another to the body, and it looks like Louis is going down."
> My race groaned. It was our people falling. It was another lynching, yet another Black man hanging on a tree. One more woman ambushed and raped. A Black boy whipped and maimed. It was hounds on the trail of a man running through slimy swamps. It was a white woman slapping her maid for being forgetful. . . .
> This might be the end of the world. If Joe lost we were back in slavery and beyond help. It would all be true, the accusations that we were lower types of human beings. . . .
> "And now it looks like Joe is mad. . . . Louis is penetrating every block. The referee is moving in . . ."
> Champion of the world. A Black boy. Some Black mother's son. He was the strongest man in the world. People drank Coca-Colas like ambrosia and ate candy bars like

Christmas. Some of the men went behind the store and poured white lightning in their soft-drink bottles. . . .

It would take an hour or more before the people would leave the Store and head for home. Those who lived too far had made arrangements to stay in town. It wouldn't do for a Black man and his family to be caught on a lonely country road on a night when Joe Louis had proved that we were the strongest people in the world.

The black press celebrated Louis's importance by devoting more attention to him than to any other black from 1935 through 1941. Sociologists St. Clair Drake and Horace Clayton, in their study of black Chicago, noted, "Joe Louis, between 1933–1938 received more front page exposure in the *Chicago Defender* than any other Negro. Three times as much as Haile Selassie, four times as much as Oscar DePriest, 1st black congressman since 1901." The *Defender* and other black papers published special editions on the nights of important Louis fights. Louis's picture popped up everywhere and anywhere in black papers, accounts of his fights occupied whole pages, and Louis appeared often in advertisements. He endorsed Murray's Superior Hair Pomade:

> Besides being a great fighter, Joe Louis is one of the best dressed men in America. He says, "I always try to be well-groomed and the last thing I do before I go into the ring before any fight is to see that MURRAY'S POMADE has my hair smooth and perfectly in place."

A mail-order house sold Joe Louis ashtrays, "an exercise in self-respect," for one dollar. The black press's obsessive interest in Louis carried over to his wife Marva, who became the first lady of black America. Black papers printed pictures of Marva in her splendid outfits, and Mrs. Louis even wrote a fashion column for the *Chicago Defender*.

The black press avoided some of the worst stereotypes that characterized white coverage of Louis, but Louis generally had the same public image in the black press as in the white. Black reporters called him the Brown Bomber and the Dark Destroyer, and they often referred to him as a killer. They didn't go in for the jungle imagery and the references to Louis's primitivism that so delighted white reporters, however. The black press also reported that Louis slept and ate a lot, that he liked to read the comics and rooted for the Detroit Tigers, but they avoided the darkie image of Louis that appeared in the white press. Black papers did not call Louis lazy; they described him accurately as an enthusiastic and hardworking fighter. And the black press studiously avoided quoting Louis in dialect. They quoted him in overwrought English or in sportswriting clichés.

The black press followed the white press closely when it came to promoting Louis's official image as a well-behaved, clean-living fighter. Black reporters were aware that Roxborough, Black, and Louis were trying to sell a good image to whites, and they did all they could to aid the process. They even criticized Louis and his managers when they strayed off the path of virtue. When Al Monroe of the *Chicago Defender* heard that Roxborough and Black were hosting a cocktail party in Louis's honor during January 1936, he was outraged:

> Perhaps managers Black and Roxborough have forgotten that the powers that be have long since decided there should be no more Race heavyweight champions and changed that decree only because of Joe Louis' record. A record that not only includes his success in the ring but his gentlemanly tactics outside the arena. Louis wishes to win the heavyweight championship and is carefully molding his life to warrant such consideration despite his Race's handicap. He knows his job is a tough one because of those handicaps and is avoiding all pitfalls that might become barriers.
>
> One incident that may offer some light on this subject occurred in New York just after the Maxie Baer fight. Joe, just married, decided to take his wife to the Cotton Club for a few hours. He had hardly arrived in the house before photographers rushed him for pictures. Joe consented to the photographs but kicked up terribly when one of the boys attempted to place some empty whiskey bottles on his table. "We only wanted to make it look like a real cabaret," one of them said. "But I am not a real cabaret man," was Joe's reply. Nor for that matter is Joe a real "cocktail party" honoree. If we as friends and well-wishers of the

Bomber must drink to his success then let's color the fete with a different name since Joe neither drinks nor permits anything alcoholic in his home.

One imaginative black reporter quoted Louis in overwrought language on why he had banned alcohol from his training camp: "Drinking brings out the objectionable traits in people and when there is a big crowd around they become annoying to others. They do to me too, because they become pestiferous and interfere no little with my daily routine of work." Although that hardly sounded like Joe Louis, it was true that Louis did not drink.

From a modern perspective, Louis's exaggerated decorum and catering to white sensibilities might be considered "tomming" and would probably draw disgust, not admiration, from the black masses. But in the 1930s, when Louis was the only black consistently winning in white America, and when most blacks understood the implacable racism of their society, Louis's official image did not diminish his popularity among blacks. The official image could not hide the nature of Louis's victories: he wasn't just defeating whites; he was beating them up in the process. As sociologist Lawrence W. Levine wrote in 1977:

> However quietly and with whatever degree of humility he did it, Joe Louis, like Jack Johnson before him, stood as a black man in the midst of a white society and beat representatives of the dominant group to their knees. In this sense no degree of respectability could prevent Louis from becoming a breaker of stereotypes and a destroyer of norms. He literally did allow his fists to talk for him, and they spoke so eloquently that no other contemporary member of the group was celebrated more fully and identified with more intensely by the black folk.

The primal, one-on-one confrontations in the prize ring lent themselves to symbolism, and the violence of boxing provided many blacks with a vicarious revenge on whites. Historian Charles S. Johnson, in *Growing Up in the Black Belt: Negro Youth in the Rural South*, wrote:

Admiration of the prowess of Negro athletes in the prize ring, indeed, provides other incidental and vicarious satisfactions. These Southern black youth, who cannot resent insults, or pit their strength fairly with that of white youth, or resist malicious aggression without incurring the danger of wholesale reprisals from the white community, are more than normally thrilled and vindicated when the special racial handicap is removed and a Negro reveals his superior physical quality. In a few areas of the South, the disposition of Negro youth to celebrate too jubilantly the fistic triumphs of Joe Louis has been brusquely and sometimes violently discouraged, indicating that the symbolism was as significant for the white as for Negro youth.

Sociologist E. Franklin Frazier wrote in 1940: "Joe Louis enables many lower class youths (in fact many Negro youths and adults in all classes) to inflict vicariously the aggression which they would like to carry out against whites for the discriminations and insults which they have suffered."

This vicarious thrill appeared in folk songs about Louis. Many of the songs contained images of white fighters on their knees before Louis. Black kids in Harlem sang this song after Louis defeated Bob Pastor for the second time in the fall of 1939:

> *Bob Pastor was on his knees*
> *Said, "Joe*
> *Don't hit me please,*
> *Just go trucking out of the ring."*

Black dock workers in Fernandina, Florida, sang:

> *Joe Louis hit him so hard he turn roun and roun,*
> *He thought he was Alabama bound. Ah, Ah,*
> *He made an effort to rise agin,*
> *But Joe Louis's right cut him on the chin, Ah, Ah,*
> *Weak on his knees and tried to rise,*
> *Went down crying to the crowd's surprise, Ah, Ah.*

During the 1930s, blues singers celebrated Joe Louis over and over, more than any other black figure from the period. Blues scholar Paul Oliver has noted the special appeal Joe Louis had for the blues singers:

> There are no blues devoted to the achievements of Paul Robeson, George Washington Carver (the Black scientist) or Ralph Bunche (Black politician and diplomat), though these figures would probably have been known to the more literate and especially the city-dwelling singers. . . . Not even Jesse Owens was commemorated in a blues, at any rate on record. . . . For the blues singer, Joe Louis was the singular inspiration of a man who had within his achievements all the drama, the appeal and the invincibility of the traditional Negro ballad hero. . . .

Louis's victories over Carnera and Baer in 1935 inspired a host of songs. Though the black artists were blues singers, the songs differed from traditional blues in subject matter and mood. The early songs about Louis were exultant and happy, and in their portrayal of Louis as a heroic figure they resembled old Negro ballads. Memphis Minnie McCoy, with Black Bob on the piano, recorded "He's in the Ring (Doin' the Same Old Thing)," and she also did the "Joe Louis Strut." Ike Smith recorded "Fighting Joe Louis," George Washington did "Joe Louis Chant," and Lil Johnson did "Winner Joe (the Knock-Out King)." All these songs came out within a year after Louis broke into the big time with his knockout of Carnera in 1935. Billy Hicks and the Sizzling Six did "Joe the Bomber" after he won the heavyweight championship in 1937, and Bill Gaither recorded a song about Louis's victory over Max Schmeling in their 1938 rematch.

The impression Joe Louis made on black music and oral culture only begins to suggest the depth of Louis's penetration into black consciousness during the 1930s. Swedish sociologist Gunnar Myrdal found a one-room black school in Georgia where the children had received no education and had so little contact with the outside world that they could not name the president of the United States. Nor could they identify the NAACP or black leaders W.E.B. DuBois or Walter White. But they knew who Joe Louis was.

Martin Luther King, Jr., remembered another example of the powerful meaning Joe Louis had for blacks:

More than twenty-five years ago, one of the southern states adopted a new method of capital punishment. Poison gas supplanted the gallows. In its earliest stages, a microphone was placed inside the sealed death chamber so that scientific observers might hear the words of the dying prisoner to judge how the human reacted in this novel situation. The first victim was a young Negro. As the pellet dropped into the container, and gas curled upward, through the microphone came these words: "Save me, Joe Louis. Save me, Joe Louis. Save me, Joe Louis. . . ." It is heartbreaking enough to ponder the last words of any person dying by force. It is even more poignant to contemplate the words of this boy because they reveal the helplessness, the loneliness, and the profound despair of Negroes in that period.

Louis's powerful image touched all blacks. To them he was hope, and pride. For Richard Wright, author of *Black Boy*, Louis was

the concentrated essence of black triumph over white. . . . From the symbol of Joe Louis' strength Negroes took strength, and in that moment all fear, all obstacles were wiped out, drowned. They stepped out of the mire of hesitation and irresolution and were free! Invincible! A merciless victor over a fallen foe! Yes, they had felt all that. . . .

Louis was not only a symbol, he was a role model. Malcolm X remembered, "Every Negro boy old enough to walk wanted to be the next Brown Bomber." Malcolm himself took up boxing at the age of thirteen, but two quick defeats ended his ring career. Malcolm was not alone. After Louis beat Carnera, poor black kids filled boxing gyms all over the country. Blacks have disproportionately dominated boxing ever since.

Louis's meaning to blacks struck home the night of June 19, 1936, when Louis lost to Max Schmeling. Lena Horne was singing with Noble Sissle's band in Cincinnati's Moonlight Gardens that night. She remembered:

Until that night I had no idea of the strength of my identification with Joe Louis.

We had the radio on behind the grandstand and during the breaks we crowded around it to hear the fight. I was near hysteria toward the end of the fight when he was being so badly beaten and some of the men in the band were crying. . . . Joe was the one invincible Negro, the one who stood up to the white man and beat him down with his fists. He in a sense carried so many of our hopes, maybe even dreams of vengeance. But this night he was just another Negro getting beaten by a white man. . . . My mother was furious with me for getting hysterical. "How dare you?" she screamed. "You have a performance. The show must go on. Why, you don't even know this man."

"I don't care, I don't care," I yelled back. "He belongs to all of us."

Schmeling himself never forgot the "hysteria and desperation" of blacks that night. After the fight Schmeling drove through Harlem on his way from Yankee Stadium to a midtown hotel. He saw black kids spitting on the passing cars of whites; some threw chunks of wood and brick at the cars. Schmeling saw members of a street band destroying their precious instruments against streetlights and fire hydrants.

The crowd was so ugly that even former black hero and heavyweight champion Jack Johnson did not escape its wrath. The Louis camp had rejected Johnson's offer to train Louis in June 1935, and after that Johnson had frequently criticized Louis as a fighter to white reporters. Before the Schmeling fight Johnson had said that Louis's stance was all wrong and had predicted that Schmeling would win. Johnson also bet heavily on Schmeling. When he flaunted his winnings in Harlem, he had to get police protection.

A black teenage girl walked into a drugstore in Harlem, picked up a bottle of poison, and tried to drink it before the druggist stopped her.

After Louis's defeat, the black press commented on the hope and pride he had given blacks and described the depression in black neighborhoods. The depression was even deeper because the loss followed close on the heels of Italy's conquest of Ethiopia and the fall of Haile Selassie, who had become a hero to American blacks. Adam Clayton Powell, Jr., then just emerging as a black leader in New York, wrote in the *New York Amsterdam News*:

> . . . along came the Brown Bomber, Death in the Evening, and our racial morale took a sky high leap that broke every record from Portland to Pasadena. Surely the new day was just around the corner. . . .
> Then along came the sudden fall of Addis Ababa and the Yankee Stadium fiasco and something died. Gone today is the jauntiness, the careless abandon, the spring in our stride —we're just shufflin' along.

It didn't help that the black press, and black society in general, had been more sensitive than the white press to the symbolic implications of the first Schmeling fight. Roi Ottley wrote, "The fight pictures will record for posterity the complete mastery that an 'Aryan' has over the 'non-Aryan,' according to the Nazi view. . . ."

Black identification with Louis was so great that there was a desperate need to explain or forget. Black papers ran headlines for weeks voicing wild rumors that Louis had been doped before he went into the ring. On June 27, the *Baltimore Afro-American* replaced the large picture of Louis that had dominated the front page the week before with a front-page picture of Jesse Owens. At the time blacks needed symbols to break the myth of inferiority, an uphill battle that could tolerate no losers.

But Louis, of course, came back, and as he did, he lifted the spirits of blacks to new heights. His championship fight with James J. Braddock was an event of signal importance. Even after Louis broke into the big time, and even as he seemed to be winning white acceptance, blacks remained deeply skeptical about Louis's chances of getting a title bout. After Louis beat Baer in September 1935, Al Monroe of the *Chicago Defender* suggested that Baer's loss to Braddock earlier that year had been intentional. According to this theory, Baer wanted to fight Louis because he knew the fight would make a lot of money, but he didn't want the title to fall into black hands. So, in effect, he loaned the title to Braddock. The theory was nonsense, but it reflected the depth of black pessimism. As late as January 16, 1937, Monroe insisted that Louis would never get a title shot. In March, after Louis and Braddock had signed contracts to fight, Monroe still wasn't sure.

As the date of the championship fight approached, the black press underlined its importance by trying to downplay its meaning, just as many white papers underlined the importance of Louis's fights by downplaying them. The *New York Amsterdam News* ran a front-page editorial the week before the fight with the headline "Win or Lose, Let's Be Sane" and said, "By all means, let us accept the fight in its true light: a great sports event and nothing else." The *Chicago Defender* downplayed the fight even more in a front-page editorial with the headline "Louis-Braddock Fight—Just Another Contest":

> Intelligent black men and white men alike regard the contest between Louis and Braddock simply as a prize fight between two contestants and not a war of races. . . .
> The Louis-Braddock fight will not disturb the equilibrium of sane and sensible people regardless of race or nationality. The less informed will be guided by the best informed. It is just a prize fight—not for fun. It has its economic value both to the winner and the loser. This paper has no concern beyond hoping that the man who displays the superior quality will be awarded the decision.

The editorial style of black newspaper coverage of Louis, with its stilted language, careful quotation marks around anything that might pass for a slang expression, and its often studied neutrality, reflected another aspect of the black reaction to Joe Louis. Black society during the 1930s was divided along economic lines as surely as was white society; blacks just had far less to divide. Each black neighborhood had its Sugar Hill where the middle class huddled, still close to the mass of poorer blacks because no amount of money could buy a house in a white neighborhood. During the Depression the black middle class was just scraping by and included virtually anyone with reliable employment.

The black middle class owned and wrote black papers, and the black press reflected the ambivalence of middle-class blacks toward Joe Louis. On the one hand, middle-class blacks were just as thrilled by Louis's victories as any other blacks. Louis was their avenger and hero, too. Like them, Louis was trying to project an image of middle-class respectability, and they could only applaud Louis's intentions. On the other hand, Louis was uneducated, and he was "just" a boxer. By the standards of the white society they were trying to imitate, sport was an insignificant diversion, and athletic achievements were hardly comparable to achievements in business, science, or the arts.

A middle-class black girl from Washington, D.C., expressed the ambivalence of her class in an interview with sociologist E. Franklin Frazier:

> Outside of fighting, I think he is a laughing stock. It is too bad he is so ignorant. I listen to his fights. When he lost I cried, I felt so bad about it, but there was so much to that Schmeling fight. After his last fight, we went down on U Street [the heart of Washington's black ghetto]; it didn't look disorderly to me. Then it seemed as if the people were having a good time. I read later of them destroying property. I did all my yelling right here in this house and on my own front. Of course, if I had been out in the street listening to the fight, I might have joined in the cheering. I think the people who went around beating up white people are just ignorant—that doesn't help a bit.

The *New York Amsterdam News* chided Pennsylvania State Athletic Commissioner Joe Rainey, who said after Louis's first big victory, over Primo Carnera, "I have never been so proud of the fact that I am a Negro." The *Amsterdam News* reminded Rainey that the black race had produced boxers before and went on:

> Dr. Carter Woodson's achievements in history, Dr. Ernest Just's discoveries in zoology, Dr. W.E.B. DuBois' new book, "Black Reconstruction," Dr. Charles Houston's victory in the University of Maryland [desegregation] case ought to give us greater pride in achievement than a victory in any sporting event.

One Scottsboro victory, one Eul Lee victory, one Federal anti-lynching law or one Herndon triumph is worth a dozen successes in the prize ring. . . . And so we wonder whether Commissioner Rainey didn't mean to say that Joe Louis' victory gave him his most exciting and thrilling moment rather than his proudest one.

Educated blacks often tried to separate themselves from other, less fortunate blacks when they downplayed Louis's importance. The *Chicago Defender* said in an editorial before the Louis-Braddock fight:

Joe Louis as a prizefighter represents the same sum total to the intelligent black people of America as James Braddock represents to the intelligent white people of America. It is assumed that white America does not regard Mr. Braddock as a leader in the social, economic, and political life in the great scheme of their existence.

In the same sense black America desires to be seen in like light. In other words intelligent black people regard Mr. Louis in no different manner than intelligent white people regard Mr. Braddock.

Not only did middle-class blacks disassociate themselves from poorer blacks; they also lectured poorer blacks for their over-enthusiastic celebrations following Louis's victories. Al Monroe of the *Chicago Defender* wrote after the Louis-Baer fight:

The powers of boxing are afraid to trust the heavyweight crown in the hands of the black race and the Race folk of New York and Chicago are responsible for this fear. They have, by their thoughtless demonstrations, caused politicians and city officials to consider the risk too great to give one of their own the topmost rung in boxing, a position Joe Louis should not be thrown into.

After Louis lost to Schmeling, the *New York Amsterdam News* printed this letter:

To the Editor of the *Amsterdam News:*
Dear Sir—Several leading newspapers in this city carried stories of disorder in Harlem and a few other leading cities after Joe Louis fought Schmeling.

This sort of thing must not be. It is not only unsportsmanlike, but it hurts the future of our boys in this particular field.

If this sort of thing keeps up every time they have a mixed bout, then they will do away with mixed bouts. . . .

It sure hurt me to go to work Saturday morning and white people telling me your people sure acted terrible after the fight. Can't you do something to cure such a social evil?

REGULAR READER

For some educated blacks, however, Louis was not an embarrassment at all. Even in the 1930s many black intellectuals had the confidence and good sense to appreciate their own culture and common black folk. To men like Richard Wright and Paul Robeson, Joe Louis was a bond to black people everywhere. Wright had written several moving novels on the black experience, and Robeson used his gifts as a singer to revive Negro spirituals. In 1940 the two men joined with Count Basie, the black jazzman and band leader, to record a song called "King Jo (Joe Louis Blues)." Wright wrote the lyrics, Basie wrote the music, and Robeson sang. "King Joe" was a tribute to traditional black culture.

> *Black eye peas ask corn bread,*
> *What make you so strong?*
> *Corn bread says I come from*
> *Where Joe Louis was born.*
>
> *Rabbit say to the bee*
> *What make you sting so deep?*
> *He say I sting like Joe*
> *An' rock 'em all to sleep.*

No matter their personal feelings about Louis, black leaders used him as a rallying point, and they used his image and popularity to appeal to whites. When the Daughters of the American Revolution (DAR) caused a national incident by refusing to let black contralto Marian Anderson sing at Constitution Hall in Washington, D.C., in the fall of 1939, Anderson immediately visited Joe Louis's training camp. Louis and Miss Anderson posed for pictures, and Louis invited her to sing the national

anthem before one of his fights. On March 30, 1941, the National
Urban League sponsored a radio program over the ABC network, a national appeal to let blacks participate in the rapidly
growing defense industry. Joe Louis dominated the program.
First two actors did a funny skit about the futility of Louis's
opponents, then a radio announcer interviewed Louis about his
first jobs as a kid—selling papers, carrying ice for a dollar a
week, pushing truck bodies for Ford. Louis said he knew blacks
could do defense work: "I've seen them do tougher things when
they get a chance." Then Louis made a carefully worded appeal
to whites on behalf of his fellow blacks. "We can defend this
country if everyone has a job to do. . . . I know America believes in fair play and I feel that America will give Negroes a
chance to work."

What did Joe Louis have to do with appealing to whites for
equal opportunity? Everything. Black leaders and writers recognized that Louis was beginning to change white perceptions of
blacks. As early as August 1935, Al Monroe of the *Chicago
Defender* wrote:

> Frankly it is hard to see how whites that greet our star
> athletes with wide open arms can turn around and wish to
> lynch, or see lynched, the brothers of these same youngsters
> who do not happen to be athletically inclined. . . .
>   A few days ago your correspondent accepted an invita-
> tion to accompany Joe Louis to a festival that had never
> before welcomed Race guests and the treatment accorded
> our party was almost unbelievable. Joe Louis was the hero
> of the assemblage. When we entered the place there was
> an air about it that did not seem so free from discrimination.
> The little fellow who met us at the door appeared a bit
> bewildered. He had not seen Joe Louis in the background.
> A few moments later we had the best of everything about
> the place—they had discovered the presence of Joe Louis,
> the Bomber.

In what was probably the most perceptive article written
along these lines, Theophilus Lewis, a black writer for the *New
York Amsterdam News*, predicted the impact Louis would have
on white attitudes. On October 5, 1935, Lewis wrote:

His place in the limelight makes Joe Louis the world's most conspicuous Negro. . . . Hundreds of stage shows and thousands of newspaper stories have associated the word "Negro" with crime and irresponsibility. In the mind of the average white man, the personal qualities of the most conspicuous Negro are merely an enlargement of the racial traits of all Negroes. . . . Give [whites] the impression that Negro is a synonym for Joe Louis and race relations will change for the better.

Confronted with a black fighter widely conceded to be an admirable person, white writers downplayed the racial aspects in Louis's fights. Joe Williams, a white reporter for the *New York World-Telegram*, wrote before the Louis-Kingfish Levinsky fight in 1935:

It is probably just as well that nobody, not even in the interest of ballyhoo, has attempted to interject the matter of racial supremacy into the Joe Louis-Kingfish Levinsky fight. Such interjections are usually sponsored by the Caucasians. In this instance the jury might find it necessary to render an embarrassing verdict.

Jim Jeffries, the man who had come out of retirement to fight Jack Johnson "for the honor of the white race," in 1910, said in an article for the *Saturday Evening Post* in 1935:

I'm not handing out that kind of hokum now. The races of mankind don't have to defend their honor by throwing a couple of prizefighters into the ring, and there never was a time when I thought they did. . . . Right now if a black fighter wins the title fair and square I'm for him, and I hope he behaves himself and keeps his nose clean while he's up there.

Whites were aware of Louis's symbolic significance to blacks. Every white sports page that carried an account of a Louis victory also carried an obligatory column or two under a headline like "Harlem Celebrates Louis Victory." Sometimes the stories were patronizing, evoking the old southern stereotype of blacks as children, but more often the stories had the ring of dispatches from a foreign country, as though blacks were strange and exotic people. A headline in the *Boston Traveler* after the Braddock fight read, "Negroes Stage Weird Parade." The story referred to Harlem as "New York's 'Little Africa.' " A Universal Newsreel feature on Harlem's reaction to Louis's victory over Max Baer made it sound as if blacks were observing some pagan rite. As pictures of blacks crowding toward the camera, smiling and waving, played across movie screens all over the country, a narrator said:

> New York's great Negro quarter and its hot spots turn into a frenzied, howling, celebrating mass of dark-skinned hysteria, when Joe Louis's gloves lay Max Baer low. . . . A people gone wild with enthusiasm, chanting the praise of the Detroit Bomber, Joe Louis, the bronze idol of his race.

Whites understood the excitement in black neighborhoods and approved of the black reaction to Joe Louis. Many white reporters wrote that Louis was a good example, that he would have a positive influence on his fellow blacks. Because Louis was taking care not to offend whites, because he was quiet and "well behaved" and undemanding and he made no waves, whites hoped other blacks would imitate Louis.

Perhaps whites would not have been so sanguine had they realized the depth of the impression Louis was making on blacks. Louis was a hero of revolutionary proportions—a black man who beat whites in direct competition before a national audience. The mood in black America was changing. As Lawrence W. Levine wrote: "For the young Malcolm X and his peers the career of Joe Louis was a testament to the fact that defeat at the hands of the white man was no longer to be taken for granted."

10

JOE LOUIS: AMERICAN

Joe Louis was enjoying a well-earned vacation and trying to patch things up with Marva, who had almost divorced him, when the Japanese bombed Pearl Harbor on December 7, 1941. Louis's reaction matched that of most Americans—anger. Like other Americans, in the next few weeks Louis had to figure out how the war would affect his life. Months before, Chicago's Local Draft Board Eight had classified Louis 1-A, eligible for service, and Louis had a low number in the draft lottery. He had been on the verge of conscription before Pearl Harbor. Now that the country was at war, Louis was sure to be drafted, and soon. Under the provisions of the Selective Service Act then in effect, Louis could have claimed a deferment as the sole supporter of his mother, wife, and several siblings. In his honest way, though, Louis never really considered applying for a deferment, even in peacetime. His mother and his wife were living well. As Louis said in his autobiography, "I mean, what could I say? 'I have to be exempted so I can work so that my wife can pay the housekeeper.'" Louis also felt a real obligation to serve his country. For months Louis repeated variations on the statement he had made over national radio in mid-1941: "As far as the army is concerned, I am ready for to go anytime Uncle Sam call me." In the superheated patriotic atmosphere after Pearl Harbor, a deferment would have been unthinkable, anyway. It would have done irreparable harm to his public image, while only postponing the inevitable. Louis would join the army; the only question was when.

The war promised to be a financial disaster for Louis. He had defended his title seven times in 1941, a record, but only the fights against Billy Conn and Lou Nova had drawn big gates. Expenses from seven training camps ate away a large portion of his earnings. When he wasn't training, Louis still supported his large entourage and continued to spend extravagantly. Louis was living from fight to fight, and within months after the Nova fight he was again borrowing from Mike Jacobs. A big tax bill on his 1941 earnings would come due in early 1942. (The IRS had not yet begun to deduct taxes directly from a fighter's purse.) None of Louis's investments produced any income. His Chicken Shack in Chicago had folded, and the Rhumboogie nightclub in Chicago he had started with his friend Charlie Glenn was just muddling along. The only other substantial investment Louis had to show for his seven years of big boxing purses was his apartment house in Chicago. Without another fight, Louis could not afford to spend money at his usual pace for more than several months without falling irreparably into debt. Characteristically, Louis did not think about what years of war-enforced inactivity might do to his finances.

Mike Jacobs also had to consider the effect of war on his business. Like the moguls of baseball and Hollywood and other entertainment industries, Jacobs must have feared that the American public would disapprove if boxing operated as usual during wartime. The government might disapprove, too. And as a patriotic American, Jacobs surely wanted to do his part to help the war effort. By happy and designing coincidence, Jacobs found a way to forestall criticisms of his sport and help his country too. Jacobs got the idea of staging a heavyweight championship fight for the benefit of the Navy Relief Society, a charity for the families of servicemen killed in action. The Navy Relief Society had the sudden responsibility of looking after the families of navy casualties at Pearl Harbor. A few days after the United States declared war on Japan, Louis was playing golf at the Hillcrest Country Club in Los Angeles when he got word that Mike Jacobs was waiting to talk to him over the phone from New York. Jacobs told Louis about his plans for a charity fight and asked if Louis would go along. Louis agreed. Jacobs asked him again, to make sure Louis understood he wouldn't get any money. Louis agreed without a second thought.

Louis and Jacobs were not alone. In the weeks following Pearl Harbor, virtually every public figure in America made some sort of patriotic gesture. Benefits and flag-waving were the order of the day. Other sports contributed to army or navy relief. The NFL held a game between the champion Chicago Bears and all-stars from the rest of the league, and over the course of the 1942 season baseball contributed well over a million dollars to wartime charities.

But Louis's charity fight particularly impressed the public. For one thing, Jacobs had moved quickly. His announcement of plans for the fight, following so closely on the heels of the Japanese attack, had a freshness and immediacy. For another, none of the other entertainers and athletes who performed for charity stood to lose anything but a little time or money. Louis was risking the heavyweight title, an asset he could not afford to lose. Jacobs lined up a dangerous opponent for Louis, six-foot-six, 250-pound Buddy Baer, who had knocked Louis through the ropes only seven months before. Baer also agreed to contribute a percentage of his purse to the Navy Relief Society.

The white press washed Louis in patriotic praise. Jimmy Powers of the *New York Daily News* put Louis's gesture in perspective. Louis was risking the heavyweight title, which Powers assessed at a value to its owner of one million dollars, for nothing:

> You don't see a shipyard owner risking his entire business. If the government wants a battleship, the government doesn't ask him to donate it. The government pays him a fat profit. . . . The more I think of it, the greater a guy I see in this Joe Louis.

Burris Jenkins, Jr., the sports cartoonist for the *New York Journal-American*, drew a cartoon on the eve of the Louis-Baer fight with Uncle Sam holding Louis's right hand aloft in the traditional boxing sign of victory, and beneath the picture Jenkins wrote, "In the most magnificent gesture ever made by a champion—to sacrifice not only his $70,000 winnings to Naval Relief but risk a million dollar title—Joe Louis tonight can't fail to win the most priceless prize ever won in the world of sports." The prize was in the headline over the cartoon—"The Undying Admiration of His Countrymen."

Even the most routine preliminary newspaper stories on the fight emphasized Louis's generosity. Dick McCann of the *Daily News* began his final preliminary story this way: "In the most generous move ever made by a boxing champion, Joe Louis tonight risks his million-dollar heavyweight championship for the total sum of $0,000,000.00 when he meets Buddy Baer in a scheduled 15-round bout at the Garden." Jack Singer of the *New York Journal-American* wrote, "A simple, quiet, unassuming colored boy who once picked cotton on an obscure Alabama plantation tonight makes the greatest gamble of all time. Joe Louis, the world's heavyweight champion, risks a million dollars against nothing. . . ."

Louis earned even more admiration from white sportswriters because he prepared for the fight without boasting or posturing. Louis had been on vacation since September; Jacobs arranged the fight in December and scheduled it for January 9, 1942. That did not give Louis time to train properly, and he was up against a dangerous opponent. But Louis trained in his quiet, matter-of-fact way, without complaint about his lack of training or worry about the fight's outcome and without much talk about the charity angle. To Louis it was just another fight. When a reporter asked Louis how he felt about risking his title for nothing, Louis supposedly replied, "Ain't fighting for nothing. I'm fighting for my country." Louis had a knack for saying the right thing, and that statement drew even more praise and affection.

Before the war the white press had noted that the public usually rooted for Louis's underdog opponents, and white reporters had often shared that sentiment. But now white reporters came out unabashedly for Louis and assumed the rest of the country was rooting for him, too. Stanley Frank of the *New*

York Post wrote before the Baer fight, "I'm rooting for Joe to win this fight and every one to which he will ever be a party." The day of the fight the *New York World-Telegram* ran a column by Joe Williams with the headline "Whole Nation Pulls for Louis in Poetic Fight."

A few blacks questioned Louis's choice of charities. The navy refused to let its black sailors do anything but service jobs. The *Pittsburgh Courier*, a black paper, pressed Louis to make a statement about discrimination in the navy before the fight, but Louis refused. Louis felt that if he quietly went ahead with the fight, he would do more to embarrass the navy and win over public opinion.

Louis's contribution to the Navy Relief Society did make some white sportswriters think about racism in the navy, if only briefly. Bob Considine of the *Washington Post* got a letter from Dan Burly, a black sportswriter who criticized Louis for fighting to benefit the navy. Considine quoted this passage from Burly's letter without comment: "There is no public record that the Navy is going to bring its colored men up from the galleys and mess halls, allow them to drop their shoe shine brushes and grab guns and help fight for it." A few days later, though, in another column about Louis, Considine brought up the issue himself. He praised Louis as "the poor boy who overcame everything to become a great and beloved champion . . . who . . . had given all the money he made out of the Baer fight to the Navy Relief Society—though the Navy will not let Negroes enlist except in servant capacities." The Broadway columnist of the *New York Daily News*, who did not usually write about sports, wrote the day before Louis fought Baer:

> Louis, who has been a great champion, and who has established marks that others will be shooting at for years to come, now has hung up a mark in generosity and patriotism that will not be challenged. . . . He is doing it for the U.S. Navy, and so it highlights the Navy's reactionary policy in refusing to let colored men serve in any other capacity than messboys in the fleet. . . . It would be a very wonderful thing if the Navy announced, after accepting Louis' dough, that it had decided to be as generous—as Joe Louis.

Despite Louis's gesture and the small pressure it created, navy policies toward blacks changed very little during the course of the war.

On January 9, 1942, close to 17,000 fans filled Madison Garden, with ticket prices starting at thirty dollars for ringside seats. In Louis's dressing room Jack Blackburn told the champion, "My heart's bad. I don't think I can make those stairs tonight." Louis was surprised. "You got to," he said. Blackburn's health was failing rapidly. During training camp Louis had noticed how old Blackburn looked. Assistant trainer Mannie Seamon, who was usually in charge of Louis's sparring partners, had handled most of Blackburn's duties. Blackburn had been in Louis's corner during every one of Louis's professional fights, and the champion, who feared no man in the ring, still felt he needed his old trainer. Louis told Blackburn, "If you get up those stairs with me, I'll have Baer out before you can relax."

Blackburn made it up the steps to the ring, but like everyone else, he had to wait a while before he saw a fight. Mike Jacobs was milking the occasion for all it was worth. Jacobs had flags hung from the rafters and on every available bit of wall space. The introductions from ringside took longer than usual, since Jacobs had gathered an impressive host of dignitaries, including Wendell Willkie, the unsuccessful Republican presidential candidate in 1940. Just before the fight began, Willkie made a speech to the Garden crowd and a national radio audience. Willkie mispronounced Louis's name and called Buddy Baer "Max," apparently mistaking him for his older brother, but no one seemed to care. Willkie praised both fighters for their generosity and wound up his speech as follows:

> Joe Louee, your magnificent example in risking for nothing your championship belt, won literally with toil and sweat and tears, prompts us to say, "We thank you." And in view of your attitude it is impossible for me to see how any American can think of discrimination in terms of race, creed, or color.

When the ring finally cleared, Louis was left alone with a giant. The six-foot-six Baer towered over Louis, and Baer came out swinging. Louis's expression never changed as Baer looped in a couple of left hooks. Louis held his ground, then began to counterpunch, reaching up to Baer's chin with a succession of sharp punches. Baer was too slow to parry Louis's quick hands, and every punch Louis landed had its effect. Before long, Baer's head was rocking backward, and he was swinging wildly, while Louis continued to bore straight in. A right dropped Baer for a nine count. Louis came out of his neutral corner and dropped Baer again. Baer struggled to his feet, and Louis again smashed him down. Baer tried to pull himself up by the ropes, but he could not get up in time. Knockout, at 2:56 of the first round. Years later Baer told a reporter, "The only way I could have beaten Joe that night was with a baseball bat."

After deducting training expenses, Louis contributed $47,100 to navy relief. Mike Jacobs donated his whole share of the gate, $37,229, and Buddy Baer kicked in $4,078.

The next day, January 10, 1942, Joe Louis volunteered for service in the U.S. Army. On January 11 Louis went to Governors Island for his army physical, followed by a crowd of reporters. Pictures of Louis expanding his chest for a doctor with a tape measure appeared the next day in papers all over the country. Not surprisingly, the army found Louis fit for service. The next day Louis reported for duty at Camp Upton, Long Island, with an even bigger escort from the press. Newsreel cameras recorded Louis's induction and a staged scene between Louis and a soldier who was typing out a form on Louis. The soldier asked Louis, "What's your occupation?" and Louis replied in a rush, "Fighting and let us at them Japs." Newspaper stories the next day quoted Louis as saying the Japanese were "all lightweights, anyway." The *New York Daily News* printed a full-page picture of Louis in uniform saluting with an American flag in the background. A huge headline over the picture read, "Joe Louis Joins Army."

Louis's enlistment was big news. It came only a month after Pearl Harbor, when the country was still in the first flush of enthusiasm for the war. The press felt a duty to support the war effort, and part of that duty was to join the War Department in publicizing the inductions of public figures. The first celebrity enlistments were particularly important symbolic acts —American heroes going off to war. They spurred other men to enlist and fed the public's sense of unity and national purpose. When Bob Feller, the star pitcher of the Cleveland Indians, enlisted in the navy two days after Pearl Harbor, his induction ceremony was broadcast live over a national radio network.

When Joe Louis volunteered for the army, he struck an even deeper chord. Louis had been America's token black ever since the summer of 1935. He had been the only black to appear consistently in the white media, to intrude on white consciousness. To whites, Joe Louis was the symbol of his race. Louis's generosity, his willingness to serve, and his patriotism reassured whites about the loyalty of all black Americans. To a country deeply divided along racial lines, yet desperately wanting to believe it was united against a common foe, Louis was a symbol of national unity.

World War II wrought a fundamental change in Louis's public image. Before the war the white press had always praised Louis as a boxer, but the praise for Louis as a person was for the things he was not, the things he did not do. Louis was not a Jack Johnson; he did not go out with white women, humiliate his white opponents, or make waves on racial issues. Louis had "never done anything to discredit his race." The phrase was shopworn. At his best in the white press, Louis was easygoing, quiet, modest, and always black. At worst, white reporters called him an Ethiopian or an African, stereotyped him as a jungle killer or a lazy nigger, and questioned his intelligence.

Now the white press rushed to embrace Louis. The same papers that had once called him an African called him a good American and wrote about him with a new warmth. The conservative *Chicago Tribune* wrote:

> There never has been a heavyweight champion who has behaved better than Joe has, in and out of the ring. . . . Joe hasn't had educational advantages and there are those who say he isn't very bright, but he has had enough education and he is bright enough to know where his duty lies. Joe is champ.

To be a good American and to know where his duty lay—
there was no higher praise in an America a month at war. The
surest indication that Louis's public image had changed came
from Paul Gallico, the former *New York Daily News* sports
columnist who had done so much to build Louis's image as a
jungle killer. In 1935 Gallico had described Louis as cruel, savage, primitive. In the intervening years before the war Gallico
had retired from sportswriting to take up a career as a free-lance
writer. In early 1942 Gallico wrote an article for *Liberty* magazine entitled "Citizen Barrow," which was condensed and reprinted in *Reader's Digest*. Gallico wrote:

> Years ago I wrote that Joe Louis was "mean." Then he
> was a primitive puncher just emerging from the pit. Some-
> where on his long, hard climb Joe found his soul. It was
> this, almost more than his physical person, that he handed
> over to his country.
> "You can't think of yourself these days," Joe said. But I
> can think of him. I write of him now, not especially as a
> hero—every unsung youth who has shouldered a gun has
> made a similar sacrifice—but as a simple, good American. . . .
> Joe has become one of the most popular of all champions,
> cheered by white and black alike. But he has won more
> than popularity. He has won respect. The simple, unlettered
> colored boy has brought to the championship a dignity it
> has too often lacked.

Gallico also revealed the insecurity whites felt about black
loyalty and Louis's symbolic role in soothing those doubts:

> "You do whatever you do for your country. That's natural.
> Your country is what made everything possible for you.
> That's how you figure." You hear many versions of that
> statement these days. But it sounds different coming from
> the mouth of a colored boy in an Army uniform who be-
> lieves it with his heart and soul.

Before the war, newsreels rarely covered Louis outside his
role as a boxer. But after December 1941, the war-conscious
reels recognized Louis's new importance as a symbol of national

unity and featured him even when he was just a spectator at some event. For instance, the cameras picked out Joe Louis as he sat watching a benefit football game between the New York Giants and the Army All-Stars. When Louis sparred in a Polo Grounds benefit that featured many other prominent athletes, a Universal newsreel described Louis as "Hero of the day." He was the only athlete mentioned in the reel's advance notices. Another Universal newsreel threw subtlety to the winds during a feature on "I am an American Day" ceremonies in Central Park in early 1942. One million and a quarter people turned out at the park, and NBC broadcast the ceremonies over its national radio network. As the camera focused on Louis, who was one of many dignitaries present, the reel's narrator said, "Yes, we are *all* proud to be Americans."

Tributes to Louis poured in. The Boxing Writers Association of New York gave Louis its Edward J. Neil Plaque, named for a reporter killed while covering the Spanish Civil War in 1937 and awarded to the man who had done the most for boxing in the previous year. The association presented the plaque to Louis at a special dinner held in Ruppert's Brewery in Manhattan, January 21, 1942. The working press attended the dinner in force, and J. Edgar Hoover and former heavyweight champions Jack Dempsey, Gene Tunney, and Jimmy Braddock were among the celebrities present. Former New York Mayor James J. (Jimmy) Walker, who had helped legalize boxing in New York twenty years before, presented the plaque to Louis and made a long speech in praise of the heavyweight champion. He concluded:

> Joe, all the Negroes in the world are proud of you because you have given them reason to be proud. You never forgot your own people. When you fought Buddy Baer and gave your purse to the Navy Relief Society, you took your title and your future and bet it all on patriotism and love of country. Joe Louis, that night you laid a rose on the grave of Abraham Lincoln.

Louis's acceptance speech was in sharp contrast to Walker's windy oration:

You don't know how you make me feel. The way I feel is good. I never thought I'd feel so good as when I won the heavyweight championship of the world, but tonight tops them all. I feel better than I ever felt in my life. Thanks for what you did for me. I want to thank Mike Jacobs for what he did for me. I want to thank the boxing commission for what it did for me. I hope I never did anything in the ring I'll be sorry for in the years to come. I'm a happy man tonight.

Newspapers all over the country quoted Walker's speech.

Louis returned to Camp Upton, where he was undergoing basic training as a private. The army had offered him a commission, but Louis turned it down. He did not feel he had the education to be an officer, and he wanted to be around men with backgrounds similar to his own. But the army could not allow Louis to serve as an ordinary private. The heavyweight champion had fought a benefit for the other service's charity, and the army wanted Private Louis to fight for army relief. Louis agreed to donate his entire purse from another title defense, and Mike Jacobs lined up Abe Simon as an opponent. Simon was another giant—six feet five, 260 pounds. Louis had knocked Simon out in thirteen rounds the year before.

Once again, Louis's generosity drew praise from the white press. The army transferred Louis to Fort Dix, New Jersey, which had a new gymnasium Louis could use for his training. Louis's preparations for the Simon fight were different from his usual routine. The army required him to do two hours of military training every day in addition to his running and boxing drills. And for the first time in Louis's professional career, Jack Blackburn was not with him. The old trainer was too sick to leave Chicago. Louis was cheered, though, by the thousands of GIs, black and white, who came to watch him train. Even though he didn't have the money to do it, Louis bought $3,000 worth of tickets for the fight and gave them to servicemen.

Jacobs and the army scheduled the Louis-Simon fight for March 27, 1942. On March 10 the Navy Relief Society held a combination dinner and show in Madison Square Garden. Louis attended as the guest of Wendell Willkie. The society set the dais in the middle of the Garden's boxing ring. During the proceedings, someone praised Louis for his contribution to the society and asked the heavyweight champion to make a speech. Harry Markson, who by then was working as Mike Jacobs's publicist, remembered forty years later:

> He [Louis] stopped at my office on the afternoon of the dinner, and I said, "You know, Joe, they're probably going to ask you to make a speech. Do you want me to write something for you?"
> And he says, "Aaahh, they're not gonna call on me."
> "What if they ask you to talk?"
> "Nah, they won't ask me." And so when they called on him, he had to make this line up from the time he jumped over the railing at the Garden up to the ring.

Louis was wearing his army private's uniform. The crowd, already overdosed on patriotism, watched as Louis slowly made his way to the microphone. Louis always spoke better when he was not bound by someone else's words. He said a few lines of thanks, then concluded in his deliberate, resonant voice, "I have only done what any red-blood American would do." The audience began a ragged clapping, but Louis cut them off. "We gon do our part, and we will win, because we are on God's side. Thank you." Louis's sincerity struck home as surely as the rhythm of his last line. The crowd gave him a loud, standing ovation.

"We are on God's side" became one of the most famous phrases to emerge from all the overblown oratory during World War II. Louis's words inspired a poem by Carl Byoir, one of Madison Avenue's best advertising men, which appeared in the *Saturday Evening Post.* "Joe Louis Named the War" was not much of a poem and its style is especially grating over forty years later, but the fact that the *Saturday Evening Post* featured it prominently indicated the impression Louis had made.

The Louis-Simon fight was another Louis love fest. Announcers Don Dunphy and Bill Corum, broadcasting the fight for the national Mutual Radio Network, devoted almost all of their prefight comments to Louis. They identified him as "Private Joe Louis of the United States Army," mentioned the absence of Jack Blackburn, who was still laid up in a Chicago hospital, and informed their audience that Louis had bought thousands of dollars' worth of tickets for his army buddies. When Louis entered the ring, the radio microphones picked up the sound of a loud ovation. When Billy Conn was introduced from ringside, the crowd cheered noticeably softer than it had for Louis. Undersecretary of War Robert F. Patterson was introduced, and he spoke to the thousands of servicemen listening over the radio: "It is an army of champions. It is engaged in a championship fight, and it's going to win. We pay a special tribute to Private Joseph Louis Barrow. He is a truly great champion. He is a credit to the ring and a credit to the army." When the ring announcer introduced Louis, the crowd roared again.

Don Dunphy incorporated the nationalistic mood of the prefight ceremonies into his description of the fight itself. He noted the "real American gameness in both boys." As Louis took the offensive early, Dunphy said, "Louis keeps moving in all the time, the American way."

Louis dropped Simon at the end of the second round, but the bell saved the challenger. The bell saved Simon again at the end of the fifth. In the sixth round Louis continued his onslaught and dropped Simon once more. Simon was struggling to his feet at the count of ten, but the referee ruled he had not made it up in time.

Dunphy interviewed Louis briefly after the fight, and Louis said hello to the servicemen listening in and wished them "godspeed." Abe Simon had sufficiently recovered to talk to Dunphy, as well. Simon complained to Dunphy that the referee should not have stopped the fight, but he was careful to compliment Louis as the greatest fighter ever.

Dunphy wound up the broadcast with another appeal to America's nationalistic spirit. Once again, Dunphy used Louis as a national symbol: "We won't stop punching, just as Louis does, till we win."

The Joe Louis media blitz began with Mike Jacobs's announcement of the Buddy Baer charity fight, in December 1941. It ran through Louis's enlistment in January, the awards dinner for the Edward J. Neil Memorial Plaque, the Navy Relief Society show, and Louis's benefit fight against Abe Simon in March. Once again, Louis's personal attributes had combined with circumstance to elevate and burnish his public image, this time to truly heroic proportions. Before the war Louis had won white acceptance. In the war's early months Louis earned genuine respect and affection from whites. Whites began to root for him in his fights against white opponents. Jack Johnson could never have imagined such a thing.

World War II did something else for Louis's public image and for blacks in general. By one of the happiest coincidences in American history, the United States was fighting against Nazi Germany, a blatantly racist regime. American racism, disgraceful as it was, was so ingrained in custom that most white Americans didn't consider themselves truly prejudiced, a contradiction that continues today. Few whites in the 1930s said they wanted to keep blacks down, but they would not hire blacks or let blacks live in their neighborhoods, and most whites shared the unchallenged assumption that blacks were inferior. Joe Louis was helping whites begin to face that contradiction, and World War II accelerated the process.

Even before the war the American media had created a negative image of the Nazi regime as totalitarian, racist, and warlike. With the declaration of war against Germany, the American people intensified those impressions in the collective process of defining their enemy. Throughout history men have needed rationalizations to kill or oppress each other. Successful murderers or oppressors usually defined their victims as different from themselves, as less human. The act of defining an enemy or a victim is also an act of self-definition, so as Americans defined Germans as totalitarian, they defined themselves as democratic; as they defined Germans as racist, they defined themselves as tolerant; as they defined Germans as warlike, they defined themselves as peaceful. Save for the influence of one aberrant individual, Adolf Hitler, there was little ground for these distinctions. The American people needed no artificial distinctions to define themselves as different from the Japanese—racism was a constant component of anti-Japanese propaganda, and Americans hated the Japanese far more than they did the Germans.

Nazi racism, so clearly offensive, was the toughest challenge to Americans who wanted to think of themselves as different from their enemy. The United States' announced war aims included freedom and equality for all peoples, and war propagandists shamelessly criticized Germany for its treatment of the Jews while ignoring or downplaying American racism. But even after sixty years of silence and naïveté about America's race problem, many whites recognized the contradiction between the country's war rhetoric and its treatment of blacks. Black writers unerringly emphasized that contradiction and used it to appeal for justice.

Had it not been for the 1936 Olympics and Joe Louis's two fights against Max Schmeling, Nazi racism would not have posed such a challenge to Americans' definitions of themselves. Those athletic events, especially Louis's second fight with Schmeling, had dramatized Hitler's theories of race and Aryan superiority as few other events had. And they revealed Nazi attitudes toward blacks that otherwise might never have become an issue because there were so few blacks in Europe.

The war against Germany confirmed the symbolism of the Louis-Schmeling fights. When Louis enlisted in the army, the *Chicago Tribune* said, "Joe has a date for a return engagement with Max Schmeling." Louis was often introduced during the war as "the first American to kayo a Nazi." In the early months of the war, sportswriters remembered Max Schmeling as a Nazi and wrote that Schmeling was the only opponent Louis ever hated. In his article for *Liberty* magazine in early 1942, Paul Gallico wrote, "Schmeling was the only opponent Joe Louis ever hated. Not only had Schmeling knocked Joe out, but by 1938, when they met again, he had become an out-and-out Nazi."

The government and the army used Louis and the symbolism of his fights with Schmeling to sell the war to blacks. Chandler Owens, a black publicist, prepared a pamphlet for the Office of War Information called "Negroes and the War" designed to boost black patriotism. The pamphlet described Nazi racism, emphasizing Hitler's snub of Jesse Owens at the 1936 Olympics. Owens put the best face possible on the situation of blacks in America, saying blacks had "come a long way in the last fifty years, if slowly. There is still a long way to go before equality is attained, but the pace is faster, and never faster than now." For the hard sell, Owens turned to the symbol of Joe Louis:

> Under the lights at Yankee Stadium, our champion knocked out the German champion in one round. Sergeant Joe Louis [Louis's promotion was rapid] is now a champion in an army of champions. Joe Louis doesn't talk much, but he talks truly. He talks for 13,000,000 Negro Americans, for all American citizens, when he says: "We're going to do our part, and we'll win 'cause we're on God's side."

In 1944 the Army Signal Corps produced a film, "The Negro Soldier," under the supervision of Col. Frank Capra. Like Chandler Owens's pamphlet, the film was supposed to drum up enthusiasm among blacks for the war. Carlton Moss, a black, wrote the script and played the lead role. In a tribute to Louis's power as a symbol, Moss explained a world war in terms of a boxing match.

The film was in the form of a sermon, with Moss playing a minister in a richly appointed church. Moss began his sermon by saying he had been at Yankee Stadium for the second Louis-Schmeling fight.

> In one minute and forty-nine seconds an American fist won a victory. (Footage from the fight) But it wasn't the final victory. Now those two men who were matched in the ring that night are matched again. This time in a far greater arena and for much greater stakes.
>
> (Footage of Max Schmeling doing military training) Max Schmeling, a paratrooper in the German Army, men turned into machines, challenging the world.
>
> (Footage of Louis doing military training) Joe Louis, training for the fight of his life. This time it's a fight not between man and man but between nation and nation. A

fight for the real championship of the world, to determine which way of life shall survive, their way or our way, and this time we must see to it that there is no return engagement. For the stakes this time are the greatest that men have ever fought for.

Moss went on to read a racist statement from Hitler's *Mein Kampf* and reviewed American history, highlighting the roles of blacks in various American wars. Somehow Moss neglected to mention slavery or the Civil War.

Despite this effort to encourage black enlistments and persuade blacks that they had a full stake in the war, the War Department remained adamantly racist. The Marine Corps and Air Corps, "elite" services by self-definition, barred blacks. The navy used blacks only in menial roles. The army was little better; blacks were assigned to segregated units, usually with white officers, and had to endure the humiliations of segregated army buses and discrimination in towns near military bases. In the fall of 1940, with the armed forces gearing up for the first peacetime draft in their history, the War Department submitted a policy statement to Pres. Franklin Roosevelt regarding blacks in the services. Secretary of War Henry Stimson believed blacks were inferior soldiers and said the army should not become a "sociological laboratory." His policy was to maintain segregation, and FDR initiated his approval of Stimson's recommendations on October 8, 1940. Throughout the war to come, FDR steadily maintained that winning the war was the first priority and that justice for blacks would have to wait until Germany and Japan surrendered. FDR had been telling blacks to wait since his election in 1932.

As a sop, the War Department on October 25 promoted its ranking black officer, Col. Benjamin O. Davis, to brigadier general. On the same day, Secretary Stimson appointed a black man, William H. Hastie, the dean of Howard Law School, to the new post of civilian aide on Negro affairs. Hastie could do little to improve the treatment of blacks in the military. The War Department assigned him only one aide and a secretary. As his aide, Hastie chose Truman K. Gibson, a black lawyer from Chicago and a friend of Joe Louis's, for whom Gibson had done some legal work years before. Hastie and Gibson were relegated to the periphery of Pentagon affairs and spent most of the war spinning their wheels.

In the private sector, growing defense industries had largely wiped out unemployment for whites by the end of 1940, but the economy's gains had not yet filtered down to blacks. Many defense contractors refused to hire blacks—a practice that was widespread and perfectly legal at the time. Meanwhile, Congress was cutting New Deal aid programs. Blacks responded with stirrings of militancy. A. Philip Randolph, president of the Brotherhood of Sleeping Car Porters, a union of black railroad employees, proposed that blacks march on Washington in force to "exact their rights in National Defense employment and the armed forces." In January 1941 Randolph organized the Negro March on Washington Committee and surprisingly won the support of the NAACP and the Urban League, organizations usually too cautious for such a move.

Roosevelt tried to stop the march, knowing that it would embarrass him politically and provide the Nazis with a propaganda coup. But Roosevelt did not offer blacks anything substantial in exchange for stopping the march, and by late spring Randolph's organization was gaining momentum. On May 29, 1941, Randolph wrote to FDR and told him that 10,000–50,000 blacks were mobilized to march. Finally, Roosevelt agreed to meet Randolph. Even FDR's considerable charm would not persuade Randolph to call off the march without some significant government concession, and FDR agreed to issue an executive order, with the wording subject to Randolph's approval. As finally approved, the order read, "There shall be no discrimination in the employment of workers in defense industries or government because of race, creed, color, or national origin." To enforce Executive Order 8802 Roosevelt created a Fair Employment Practices Committee (FEPC). It was the U.S. government's first halting step toward ensuring equal opportunity for blacks.

Despite Roosevelt's order and all the wartime rhetoric about American tolerance, things didn't change all that much. The booming wartime economy did eventually employ blacks, but blacks continued to encounter problems getting promotions and equal pay and were often barred from white unions. The FEPC never had the authority or budget to enforce Roosevelt's executive order. It could charge a contractor with discrimination in a public hearing, hoping to embarrass the contractor into hiring blacks. But the FEPC couldn't handle all the complaints it received, and many companies refused to yield to the commission's weak powers of suasion.

As blacks and whites crowded together in the cities, wartime shortages created tense competition for housing and recreational facilities, and racial hostilities flared. In Detroit, competition between black and Polish immigrants for space in a government housing project led to a two-day race war in the streets. Twenty-five blacks and nine whites died before the National Guard restored order.

Segregation persisted in the armed services. William Hastie eventually resigned in disgust from his post as civilian aide to the War Department on Negro affairs. Louis's friend Truman Gibson replaced Hastie but was often powerless to redress the grievances of black servicemen. This letter from a black GI at Camp Lee, Virginia, forwarded to Gibson, reflected the almost-universal experience of blacks serving their country during the war:

> We the colored soldiers here would appreciate so much if you or one of your assistants could come down here and let us explain just how bad the conditions are. The prisoner of war gets much better treatment than we do even when they go the dispensary or hospital and it is really a bearing down to our morale as we are suppose to be fighting for democracy. Yet we are treated worse than our enemies are. I must say all of us feel the same and it has gotten so bad that we have lost all interest in this so called Democracy. If something isn't done quick, I am afraid a great disaster will surely come.

As Uncle Sam's most famous private, Joe Louis enjoyed considerably better treatment. After his charity fight with Abe Simon, Louis asked for, and got, a five-day furlough to visit Jack Blackburn, who was down with pneumonia in Chicago's Provident Hospital. Louis visited his trainer every day of the furlough, and they talked about Louis's old fights. Several days after Louis returned to camp, Blackburn died. Louis returned to Chicago for the funeral. Nearly 10,000 people attended. Louis's life was changing. Blackburn, a father figure to Louis, was dead, and John Roxborough, a fatherly protector, had been indicted in an investigation of municipal government corruption in Detroit and was serving a term in jail for policy operating. Louis was on his own more than ever before.

The army was still unsure what to do with Louis. Louis's friend Truman Gibson told Undersecretary of War Robert Patterson that Louis loved horses and suggested that Louis train with a cavalry unit. Patterson agreed, and Louis was assigned to Fort Riley, Kansas. His unit was all black, and the experience had a beneficial impact on Louis. He became more familiar with the problems of ordinary black servicemen, who did not get the special attention Louis was accustomed to receiving. Whenever he could, Louis used his privileged position to help out. One of the first men to approach Louis for help was Jackie Robinson, who had been an all-American football player at UCLA. Robinson, of course, played a little baseball, too. In the army, however, Robinson was allowed to play on the camp football team but not on the baseball team. Football had at least something of a tradition of integrated play, while baseball had been rigidly segregated for more than sixty years. Louis went to the commanding general of Fort Riley, Donald Robinson, and the general eventually let Jackie Robinson play on his baseball team.

Jackie Robinson and nineteen other black college graduates at Fort Riley had applied for officer candidate school (OCS). Years later, Robinson remembered that the applications had been stalled and that Louis successfully interceded. Louis gave the same account, but Truman Gibson, a sharp man with a vivid memory who still practices law in Chicago, insists that Louis's influence was not decisive, that Robinson would have gotten into OCS, anyway. But Gibson remembered another occasion in which Louis helped Robinson:

Toward the end of his [Robinson's officer] training, he was on a drill field, and a white officer referred to a black soldier as a "stupid nigger son of a bitch." Whereupon Jackie went to him and said, "You shouldn't address a soldier in those terms." And he [the white officer] says, "Oh, fuck you; that goes for you too." Well, that's the last this guy knew. Jackie had an explosive, terrible temper. He almost killed the guy. So Joe, concerned with Jackie's busting out of officer candidate school, called me. Together we went to the commanding general. Joe gave him some very expensive gifts, and Jackie was permitted to finish officer candidate school.

But that wasn't the end of Jackie Robinson. Jackie went to Camp Swift [Texas] and was getting on the bus going back to camp when the bus driver, who along with most of the white bus drivers in the South was deputized and carried a pistol and whose firm resolve was to see that Negro soldiers would get to the back of the bus, said, "All right, nigger, get to the back of the bus."

Jackie said, "I'm getting to the back of the bus. Take it easy."

"You can't talk to me like that."

Jackie said, "Well, I can talk to anybody any way I want."

So he [the bus driver] pulled his pistol, and Jackie said, "That's a fatal mistake." He says, "You're gonna eat that son of a bitch." So Jackie took it and broke every tooth in the guy's mouth, and they discharged Jackie for the good of the service. That's the Jackie Robinson story.

While Louis was still at Fort Riley, in September 1942, Mike Jacobs arranged with the army to hold a Louis-Conn rematch for the benefit of the Army Relief Fund. It had been over a year since Louis and Conn fought. The public was eager to see the rematch, and it was a certain million-dollar gate. Jacobs enlisted a committee of sportswriters to promote the fight in the public interest, but Jacobs had some private interests in mind, too. Louis had not made any money from fighting for a year, but his spending never slowed. Louis had borrowed $59,000 from Jacobs and $41,000 from John Roxborough. Conn, who had joined the army in early 1942, also had borrowed heavily from Jacobs, to the tune of $34,500. Jacobs persuaded the army to let Louis and Conn pay their debts off the top of the purse. When Grantland Rice, one of the sportswriters Jacobs had recruited to promote the fight, heard about this special arrangement, he quit the committee with his nose high. But John Kieran of the *New York Times* defended the arrangement. He pointed out that even after deducting expenses and the fighters' debt payments, the Army Relief Fund stood to profit by at least $750,000.

Both fighters started training in mid-September, Louis at Greenwood Lake, New Jersey, and Conn at Mike Jacobs's estate in Rumson, New Jersey. After two weeks, though, Secretary of War Stimson called off the fight. Stimson was careful to say that neither fighter was at fault, but he said that the fight would not be fair to other servicemen who did not have a chance to work off their debts while in the military. Conn and Louis then offered to fight for free, but Stimson still refused. He banned further fund raising by the Army or Navy Relief funds, saying they had enough money.

Jacobs would have had to postpone the fight, anyway. Conn had taken time off from training to attend a family party. Apparently Conn's father-in-law still disapproved of his daughter's choice; he provoked Conn into a fight. In the melee Conn broke his hand on his father-in-law's head. Whenever he got a chance, Louis kidded Conn about the incident. "Your father-in-law still beating you up?"

The abortive benefit fight did not really damage Louis's public image, but the controversy did reveal, for anyone who cared to see, the sorry state of Louis's finances. In truth, Louis's financial situation was even worse than his debts to Roxborough and Jacobs indicated. In early 1942 the IRS assessed Louis a $117,000 tax bill on his 1941 earnings. Louis did not have the money. Fortunately, the government allowed men in uniform to wait until they got out of the service to pay any outstanding tax bills and did not charge interest in the interim. With the $117,000 he owed the government, the $59,000 he owed Jacobs, and the

$41,000 he owed Roxborough, Louis was already over $200,000 in debt by the fall of 1942. He had no income save for his paltry army salary, and he was still supporting his mother. His wife was living like a queen in Chicago. Worse yet, Louis had only a vague sense of his own disastrous situation. Mike Jacobs lent him money whenever he asked, and Louis assumed that when he got out of the service and started fighting again, everything would be fine. Louis enjoyed his expansive role as the rich, free-spending heavyweight champion of the world, and so he continued to spend borrowed money, treating soldiers to steaks at almost every PX he visited.

Truman Gibson estimates that Louis spent over a quarter of a million dollars on soldiers. Gibson doubtlessly exaggerated the actual amount Louis spent on his fellow soldiers, but by the end of the war Louis did owe Jacobs well over $100,000.

Louis's responsibilities were about to grow. His wife Marva was expecting a baby in early 1943. In the late summer of 1942 Louis set Marva up in an apartment near Fort Riley, hoping they could be together when she had the baby. But Mrs. Louis did not like the Kansas heat, and she missed her friends and family in Chicago. She returned home and there gave birth to a daughter, named Jaqueline in honor of Jack Blackburn. Louis got a two-week furlough and rushed home to see his new baby.

Even the baby could not keep the Louises together. As usual, Louis had places to go. In early 1943 he went to Hollywood for a role in *This Is the Army*, starring Ronald Reagan, among others. *This Is the Army* was a gushy war-propaganda feature about a traveling variety show with a cast composed entirely of soldiers. One number in the show was a southern scene complete with white performers in blackface. Louis appeared just long enough to make a patriotic speech and to be used as a symbol in a black musical number. The number featured black dancers singing "That's What They're Wearing in Harlem This Year," saying that military uniforms were in fashion with blacks and suggesting that blacks were behind the war effort. One line in the chorus went, "If you want to know, / Just ask Bomber Joe," and the cameras switched from the dancers to catch Louis punching a speed bag and looking serious.

The film took six months to complete, and despite his small role Louis stayed in Hollywood during the filming and renewed intimacies with a number of starlets. While Louis was carrying on in Hollywood, Marva was shuttling back and forth from Chicago to New York for voice training to work up a nightclub act. Marva opened successfully in New York and from there went on a tour of the South. But after three months of eating and sleeping in her chauffeured car because restaurants and hotels would not serve her, Marva Louis gave up.

Back at the War Department, Truman Gibson suggested that Louis head up a traveling troupe of black boxers to tour army bases and build morale. The War Department approved, and in late 1943 Louis set out for a tour of U.S. Army bases with his old sparring partner, George Nicholson, and Sugar Ray Robinson, born Walker Smith in Detroit. As a kid, Sugar Ray's idol had been an older amateur light-heavyweight fighter from his neighborhood—Joe Louis Barrow. Sugar Ray moved to New York, where he won a Golden Gloves championship in 1940 and then turned pro. By 1944 Robinson was a leading contender in both the middleweight and welterweight divisions.

Louis's boxing troupe visited countless military camps in the United States and went overseas to visit GIs in England and Italy. Louis even did a tour of the Aleutian Islands in wintertime, clearly service beyond the call of duty. In his forty-six months of army duty, Louis fought ninety-six exhibitions, visited hospitals, and traveled over 70,000 miles. He saw firsthand the deplorable treatment of black GIs. Unlike other black soldiers, Louis had a friend in Washington. Louis would call Truman Gibson:

> Joe, who had a very keen sense of justice and injustice, would report on conditions in these camps from everyplace that he went and even overseas. And he was responsible for a lot of changes in the army. . . .
> I remember very vividly the situation at Fort Bragg. Joe had called up—he called from practically every post, every camp—and said, "They've reached the limit here. They don't have Jim Crow buses [where blacks had to sit in the

back]. They don't let Negroes *on* certain buses." So I went
in and told [Under-]Secretary [of War Robert] Patterson.
He said, "That's impossible."

I said, "It is, huh?" I said, "Why is it impossible?"

Patterson called in another general, and after discussing
the situation promised to call the commanding general at
Fort Bragg.

I said, "Well, call him now."

So they called him, and Joe was correct, and they then
and thereafter barred all segregation on army posts, camps,
and stations, period.

Orders against segregation had little effect as long as the War
Department continued its basic policy of assigning black soldiers
to all-black units and so long as the rest of society remained
segregated. But Joe Louis did play a small role in alleviating
some of the worst conditions at the camps he visited.

Louis enjoyed a privileged status, above segregation, in his
private life. He also had followed the example of his managers,
who did not challenge the color line. Julian Black and John
Roxborough maintained their dignity by simply avoiding embarrassing situations. But in the service Louis had to confront
the issue on his own, and he came to his own decision. He would
obey Jim Crow in towns, but on army bases he would insist
on his rights. Louis's newfound assertiveness caused a dangerous
scene at Camp Sibert in Alabama. Louis and Sugar Ray Robinson
were sitting at the camp bus depot, waiting for a taxi to take
them to town. A military policeman ordered them to move to a
bench in the rear. "That's for people like you," the MP said.

"We ain't moving," Louis said.

The MP recruited help to arrest Louis and Robinson. Louis
kept his cool, but Sugar Ray bear hugged one of the policemen
and started yelling. The MPs took Louis and Robinson to the
provost marshal, who bawled them out for disobeying a military
policeman. Louis would not back down. "Sir, I'm a soldier like
any other American soldier. I don't want to be pushed to the
back because I'm a Negro." When the provost marshal continued to bluster, Louis said, "Let me call Washington." The

marshal didn't let Louis make the call, but he let Louis and Robinson go. The incident caused embarrassing publicity, and the army issued yet another directive against segregated buses.

On tour in England, Louis discovered that the American military establishment had brought Jim Crow overseas. When he took a group of black GIs to a theater in Salisbury, England, the ticket taker pointed them in the direction of a special section. Louis demanded to see the theater manager, who recognized the world's heavyweight champion, apologized, and told Louis he had segregated his theater under orders from the local American military commander. Louis called another friend, Gen. John C. H. Lee, who served on Gen. Dwight Eisenhower's staff. Lee corrected the situation.

Doing so much traveling, asserting himself in new ways, living outside the cocoon his managers had woven for him most of his adult life, dealing with crowds of strangers each day, Joe Louis was maturing. He looked older. His face was fleshing out, and his once-hard body was softening, its outline blurring. But just as Louis was coming into a greater confidence and a new understanding of his role as a public figure, he began to worry for the first time about his personal life. Louis was falling deeper and deeper into debt and finally became anxious about his finances. He had reason to hope a rematch with Billy Conn would be his moneymaking salvation, but beyond that he did not know how long his boxing career would last. Every year he spent in the service was a year taken away from his athletic prime.

Louis's new maturity did not extend to his relationship with his wife and family, however. Part of the problem, as usual, was not his fault—he had to travel for the army, just as he had to leave home to train for his fights. But Louis made little effort to make up for his absence. It was one of the worst flaws in Louis's character that a man so considerate and friendly with hundreds of casual acquaintances was so careless with the people he loved most. Louis still took Marva for granted. When he got a furlough and was in the States, he expected Marva to pack her bags and meet him somewhere. He did not go to her. And he never considered Marva's feelings as he continued his unrestrained pursuit of pleasure with other women. In March 1945 Marva Louis Barrow sued her husband for divorce on the grounds of desertion, and Louis did not contest the action.

The divorce did not get much attention from the press. As long as Louis avoided public scandal, the press paid no more attention to his private life than it had in the 1930s. And by 1945 Louis was such a well-loved figure, and so important symbolically to the war effort, that the divorce hardly dented his public image. Even as the War Department was breaking up black combat units or assigning them to labor duties because it felt blacks were inferior soldiers, the army was using Joe Louis's morale-building tours as a symbol of America's racial tolerance and unity.

Life magazine did a story in the fall of 1943 on Louis's tour of army bases, describing it as "a quiet parable in racial good will, for hard-working Joe makes a good impression and hundreds of white soldiers, officers and men, are proud to shake his hand." The anonymous *Life* writer, like many other writers during the war, noticed a change in Louis's personality: "To those who remember the tongue-tied, taciturn title-winner of six years ago, Joe's present personality is a revelation of what metamorphoses public life and Army life can work." In October 1944 the *New York Times* editorially praised Louis as "a real champion . . . whether or not he ever fights again for a purse and title." And Al Laney of the *New York Herald-Tribune* commented, "The dignity of the man is enormous and goodness envelops him." Louis's new image as a dignified citizen and a friendly, personable, faultless character was solidifying.

In 1945 a young white journalist named Margery Miller wrote *Joe Louis: American*, a biography of Louis that reflected the positive image Louis had acquired during the war. Miller wrote a standard account of Louis's career, beginning with John Roxborough's dream "of one day finding a Negro boy with a particular gift—preferably an athletic gift—that would make him outstanding, and of molding this boy into a veritable ambassador of good will from the Negro race to the white race." Miller wrote the standard inaccuracies about Roxborough, describing him as a college graduate and a lawyer. Even though

Roxborough was still in jail, Miller never mentioned his role in Detroit's numbers racket. Miller went on to describe Louis's generosity and patriotism, his fights for the Army and Navy Relief Funds, and his military service. Miller had no doubts that Louis had changed white attitudes: "Joe's accomplishments in causing good feeling between the white and Negro races are established facts. It is these, more than his accomplishments in the ring, that Joe would have people remember."

World War II ended in August 1945, when representatives of Japan surrendered aboard the U.S.S. *Missouri*. With the war over, Louis, like most of America's GIs, was eager to get out of the service. Though the War Department began a rapid demobilization, the process seemed painfully slow to Louis and his fellow soldiers. The army discharged its men on a points system based on length of time served and decorations for meritorious conduct. Louis's friend Truman Gibson took it upon himself to get Louis out of the army early, pointing out to John J. McCloy, assistant secretary of war, "At the age of 32, he has before him only a very short time in which he can engage in commercial prize fights. Through his generosity to Army and Navy Relief Funds, he has accumulated personal debts, the largest of which is $150,000 which he owes the United States Treasury for back income taxes." Gibson recommended that the army award Louis the Legion of Merit and discharge him early. McCloy passed Gibson's recommendations on to Maj. Gen. S. G. Henry, assistant chief of staff, and in a confidential memo Henry informed McCloy that the army was about to give Louis the Legion of Merit, which would make Louis eligible for discharge October 1, though that information had not yet been made public. McCloy passed on this information to Truman Gibson, who decided to surprise Louis.

All Louis knew was that the army would hold a formal ceremony to present him with the Legion of Merit on October 1. Louis and Mike Jacobs were now desperate. If Louis had to wait the expected six months to get out of the service, he would have difficulty getting ready for a second fight with Billy Conn the following summer. Gibson remarked that Mike Jacobs was not above bribery to solve his problems, and Louis was a willing agent:

> I had gone to New York to tell both Mike [Jacobs] and Joe that Joe was to be discharged from the service. I went up the day before Joe was to be given the Legion of Merit [but] I didn't get an opportunity to tell Mike. . . . Joe said, "Let's go up to Camp Shanks to see Mercer Ellington." So on the way up to Shanks . . . Joe pulled over and said, "Say, I want to ask you something."
>
> I said, "What? What's this all about?"
>
> He said, "Well, it's time I got out. Guys that went in with me got sent home from Europe."
>
> I said, "Joe, take it easy."
>
> He said, "Well, there's ten thousand in it for you."
>
> I said, "Forget you said it." I said, "Meet me in Jacobs's office at ten o'clock tomorrow morning, ten sharp."
>
> So he was there the next morning, and I said, "Joe, as of an hour ago, you're discharged from the service, so tell Jacobs to take his ten thousand and shove it."

World War II had been, as James Baldwin wrote, "a turning point in the Negro's relation to America." It marked the end of sixty years of silence about America's race problem. In the process of defining itself in opposition to a racist enemy, white America slowly began to confront its own racism. War rhetoric about freedom and equality also had its effect on black Americans. The continuing contradiction between American ideals and America's treatment of its black citizens, so grating during the war, led to a more militant mood in black America. In World War I, W.E.B. DuBois had urged blacks to postpone their campaign for justice and join in wholehearted support for the war. That strategy won blacks nothing. This time black Americans, while supporting the war effort, stepped up their demands for equality. The *Pittsburgh Courier* campaigned for the "Double V"—"victory over our enemies at home and victory over our enemies on the battlefield abroad."

Beginning with A. Philip Randolph's threat of a march on Washington, blacks slowly began to try more militant tactics.

Two organizations, the Fellowship of Reconciliation (FOR) and the National Committee (later Congress) of Racial Equality (CORE), staged sit-in demonstrations to desegregate movie houses and restaurants in northern cities. In April 1944 students from Howard University successfully integrated Thompson's, a downtown restaurant in Washington, D.C. The demonstrators used war ideals as part of their appeal. They signed a pledge endorsing tactics of nonviolent resistance, which also said, "I oppose . . . discrimination . . . as contrary to the principles for which the present World War is being fought." While some of the black demonstrators patiently waited for service inside the restaurant, other students picketed outside with signs saying, "Are You for Hitler's Way or the American Way? Make Up Your Mind."

The sit-in demonstrations served notice that the black movement for equality would become a national political issue after the war. They also indicated that there would be more to the movement than just black militancy. FOR and CORE were biracial organizations, with both black and white leadership. In the North at least, white participation, funding, attention, and support fed the civil rights movement. Growing white tolerance led to increased black militancy—a strategy impossible just a few years before, when virtually all whites intractably opposed any change in the racial status quo.

Joe Louis had a great deal to do with this new white tolerance. Before the war, Louis had been the one man who consistently made whites think about blacks. At the beginning of the war Louis's fights for military charities, his enlistment in the army, his patriotic statements, the memory of his second fight with German Max Schmeling, and the color of his skin made Louis a symbol of national unity. For whites eager to prove that they were more tolerant than their racist enemies, Joe Louis was a familiar and comfortable figure to love. White Americans found it easier to give Joe Louis a medal than to integrate the army, easier to write an editorial praising Joe Louis than to hire a black reporter. But perhaps whites needed to accept a Joe Louis before they could begin to think about justice for all blacks.

11

SWAN SONG

Joe Louis came out of the army eager to return to his idea of a normal life. During the war Louis had less free time and fewer opportunities to disappear for long periods, and he looked forward to resuming his hedonistic habits. But Louis had spent a fortune while in the army, borrowing what he needed from Mike Jacobs. Estimates of Louis's debt to Jacobs vary, but one writer with sources in the 20th Century Sporting Club claimed that Louis owed Jacobs $170,000 by the end of the war. Louis also borrowed $41,000 from his manager, John Roxborough, and had a deferred tax bill of about $115,000. When Marva Louis divorced him in 1945, she agreed to accept their apartment house in Chicago and $25,000. Louis still owed his ex-wife the $25,000. This accumulation of debts was so large that it worried even the usually unflappable Louis.

The long-awaited rematch with Billy Conn promised to be one of the most profitable fights of all time, and Louis hoped it would be his financial salvation. In fact, Louis's finances were hopeless no matter how large the Conn gate. During the war Congress had raised tax rates, pegging the highest bracket at 90 percent. Those high rates remained in effect for the rest of Louis's career. There were no provisions for income averaging then, and the tax code had fewer provisions for sheltering income. If his share of the Conn purse reached $600,000, a fantastic figure for the time, Louis would net less than $200,000.

There was no way Louis could make enough after taxes to pay $300,000 in debts.

Taxes had always mystified Louis. The IRS did not withhold taxes from a fighter's purse in those days. Mike Jacobs, with his accountant, Nath Ellenbogen, and his lawyer, Sol Strauss, always calculated Louis's taxes at the end of the year. If Louis did not have enough cash on hand to pay his tax bill, he borrowed the money from Jacobs, and Jacobs deducted the loan from Louis's purse from the next fight.

At some point during the war Jacobs must have realized that Louis could not hope to pay both his deferred tax bill and his personal debts. Jacobs could have explained the situation to Louis and cut off Louis's credit. This might have angered Louis, but it would have been in his best interests. Instead, Jacobs continued to lend Louis money and concocted a scheme whereby Louis would pay Jacobs before he paid the IRS. Jacobs's ploy was to list the money Louis had borrowed as business expenses on Louis's tax return, deductible against income Louis would earn in the future. Jacobs knew that Louis's wartime expenses were for entertainment and gifts and were therefore not legally de- ductible, but he also knew it would be some time before the IRS would catch up with Louis's return. In this way Jacobs could claim that Louis owed no taxes on his income from the Conn fight and take what Louis owed him from Louis's purse. By the time the IRS figured out that Louis's claimed deductions were not legitimate and that Louis owed full taxes on his Conn purse, the money would be in Jacobs's hands. The IRS would have to go after Louis with a tax bill Louis could not possibly hope to pay in his lifetime, but Jacobs did not see this as his problem. The scheme was illegal and odious.

Louis knew none of this when he got out of the army in October 1945. But he knew he needed money. It was too late to stage an outdoor fight with Conn in 1945, so Louis signed with Jacobs to fight Conn in June 1946. Louis figured that his debts to Jacobs, Roxborough, and the IRS could wait until after the Conn fight. He wanted to pay the $25,000 he owed his ex-wife immediately, though. Louis was already so deeply in debt to Jacobs and Roxborough that he turned to his other manager, Julian Black. Black and Louis were good friends—Black had been Louis's best man—and Louis had also made Black a fortune. But Black did not want to lend him the $25,000, claiming he didn't have the money. Louis thought Black was lying. The two argued violently, and Louis never forgave Black.

His falling out with Black and his need to pay his ex-wife caused Louis to reshuffle his contractual arrangements with his managers. The original ten-year contract Louis had signed with Roxborough and Black had expired, so Louis felt no compunction about ending his arrangement with Black. John Roxborough was another matter; Louis remained grateful to Roxborough for discovering him and getting him started. He owed Roxborough money, and Roxborough was still serving time in prison. Louis felt obligated to keep Roxborough as a manager, but he also needed a manager to arrange his exhibition tours and personal appearances, to run his training camps, and to help him discharge his public relations duties in the buildups for his fights. Louis turned to a good friend of Roxborough's, Marshall Miles, a real-estate investor from Buffalo. Louis cut Miles in on part of Roxborough's 25 percent share of Louis's boxing income, and Miles took over the day-to-day supervision of Louis's professional affairs. To clear his debt to his ex-wife, Louis gave her a share of his future ring earnings.

Louis went on an exhibition tour in the winter of 1945–46 to get in shape and make some spending money. After a break of several months, Louis then went to Pompton Lakes to begin serious training for the Conn fight. Manny Seamon, who had been Jack Blackburn's assistant, became Louis's trainer. Seamon did not command the same authority as Blackburn had. He was white and had joined Louis's camp after Louis became champion. Trusting Louis to pace himself, Seamon served more as an adviser than a taskmaster. Louis did not need pushing, anyway. After three years without top-flight competition, Louis's timing was off. He was now thirty-two years old, and his reflexes were slower. Feeling the pressure from his long layoff and realizing that he could not afford to lose the heavyweight title, Louis worked hard to lose weight and rebuild his stamina. Louis emphasized roadwork, running religiously every morning. In the ring he worked steadily on his timing. As usual, he did not try to put on a show for the press at the expense of his sparring partners. Louis looked bad in training, and many reporters wondered in print whether Louis was over the hill.

Mike Jacobs was happy that Louis was training slowly. Though Billy Conn was only twenty-seven, the war years had affected Conn more than Louis. Conn had put on a lot of weight and was much slower. Jacobs's publicity man in Conn's camp put out glowing press releases on Conn's workouts, trying to build Conn up. Conn, too, was working hard, sparring more than usual in an attempt to regain his lost speed and timing.

Despite warnings from the press that neither fighter was likely to reach pre-war form, public interest ran high. The Louis-Conn rematch was one of the first big sporting events signaling the return of peacetime normalcy and the return of first-class athletes from the service. The 1941 Louis-Conn fight had been one of the greatest of all time, and boxing fans had waited five years to see if Conn could outbox Louis again; maybe this time he could avoid getting knocked out. Close to 700 correspondents would cover the fight, filling the first seven ringside rows and overflowing into the stadium press box.

When Joe Louis stepped on the scale the morning of June 19 at the weigh-in for his fight with Conn, his hair was thinner than in the old days, but his stomach was flat. Louis looked out at the press of photographers and reporters filling the room, his lips tightly pursed. New York Athletic Commissioner Eddie Eagan announced Louis's weight. "Two-oh-seven," only a few pounds over his prewar fighting weight. He had done a remarkable job of getting in shape after four years away from his profession. Louis stepped off the scale, his eyes down. Several photographers demanded, "Wait a minute, stay there, stay there."

Louis stood behind Conn when the challenger got on the scale. Louis whispered something to Conn. Conn smiled and said something back. Commissioner Eagen announced Conn's weight at 182, at least ten pounds over Conn's weight for his first fight with Louis. The newsreel men yelled, "Announce it louder, will ya?" The photographers were yelling, "Wait a minute, wait a minute." Louis looked uncomfortable and a little irritated.

Louis arrived at his dressing room in Yankee Stadium at 7:45 P.M. Conn had almost beaten him five years before, and Louis felt he could not afford to lose the title. The champion responded to all that pressure as he always had, with unnatural calm. He went to sleep for an hour.

Above him, Yankee Stadium slowly filled. The $100 ringside section on the infield sold out, but the intermediate $50 and $30 seats in the lower deck were sparsely populated. The bleachers were almost full. Altogether, over 45,000 fans paid their way into the Stadium—a good crowd but far below Jacobs's prediction of 70,000.

Bernard Baruch and Andrei Gromyko sat together at ringside. Trygve Lie, the general secretary of the newly formed United Nations, was on hand, as was Thomas Dewey, New York's governor. In Washington, a select group of congressmen, bureaucrats, and statesmen gathered in a hotel to watch the fight on a small television screen. The Conn-Louis fight was the first boxing match broadcast on television. In the summer of 1946 there were fewer than 10,000 sets in the country. Harry Balogh introduced the principals:

> This is the stellar presentation. Of fifteen rounds' duration for the heavyweight championship of the world. From Pittsburgh, Pennsylvaneeeaaa, weighing one hundred eighty-two pounds, wearing black trunks, undefeated light-heavyweight champion and the very capable challenger for the heavyweight crown, Billy . . . Conn! . . . And his opponent, weighing two-oh-seven, he's wearing purple trunks, the internationally famous Detroit Brown Bomber. . . . Always a great credit to his chosen profession and the race he represents, the heavyweight champion of the world . . . Joe Louis! . . . And may the best man emerge victoriously.

Billy Conn and Joe Louis were friends. Before their first fight they had not known each other, and that great fight had a special chemistry, with Conn supplying most of the spark. He was then a young fighter at his peak, gifted with hand speed, stamina, and courage. He had been confident and hungry, and Louis had been an impersonal obstacle between Conn and a fortune. To Louis, Conn had been just another challenger. In the middle rounds of their first fight Conn fought like a demon, throwing three punches to every one from Louis, dancing around the champion, not afraid to move in. Conn had come out of clinches punching and scored often on Louis from close range. Conn's hand speed had been too much for Louis, and only Louis's patience and great punching power had saved his title.

Now the chemistry was different. While Conn had not won the title in the first fight, he had earned fame and the promise of a rematch. Because of the war, Conn had enjoyed the status of number-one contender for five years. He and Louis had become friends because they shared a unique status and knew that their second fight would earn them both a fortune. Conn was no longer as hungry, Louis no longer as complacent.

Billy Conn was a slow starter. He planned to dance away from Louis for the first few rounds, both to warm up and to tire Louis. Conn then hoped to pick up the tempo and outpoint Louis as he had in their first fight. But when the fight began, Conn realized his plan could not work. Louis bore in, and Conn could only dodge and move away. Conn didn't have it. Somehow he knew that his hands were not quick enough to match Louis's, and he could not hope to match Louis's power. This loss of confidence made things worse; Conn couldn't bring himself to take the risks necessary to win the fight.

The long-awaited Conn-Louis rematch was a bomb. The crowd hooted for action while Conn ran from Louis for seven rounds. Conn did not have the confidence to set himself long enough to throw a good jab, so most of his punches were left hands on the run with no weight behind them. Louis pursued Conn, occasionally jumping at Conn with a left hook, landing an occasional punch when he managed to catch Conn. Then Conn would dance away again.

In the fourth round Conn slipped trying to dodge Louis and fell to the canvas. Louis let him up without trying to hit him, and the two touched gloves before resuming. At the end of the round Louis gave Conn a friendly pat on the side as the two passed each other on the way to their corners. In the sixth Conn slipped again, and again Louis let him up, and the two fighters touched gloves.

Before the eighth round Louis told his cornermen that he was going to pick up the pace and see if Conn could take it. The two men touched gloves again at the beginning of the round. After chasing Conn for a while, Louis got close enough to throw two successive jabs. This time Conn held his ground and bent at the waist as if to clinch, but Louis hit him with a quick flurry—right uppercut, left hook, right cross. Conn missed with two lefts and clinched. As they broke, Louis missed a jab. This time Billy Conn moved in instead of running. Louis hit Conn with a right cross, jabbed, landed a right cross, missed another, and blocked two jabs from Conn. Conn tried an overhand right, and Louis ducked it into a clinch. As they broke, Louis jabbed, jabbed again, and landed an overhand right. Conn's knees buckled, and he tried to hang on to Louis, but Louis backed away and landed a right uppercut and a left hook, and Conn fell flat on his back.

Conn was just getting to one knee when referee Eddie Josephs counted ten. Josephs helped Conn up as the challenger shook his head. Louis smiled and waved to the crowd, which was standing and cheering, perhaps with relief. Louis put his left arm around Conn's shoulders.

In his dressing room, Louis was cocky at first. He stood on a bench and raised his hands to get the attention of the reporters who were crowding in on him. "Everybody seemed to be wondering whether I would still be as good as I used to be." Louis smiled. "Seems as if I am, don't it?" As the reporters asked more questions, Louis got tired and more restrained. When asked whether he was still as good as he had been before the war, Louis answered with sober honesty. "I don't know. I wasn't tested."

Press accounts understandably called the fight a disappointment. After five years of anticipation, even a good fight would have had trouble meeting expectations. Mike Jacobs's predictions of a $3 million gate and 70,000 attendance also created great expectations. The fight drew $2 million, and even though it was the most profitable of Louis's career and the second most profitable of all time, reporters described the fight as a financial disappointment, as well.

Louis's share of the gate came to about $600,000. His managers received $140,000 of that; his ex-wife, Marva, $66,000. The state of New York deducted $30,000 in state taxes immediately. Jacobs followed through on his seedy ploy, so instead of paying federal taxes on the Conn purse, Louis paid his debts to Jacobs and Roxborough, a total close to $200,000. Louis also paid his outstanding tax bill from 1941, approximately $115,000. Louis had made $600,000, but he had very little of it left, and he had paid no taxes on the income. He was running on quicksand.

Marshall Miles, Louis's new manager, realized his boxer was in trouble. Miles was one of the first people around Louis to try to salvage his finances. Miles arranged a fight for Louis in September, with Louis to get the whole purse, after expenses. Miles was giving Louis his own share of the purse and persuaded John Roxborough to do the same.

Louis's ex-wife still had a contractual share of Louis's income, but Louis took care of that problem himself. Although divorced, the couple still felt a stronge attraction and love for each other. When he got out of the service in October, Louis went back to Marva, and she did not lock him out. Louis spent more time with her before he went into training for the Conn fight, and after the fight Louis asked Marva to marry him again. Louis did not intend to be faithful to his wife, but perhaps he promised Marva that he would pay more attention to her and forget other women. Marva probably knew that Louis would not change, but she said yes, anyway. The couple remarried weeks after the Conn fight.

The honeymoon was soon over. Louis had to return to training for his September 18 fight. His opponent was Tami Mauriello, who had emerged as the best of a mediocre lot of heavyweight contenders. A strong puncher with many knockouts to his credit, Mauriello had also lost twelve fights. Mauriello was shorter than Louis. Though he was stocky and barrel chested, Mauriello weighed 198 pounds to Louis's 212. Louis's weight was up, and that was an indication of an impending decline in the champion's conditioning and his skills. After the Conn fight Louis regained his confidence. Without Blackburn to drive him, Louis started to slack off in his training. Training bored Louis and no longer came easy for him.

At the bell Louis and Mauriello came out of their corners and cautiously circled each other. Mauriello, determined to be aggressive, tried one of the most basic combinations in boxing. He feinted with his right hand and started a left hook around Louis's guard. Louis, the old pro, warded off the left just as Mauriello put all his weight into an overhand right that landed flush on Louis's jaw and sent Louis reeling off balance into the ropes. The Yankee Stadium crowd broke into a surprised roar, and Mauriello rushed in after Louis as the champion bounced off the ropes. Mauriello threw another hard right, but Louis was conscious enough to get his gloves up and partially block the punch. In close Mauriello tried to bring up a left uppercut, but Louis smothered the punch by putting both arms around Mauriello and holding on in a bear hug. Mauriello desperately tried to shake Louis off and succeeded just as referee Arthur Donovan was moving in to break the two fighters. Mauriello threw another overhand right that almost hit Donovan. Louis got his left hand up in time and then ducked into Mauriello. Louis was shaken, but he was now fully conscious and was no longer taking his opponent for granted. Worse yet for Mauriello, Louis's professional pride was stung. Louis pushed Mauriello away with both hands and stood erect, looking perfectly composed.

Mauriello waded in to continue his offensive, still thinking Louis was in trouble. Before a minute passed, Louis floored Mauriello with a left hook. When Mauriello got up, Louis put him down again with a left hook and glancing right. Arthur Donovan counted ten over Mauriello as the challenger hung over the middle strand of the ropes. Donovan helped Mauriello up, and Mauriello rubbed his face with his left hand as he walked back to his handlers. Joe Louis was smiling broadly, a real smile he rarely allowed himself in front of the white public. In his autobiography Louis said the Mauriello fight was "the last time I really felt like my old self. I had complete control, energy, power." It was Louis's last great fight.

In a radio interview right after the fight, Louis said, "I'll see you in a few days, Roxy." John Roxborough had been granted parole and would be released from prison early in October. Governor Dewey came into Louis's dressing room to congratulate Louis and the two men posed for the newsreel cameras. A white policeman standing on Louis's right side said something to Louis. While Governor Dewey smiled uneasily at the cameras, Louis smiled and talked with the cop.

Mauriello caused a scandal that made the radio networks briefly consider doing away with live post-fight interviews. "I got too god-damned careless," Mauriello told the national radio audience. Then he cried in his dressing room, saying over and over, "The first round." Mauriello was broken up about losing so quickly. He had had his chance, he had almost beaten Joe Louis, and he knew he would be remembered as a bum who lost in the first round. It is the special pressure of sport that the loser thinks about a lost moment and can never get it back.

Boxing was enjoying a postwar boom, and the Mauriello fight drew surprisingly well. Close to 40,000 fans saw the fight, paying a gate of $335,000. After expenses, Louis's share came to slightly over $100,000. In a naive attempt to help Louis avoid paying taxes on the income in 1946, Marshall Miles told Jacobs to hold the money for Louis until January. Since Louis actually earned the money in 1946, the money was taxable to him in 1946, no matter when he collected it. But the people doing Louis's tax return did not report the Mauriello purse as income to Louis in 1946. It was one more deception awaiting an IRS audit.

In early October, John Roxborough got out of prison, and Louis planned to meet him at the gate. But Roxborough, always conscious of Louis's public image, nixed the idea. Roxborough was not ashamed of being a numbers man, but to avoid bad publicity, he distanced himself from Louis after leaving prison. When Louis had become famous in 1935, Roxborough had told white reporters that he hoped Louis would be an ambassador of goodwill for the black race. Justifiably proud of his role in Louis's career, Roxborough did not want to jeopardize the success of Louis's symbolic mission.

Instead of meeting Roxborough at the prison gate, Louis attended a private party for Roxborough the day of his release.

The meeting with Roxborough illustrated Louis's most impressive characteristic: Louis accepted and liked other people as he found them. He embraced Roxborough warmly. But the meeting with Roxborough also illustrated Louis's greatest personal failing —his carelessness with the people he loved most. Louis was late to the party. He had played thirty-six holes of golf that day.

Louis's spending habits didn't improve, either. In January, Marshall Miles asked for the $100,000 that Jacobs had put aside after the Mauriello fight. Jacobs had suffered a stroke, and Sol Strauss was in charge of the 20th Century Sporting Club while the old promoter was convalescing. Strauss showed Miles a litter of canceled checks and money orders made out to Louis. In three months Louis had spent all but $500 of the money.

It took Miles three days to find Louis, who had disappeared on one of his sprees. When Miles finally found the champion, he asked what had happened to the money. Louis explained that he had invested another $40,000 in the Chicago Rhumboogie Cafe, which was suffering from a general decline in the entertainment industry and eventually folded. Louis could not account for the rest of the money. He had spent it on friends, women, and good times. Miles asked Louis why he hadn't withdrawn the last $500. Louis laughed.

Louis went back to exhibition tours to earn more money. In the fall of 1946 he traveled to Honolulu and Mexicali, Mexico. In early 1947 he toured Central and South America. Louis was a special hero to oppressed peoples the world over. The tours drew well, but Louis cleared very little from them. He paid the expenses of his entourage, which always included a few friends along for the ride. Louis and his wife spared no expense on tour. Taxes took most of the money that was left after expenses.

Marva Louis wisely kept her money separate from her husband's. With her share of the Conn purse, she set up a trust fund for their daughter, Jaqueline. And she was expecting another child. Typically, Louis was on the golf course when Marva gave birth to a son, Joseph Louis Barrow, Jr., on May 24, 1947. With a growing family to provide for, Louis felt even more financial pressure.

Louis needed a big gate from a championship fight. No legitimate contenders had emerged after Louis disposed of Conn and Mauriello. The most likely candidate for an outdoor summer fight in 1947 was Joe Baksi, a mediocre white fighter. But Baksi didn't want to fight Louis, and with no other contenders in sight, Louis went back on tour. In the late fall Sol Strauss tried to arrange a ten-round exhibition with another heavyweight contender, Jersey Joe Walcott. Walcott had an awful record. Like most black fighters before the war, he lacked adequate financial backing and never had had the resources to even eat properly, never mind train properly. He had lost to many bad fighters and had been knocked out by two of Louis's victims, Al Ettore and Abe Simon. Walcott did not even have an edge on Louis in age—he was actually several months older. In 1945 a white businessman, Felix Boccichio, had discovered Walcott and became his manager. Since then, Walcott had won three fights in a row.

The New York Athletic Commission announced that any ten-round fight would have to be for the championship. With no other opponent available, Strauss decided to promote the fight with Walcott as a full-blown, fifteen-round title match in Madison Square Garden in December. Twelve years before, when Louis had been on the verge of breaking into big-time boxing, many promoters and boxing writers had considered a black fighter risky, on grounds that white fans might not pay to see a black man fight. In 1947 no one seemed to wonder whether white fans would pay to see two blacks fight each other. White reporters largely ignored the fight's racial angle. Gradually, Louis had calmed most doubts about allowing blacks to compete, at least in sports.

White reporters questioned the fight on other grounds. Walcott's record was so bad that most writers thought he didn't belong in the same ring with Louis. Walcott was a ten-to-one underdog. Walcott caused a publicity stir when he claimed that he had knocked Louis down while serving as Louis's sparring partner before Louis's first fight with Schmeling. Walcott claimed that Louis's managers had fired him because he had embarrassed Louis. Press releases and news photos revealed the real story. In his first day sparring with Louis, Walcott clearly had the better of the fighting. The next day Louis knocked Walcott down after some spirited exchanges. Walcott left the next day. The Louis camp claimed he quit.

Louis weighed in at 211 on December 5, 1947. The weight was deceiving. Louis weighed 214 several days before the fight, and to come in at what he considered a respectable weight, Louis ate and drank little in the two days before the fight. Louis said later that because he hadn't eaten properly, he felt weak when he entered the ring. Given the decline of his athletic talents, Louis could hardly afford to feel weak. He was up against a smart, resourceful fighter who was hungry for the heavyweight championship.

When the bell rang, Louis followed his regular pattern. He walked after his opponent, keeping the pressure on and feeling the challenger out. Walcott had no intention of swapping punches on Louis's terms. He danced away, circling when Louis got too close. Walcott did not hesitate to throw punches as he moved, though. He hit Louis with a few jabs at the beginning of the round and then stood his ground long enough to floor Louis with a right hand.

Louis got up quickly. He was angry, and again his pride was stung. Walcott had no chance to follow up his advantage as Louis furiously chased him, trying for a quick knockout. Walcott danced away for a few rounds as Louis spent his fury. In the fourth round Walcott nailed Louis with another solid right. This time Louis stayed down for a seven count, and more than his pride was hurt. Walcott scored heavily when Louis got up.

The fight followed this pattern through the middle rounds as Louis pursued Walcott with more caution. Louis was clearly the aggressor, though Walcott landed more punches while still avoiding a wholesale exchange. Louis was too slow to corner Walcott. When he did get Walcott in range, he couldn't hurt the challenger. Louis's once-remarkable reflexes had slipped away. He could not counterpunch sharply, could not string his combinations together as he once had, and was slow to start his punches when he saw an opening. Louis was still strong and competent, but he was no longer great.

In the ninth round Louis maneuvered Walcott into the ropes, got his first clear shot with a right, and threw the punch a little high, bouncing his glove off the top of Walcott's head. Walcott weathered the storm and was counterpunching by the end of the round. In the later rounds Walcott continued to avoid Louis, and the champion did not have the energy to cut off the ring. Walcott believed he was so far ahead on points that all he had to do to win was avoid getting knocked out. He hardly bothered to throw a punch in the last round.

When the fight ended, the Madison Square Garden crowd buzzed. Most of the fans thought Walcott had won, and radio announcer Don Dunphy's play-by-play made the fight sound like a one-sided victory for Walcott. Walcott had landed more punches and had done more damage. He had knocked Louis down twice.

New York used a strict round-by-round scoring system. The fighter who won the most rounds won the fight. One fighter could win eight rounds by narrow margins, lose seven rounds decisively, and still win the fight. Harry Balogh announced the decision:

> Judge Frank Forbes scored the fight eight rounds to six, one round even . . . Louis! [The crowd booed.] Referee scored seven rounds to six, two rounds even . . . Walcott! [Cheers] And Judge Marty Monroe scored it nine rounds to six . . . Louis! The winner by split decision and still the heavyweight champion of the world, Joe Louis!

Walcott was shocked. The crowd booed as the two fighters briefly met in the center of the ring to shake hands. Louis said, "I'm sorry, Joe." Walcott later claimed the statement meant that Louis thought he had lost. Louis insisted that he had apologized only for fighting so poorly. Walcott stayed in the ring as the crowd continued to boo. Louis rushed back to his locker room. He told trainer Manny Seamon, "Get everyone out of the room." Louis's considerable athletic pride was smarting. The booing particularly upset him. Boxing crowds had been with him for years. Louis did not want the reporters to see how bruised he was. His handlers applied ice packs to his face, and Louis soaked his hands in ice while the reporters waited. After half an hour Louis let the press in. Louis insisted he had no doubts that he had won the fight. "Can't win the title running away," Louis said. Asked if Walcott was a second-rate fighter, Louis replied, "No, I am." A photographer asked Louis to smile. "Wider. Make it wider, Joe."

"Can't open my mouth no more," Louis said through bruised lips.

The Walcott fight made Joe Louis confront his uncertain future. He had no delusions about the decline of his boxing skills. He had told reporters that he was not the fighter he had been before the war. The problem was that Louis had thought that two-thirds of the real Louis was still enough to beat any fighter in the world. Louis was too embarrassed to quit after the Walcott fight. He knew he could still beat Walcott and could partly excuse his performance because he hadn't eaten properly before the fight. But Louis sensed that more embarrassments might await him. He decided that a rematch with Walcott would be his last fight.

Louis got over $80,000 for the Walcott fight. Even before taxes the money could only temporarily stanch Louis's financial bleeding. After fighting an exhibition in Chicago and signing to fight Walcott again in June, Louis sailed for England. He appeared at a Health and Holiday Show in London, then toured England and France. The promoters had promised him $80,000 for the tour but went broke and paid only $40,000. Living expenses for Louis's entourage soaked up most of the money. Marva called home every day to check on the children and bought expensive French clothes and perfumes. Louis could not deny her anything because Marva caught him fooling around with two English women in London. His old habits hadn't changed; Louis still liked to get away from Marva, disappearing for days at a time. Louis's marriage was on the rocks again, though Louis was oblivious to his wife's discontent.

When Louis returned from Europe, he went into training for

his June fight with Walcott. Louis was determined to beat Walcott and retire with his title intact, but his enthusiasm had waned with age. Training was boring and difficult, and Louis could no longer lose weight easily. Louis also had lower expectations of himself. He was thirty-four years old. In the 1940s boxing experts considered that ancient for a fighter, and no one expected Louis to train as hard as he once had.

Louis weighed in at 214. At the weigh-in ceremony State Athletic Commissioner Eagan, sporting a big Dewey button on his coat lapel, told Louis and Walcott, "You are members of a race that has progressed more than any other in the last 150 years."

Despite rain delays that postponed the fight for two days, over 40,000 fans showed up at Yankee Stadium on June 24. The crowd cheered loudly for Louis during the introductions and rooted for him throughout the fight. The second fight followed the pattern of the first. Walcott dropped Louis in the third round with a left-right combination, but Louis got up before referee Frank Fullam could start a count. Louis did not chase Walcott as much as he had in the first fight, trying to make Walcott lead. Walcott dodged in and out. The result was boredom, and the crowd voiced its disapproval for nine rounds. In the tenth referee Fullam finally said, "Hey, one of you get the lead out of your ass, and let's have a fight."

Fullam continued to badger Walcott, trying to get the challenger to mix it more. In the tenth and eleventh, Walcott obligingly stopped dancing away as much, and Louis's greater strength asserted itself. At the end of the eleventh, Louis drove Walcott into the ropes and let loose with all he had. Louis was no longer as quick and as calculating a finisher as he once had been, but he landed enough punches to put Walcott down for good. Fullam counted Walcott out with four seconds left in the round. The crowd was happy with the result, if not the fight itself. It gave Louis a standing ovation. Louis announced over the radio he would not fight again.

Louis knew it was time to quit. He was tired of fighting, and he realized he had reached an appropriate resting place. After his embarrassment during the first Walcott fight, Louis had come to accept the decline of his skills and the possibility of defeat. He had not accepted his own bankruptcy, however, because the IRS had not caught up to him yet for the inaccuracies in his past tax returns. Louis had enough difficulties just paying his current tax bills. Louis never adjusted to the change in tax rates. He still spent most of his income as it came in, without putting away enough for taxes, and still borrowed money from Mike Jacobs to pay his taxes and indulge himself. Because of his failure to comprehend the tax code, Louis still searched for the big payday that would pay all his tax bills and his personal debts. He was also looking for some arrangement that would guarantee him a regular income in the future.

After announcing that he would retire, Louis became coy with the press. He said he wasn't sure he would retire. With the aid of Truman Gibson, his old friend from the War Department who was serving as his lawyer, Louis negotiated with the 20th Century Sporting Club for a retirement package. John Reed Kilpatrick, chairman of the board of the Madison Square Garden Corporation, wrote a memorandum summarizing a meeting between Louis and Sol Strauss in December 1948. Louis was thinking of returning to the ring for another fight. He wanted a $100,000 payment under the table, to avoid taxes. Kilpatrick related in the memo:

> Sol said that Joe had a terrific fear of being beaten and he asked Sol what he could expect if he were beaten. Sol said that in that event he would put Joe on the 20th Century payroll for $25,000 per year. Joe asked what he would be expected to do and Sol said assist in making matches, to assist in publicity at training camps and talking to newspapermen and so forth. Joe then said, "You mean I will have to work?" Sol said, "Yes." Joe said, "Then I will work one day a year. . . . I want to play golf, I don't want to work."

Louis and Gibson were also negotiating with the Hearst newspaper chain and a man named Harry Voiler to set up a boxing promotion company to rival the 20th Century Sporting Club. Louis would give up his title, sign the leading heavyweight contenders to exclusive contracts, and promote a tournament to choose the next champion. Louis would in turn sell the exclusive contracts with the leading contenders to Hearst and Voiler for cash and a share of future profits. The deal with Hearst fell through because Voiler could not arrange financing.

Harry Mendel, a man who had worked for Mike Jacobs publicizing some of Louis's fights, suggested that Louis and Gibson sell their package to Jim Norris and Arthur Wirtz instead. Norris and Wirtz were millionaires. Norris owned Chicago Stadium and the Chicago Black Hawks and Detroit Red Wings hockey teams. He also had considerable stock in the Madison Square Garden Corporation. In February Norris and Wirtz agreed to buy Louis's ambitious scheme. They formed the International Boxing Club (IBC), which would soon monopolize boxing as Mike Jacobs and the 20th Century Sporting Club had before it. Gibson went out and signed the leading heavyweight contenders, who were only too happy to get a shot at the heavyweight title without having to fight Louis. The IBC paid Louis $350,000 for those contracts, and for giving up his title. Norris and Wirtz promised to pay Louis $20,000 a year in the future, and gave him a chunk of IBC stock.

On March 1, 1949, Louis wrote a letter to Abe Greene, the president of the National Boxing Association, announcing his retirement. The IBC named Jersey Joe Walcott and Ezzard Charles the two top heavyweights and announced they would fight in June. Green accepted Louis's resignation. The NBA, a federation of state athletic commissions, also agreed to sanction the Charles-Walcott fight as a title bout. Walcott and Charles were indeed the two leading contenders—Walcott had made two good showings against Louis; Charles had given up the light-heavyweight title to become a heavyweight and had beaten the heavyweight challengers in front of him. It was a sign of the times in boxing that both Walcott and Charles were black and that few people seemed to care about their race.

Louis's announcement caught the 20th Century Sporting Club by surprise. Louis had effectively shouldered Mike Jacobs out of the promoting business. Louis did not regret striking out on his own because Jacobs was old and sick and would not have been able to continue as a promoter, anyway. Louis needed money, and he had the sense to realize that his relationship with Jacobs had always been primarily business. The IBC did not disturb things too much anyway. The 20th Century Sporting Club had worked through Madison Square Garden for ten years. The IBC moved into the Garden and paid Jacobs $150,000 to step down as the Garden's promoter.

Several weeks before Louis announced his retirement, his wife Marva quietly divorced him in Mexico. Marva had again tired of Louis's traveling, his playing around, and his carelessness with her and the children. Louis did not contest the divorce, though he pleaded with Marva to reconsider. The two remained on friendly terms after the divorce, but this time Louis knew there was no chance of a reconciliation.

Louis's marriage had ended for good, but his retirement was short-lived. In 1950 the IRS finally conducted a full audit of Louis's past returns and unturned all of their various deceptions. The IRS disallowed the deductions for Louis's wartime expenses, which meant Louis owed back taxes on over $200,000 of income from 1946. In late 1947 Truman Gibson and Ted Jones, Louis's accountant, set up a personal service corporation for Louis with IRS approval. Joe Louis Enterprises, Inc., was a dummy corporation that was to collect all the income from Louis's services and pay Louis a salary. Had Louis accepted only his salary, much of his income would have been sheltered by the corporation and subject to lower corporate tax rates. In its audit, however, the IRS discovered that Louis had drawn far more than his salary from the corporation. The IRS ruled that all of the corporation's income was taxable to Louis. When the IRS finished adding its bill and assessing interest and penalties, Louis owed over $500,000.

Louis was to blame for the staggering tax bill. The root of his financial difficulties was his own overspending. For ten years Louis had outspent his income. Mike Jacobs and Louis's managers shared the blame. Louis was a spoiled kid who did not understand the details of his financial situation. He sorely needed good advice but never got any. And Mike Jacobs had given Louis the rope to hang himself. Jacobs's free loans assured that

Louis would not come to grips with his finances until too late. Jacobs had also arranged for Louis to pay him first and owe the IRS later. Thanks to Jacobs, Louis would owe the government until he died.

Truman Gibson tried to get the government to accept a compromise offer for Louis's back taxes. Gibson argued that Louis could not pay the full amount and that Louis had merely followed the advice of his accountants. Louis needed money quickly to pay the compromise offer, and the only way for him to make big money was to return to the ring. Ezzard Charles had beaten Walcott in June 1949 and still reigned as heavyweight champion. In August 1950, Louis signed to fight Charles on September 27. He had only six weeks to train.

Charles was a competent, quick boxer, but he did not have the punch to be a great heavyweight. The public had never fully accepted him as champion both because of his lack of a knockout punch and because he had inherited a vacant title instead of winning it from Louis. Charles saw the fight with Louis as a chance to prove himself. Even though Charles was champion, Louis was still king. Charles had to accept a challenger's cut of 20 percent. Louis got 35 percent.

Louis was thirty-six years old and had been away from competitive boxing for two years. He was fighting because he had to, and the money he earned would go to the government. His enthusiasm for boxing was gone. This fight would be work. Louis cut back on his usual training routine, running three miles a day instead of six. He added an extra day of sparring, but that could not compensate for lost roadwork. Louis weighed in at 218, ten pounds overweight.

The extra weight and lack of training probably didn't matter. Unlike Muhammad Ali, for one, Louis did not age well as a fighter. Louis had been a great boxer because he was fundamentally sound and because his hands were quicker and stronger than anyone else's. He was still strong, but his reflexes had deserted him. Louis was fighting on pride alone.

Against Charles, Louis's decline was obvious. Charles danced around Louis and was not afraid to trade punches in close. Charles repeatedly beat Louis to the punch. Louis landed a few punches and managed to give Charles a black eye, but anytime Charles got hurt, he moved away. Louis was too slow to follow. Charles was not a strong puncher, but he stung, bruised, and cut Louis. Charles won all but three rounds, many convincingly. In the fourteenth round Charles had Louis out on his feet and almost knocked Louis down. Louis was so exhausted that his handlers had to lift him off his stool for the fifteenth. Out of respect for the man who had been his childhood idol, Charles held back in the fifteenth round, and Louis finished on his feet. At the end of the fight Louis bled from cuts over both eyes. One eye had swelled shut. Blood ran from his nose and spread over his upper lip.

Louis cried when the ring announcer declared Charles the winner by unanimous decision. He brushed past a radio interviewer and went back to his locker room, the loser for only the second time in his professional career. He kept the press waiting a long time while he composed himself, holding ice bags to his face. When the reporters finally came in, Louis was gracious and dignified. "I enjoyed the fight, and I want to thank you all. I done the best I can. I'll never fight again."

The fight with Charles raised nowhere near enough money to pay Truman Gibson's proposed compromise offer. Jim Norris had accepted $200,000 for radio and television rights. Local TV blackouts and closed circuit television were ideas of the future. With the fight on TV for free, only 13,562 paying spectators showed up at Yankee Stadium. The gate totaled $205,000. Louis's purse was a disappointing $100,458. He owed taxes on that income, of course.

Louis had no choice but to continue his comeback. In the winter and spring of 1951 he won five fights against mediocre opposition. Louis had lost his championship form, but he was still too good for all but the top heavyweights. Fighting and training continuously, Louis got his weight down to 208. In June, Louis knocked out Lee Savold, the British heavyweight champion, who at thirty-five was even slower than Louis.

That summer Joe Walcott got a rematch with Ezzard Charles and knocked Charles out in the seventh round. Walcott showed no inclination to fight a serious contender that year. He was an old man in possession of the heavyweight title, and he wanted to relish it for as long as he could. Louis went back to fighting middle-level fighters, beating Cesar Brion and Jimmy Bivens in August.

Jim Norris and the International Boxing Club were desperate to shake up the heavyweight division. Boxing was enjoying a boom period, but in the big-money division too many of the top fighters were old or unexciting. Norris and the IBC were pushing a white hope named Rocco Marchegiano, who changed his name to Rocky Marciano. Marciano was not a polished boxer, but he was strong, and he had that most important asset as a gate attraction—a knockout punch. Marciano had won all thirty-seven fights in his two-year pro career, thirty-two by knockout.

Norris wanted Louis to fight Marciano. He offered Louis a $300,000 guarantee. Louis must have known he was being set up for a fall, but he could not afford to turn down a big money fight. Louis also thought he could outbox Marciano.

On October 26, 1951, Louis and Marciano met in Madison Square Garden for a scheduled ten-round fight. The fight sold out the Garden, even though it was televised nationwide. Marciano took the fight to Louis, swinging a vicious right hand whenever he got the chance. Even at thirty-seven, Louis was able to block or dodge Marciano's punches, and he kept Marciano off balance with his jab. On the strength of his jab, Louis won three of the first five rounds. Against a puncher like Marciano, though, Louis was too slow to take a chance with a left hook or a hard right hand. Marciano crowded Louis, wearing the old man down. In the sixth round Louis's legs suddenly gave out. Age and poor conditioning had caught up to him. Marciano got bolder, and Louis's jab had lost its sting. At the end of the seventh round Louis took a chance and threw his left hook, opening himself up for a right. The hook landed squarely, but it didn't even slow Marciano down.

In the eighth round Marciano floored Louis with a left hook. Louis got up at the count of eight, and Marciano drove him against the ropes. Marciano threw a looping right that caught Louis on the neck and knocked him through the ropes. Louis lay on the ring apron, his legs still in the ring, the bald spot on his head now clearly visible. Referee Ruby Goldstein stopped the fight.

Everyone watching sensed that this really was Louis's last fight. Afterward the television audience was shown the film of Louis's one-round knockout of Max Schmeling. Josephine Baker, the black singer and entertainer, waited in the corridor outside Louis's locker room. She had made headlines that week when the Stork Club refused to serve her because she was black. Joe Louis, on the other hand, was always welcome in the Stork Club. Baker told a reporter, "Oh yes, just to wait and shake his hand so he knows . . . you know, this is the kind of moment to show . . . just to shake his hand it's so important."

Inside Louis's dressing room the crowd of white reporters was quiet. Sugar Ray Robinson wept. Marciano came in crying, too. He told Louis, "I'm sorry, Joe." Louis himself was calm. He called out to Ezzard Charles when Charles came in the room and touched Sugar Ray gently on the cheek.

"What's the use of crying," Louis said. "The better man won. That's all. Marciano is a good puncher and he's hard to hit. I'm not too disappointed. I only hope everybody feels the same way I do about it. I'm not looking for sympathy from anybody. I guess everything happens for the best."

At one time in Joe Louis's life, that had been true.

When Joe Louis fought Billy Conn for the second time, in 1946, he was still a dominant athlete. At the time of his last fight, against Rocky Marciano in 1951, Louis was a pathetic shadow of his past greatness, and everyone knew he was broke. Yet in the period between those two fights Louis's public image did not change significantly. The white media's treatment of Joe Louis had improved markedly at the beginning of World War II. Louis had won genuine affection from the white press and public, and the decline of his boxing talents and the revelations of his boxing difficulties did not diminish that affection. The war had confirmed Louis's symbolic importance both as America's most prominent black and as the democratic conqueror of a Nazi boxer, Max Schmeling. The immediate postwar years confirmed

Louis's impact on white attitudes. A growing white willingness to let blacks participate in sports ushered in an era of tokenism in America that was as revolutionary as it was limited.

From the beginning of Louis's career, his managers had tried to sell an "official" image of Louis as a well-behaved, inoffensive fighter who was trying to make a good impression on the white public in order to improve race relations. This official image had always been a component of white press coverage of Louis. During the war Louis's official image had come to dominate the press coverage, and after the war the official image remained in place as though set in concerte. The white press complimented him in the same terms again and again, overpraising his good behavior and sterling character.

In 1948, after Louis knocked out Walcott in their second fight and announced his intention to retire, Sec Taylor of the *Des Moines Register* wrote, "He has worn the kingly robes with dignity. His conduct has been exemplary. He has been a credit to his race and to boxing. He has been untainted by scandal." The same year Arthur Daley of the *New York Times* wrote, "Louis has been the most considerate, gentlemanly, and methodical champion of them all."

In 1949 an anonymous writer for the *St. Louis Post-Dispatch* wrote, "He has been a wonderful champion and his enormous activity as champion and his fine behavior in and out of the ring have won public confidence. . . . Louis may have expanded in girth but he hasn't shrunk in public estimation."

This praise of Louis, so consistent over time, was also consistently overblown and artificial. It exaggerated aspects of Louis's character and behavior. For instance, when Billy Conn slipped twice during his second fight with Louis in 1946, Louis did not try to hit Conn as he fell and let Conn stand up before continuing the fight. Most boxers would have done the same thing; Conn fell too quickly for Louis to hit him on the way down anyway, and the rules of boxing forbade Louis from standing over Conn as Conn tried to stand up. Yet the press praised Louis's sportsmanship. Arthur Daley of the *Times* wrote, "An amazing man is this Louis. He grows in stature and dignity with every performance. . . . His inherent sense of decency and fairness is so deeply imbedded in his nature that he wouldn't take advantage of his opportunity [to hit Conn when he slipped]."

Louis's official image not only exaggerated his good qualities, but ignored his bad ones. In all the tributes to Louis's wonderful behavior, none of the white writers mentioned that Marva Barrow had divorced her husband twice. Press coverage of the actual divorces was slight. Louis did not contest the divorces; there were no messy courtroom scenes. Both times Marva tried to be as inconspicuous as possible. She obtained the divorces in Mexico, at times when her husband was not in training for an upcoming fight. As a result, only the wire services covered the divorces. Newspapers printed the brief wire stories at the back of the sports pages.

Louis's divorces were hardly the kind of news events likely to provoke an editorial or even a sportswriter's column. Nonetheless, when sports reporters covered Louis in training for one of his fights, they had many opportunities to comment on Louis's marital failures in their frequent analyses of his character but hardly ever made even passing references to them. In part, the white press' silence on Louis's marital problems resulted from the journalistic style of the day. The press then still tried to accent the positive. Many reporters doubtless thought Louis's private life was off limits. It was one thing, though, not to write stories about Louis's private foibles and another to write stories complimenting Louis's character as if those foibles did not exist. In the 1940s, American society did not tolerate divorce as easily as it does now.

The white press could not entirely ignore Louis's financial problems. The press covered the financial details of boxing closely; promoters released figures on attendance and each fighter's purse after every fight, knowing that part of boxing's appeal to the public was its aura of big and easy money. Boxing writers did not consider a fighter's finances off limits.

When Secretary of War Stimson called off the proposed Louis-Conn charity fight scheduled for 1943, the full extent of Louis's debts came out. In 1943, the press knew Louis owed the government about $115,000 and Mike Jacobs close to $100,000.

It was simple arithmetic to look at the tax rate and conclude that Louis was hopelessly bankrupt. *Ebony* magazine did the math and revealed in its May 1946 issue that Louis was broke.

Yet the white press never clearly reported the facts about Louis's debts. Reporters wrote about the subject in vague, often confused generalities and seemed to ignore the upper-bracket tax rates as much as did Louis himself. For instance, before the Conn fight John E. Wray of the *St. Louis Post-Dispatch* wrote that Louis was "poor, if you judge by what he owes Uncle Mike." Two days after the fight, Wray wrote, "Louis has property, and having cleared up his cash obligation by his recent show, he has plenty of leftover." The knowledge of reporters varied. An Associated Press reporter wrote a story on what the government would take from Louis and Conn in taxes and concluded, "Joe Louis and Billy Conn are not likely to retire from work the rest of their lives on what they net from their world heavyweight championship fight Wednesday night."

Louis contributed to the confusion. Being rich was a vital part of Louis's self-image, and until almost the end of his career he was still hoping or assuming that he would make enough money to pay his debts. When reporters questioned Louis about his finances, he lied. In an autobiographical article for *Life* magazine, written with the assistance of Meyer Berger and Barney Nagler, Louis claimed that he was well off and ticked off a list of worthless business interests. He often reacted angrily to suspicions of the truth. He sued *Ebony* for its May 1946 article that revealed his massive debts.

When he came out of retirement to fight Ezzard Charles, Louis had to admit he was fighting to pay his back taxes. The truth about his financial plight began to sink in about that time, but white writers still hoped that Louis's purse from the Charles fight was enough to pay his tax bill. Louis never told anyone exactly how much he owed. Sec Taylor of the *Des Moines Register* noted that estimates of the amount Louis owed in back taxes ran from $40,000 to $260,000. The upper figure in the range was short by half. Nevertheless, Tony Cordaro of the *Register* staff asked Louis if the fight with Charles cleared him financially and printed Louis's answer without editorial comment—"Yeah." In an editorial the *Detroit Free Press* said, "We hope he got enough to meet the exacting demands of the Internal Revenue department." Few writers understood the situation with the clarity of Lester Rodney of the *Daily Worker*: "The money he got when everything was trimmed off was not nearly enough. He needs more."

Four factors contributed to the exaggerations and omissions of Louis's official image. The first factor was the genuine warmth of the white press and public toward Louis. White sportswriters liked him. That affection partly explained why they overwrote their praise of Louis and ignored his personal problems. Arthur Daley wrote in the *New York Times Magazine*:

> It was the second Schmeling match that seemed to change Louis from a duckling into a swan. After that, even the unsusceptible gentlemen of the press came away from interviews warmed and pleased. The Louis brand of unspoiled naturalness, attached as it was to a celebrity, was an intoxicating experience.

Harry Markson, reporter and publicity man, as well as matchmaker for Madison Square Garden, said in a recent interview, "I suppose that in my time, and I've been around boxing for half a century, I've never felt more affection for any fighter in the ring than I had for Joe Louis."

The affection of white sportswriters for Louis came out in print. Arthur Daley of the *New York Times* noted that the boxing writers were pulling for Louis against Walcott. When Louis knocked Walcott out, "Even the boxing experts, a cold-blooded and unemotional breed of men, bounced up and yowled in unrestrained glee." White writers rooted for Louis in other fights. Lyall Smith of the *Detroit Free Press* wrote after the Charles fight, "I don't know if I was the typical television viewer of the fight. But I was pulling for Joe. . . ."

In addition to describing their own feelings, white sportswriters also described their perceptions of the feelings of the general public. Before the war white reporters had assumed that the public was rooting for Louis's white, underdog opponents. After the war, sportswriters noted that the public rooted for Louis. In the interplay between the media and the public, the affection of white reporters simultaneously fed the public's affection for Louis and reflected that public sentiment.

The strongest evidence of public affection for Louis came when he fought the first real white hope in fifteen years, Rocky Marciano. The Madison Square Garden crowd rooted for Louis. *Time* magazine reported, "A vociferous claque of rooters burst into an excited hubbub when Rocky Marciano came bouncing into the ring. But the real roar of the crowd in Madison Square Garden came for the man with the magic name: Joe Louis." The *Time* writer described Marciano's knockout of Louis: "No one in the crowd . . . saw what was coming. And no one in the crowd, even the most rabid of Rocky's fans, really wanted to see it."

When Louis went down for the count, A. J. Liebling of the *New Yorker* magazine noticed a blonde woman watching the fight with her date:

> The tall blonde was bawling, and pretty soon she began to boo. The fellow who brought her was horrified.
> "Rocky didn't do anything," he said. "He didn't foul him. What you booing?"
> The blonde said, "You're so cold. I hate you, too."

The second factor behind Louis's uniformly favorable official image after the war was an increasing appreciation of Louis's athletic talents, even as those talents declined. Although America often roots for the underdog, America loves a winner. The sportswriters and the public would never have admired and liked Louis if he had not also been a great athlete. Louis's devastating victory in his second fight with Max Schmeling had overwhelmed most doubts about Louis's boxing greatness. There was a general consensus in the white press that Louis was one of the greatest, if not the greatest, heavyweight boxer of all time. Louis held the title longer, and defended it successfully more often, than any fighter before him. Louis also won most of his fights decisively.

Until Louis's first fight with Walcott, many white reporters did not detect any chinks in Louis's boxing armor, and Walcott's near upset of Louis in December 1947 shocked the press. Northern papers featured the story prominently, often with front-page headlines. Louis fought so badly that reporters could not describe his performance as a fluke. The decline of his skills was obvious. One writer described Louis as "slower than a peg-legged man crossing a swamp." Most reporters thought Walcott had won the fight. Sec Taylor of the *Des Moines Register* wrote that Louis's "crown was saved by the decision of two magnanimous and apparently sightless judges."

Despite his boring rematch victory over Walcott, the majority of white sportswriters picked Louis to beat Ezzard Charles when Louis came out of retirement. Even the oddsmakers, who couldn't afford to be sentimental, picked Louis to beat Charles. When Louis lost to Marciano, white reporters wrote that Louis in his prime would have beaten Marciano easily.

Writers could not help but compare Louis's great performances of the past with his poor showings as he got older. In comparison, Louis seemed pathetic, a sad figure. Tony Cordaro of the *Des Moines Register* said after the Charles fight, "It seemed a terrible punishment to take for the income tax." An AP reporter described Louis's locker room after the loss to Marciano:

Middleweight champion Ray Robinson sobbed softly. Ezzard Charles blinked and blinked. Others in the sweaty room, some of them veteran newspaper men, had lumps in their throats. . . . They all realized it was the end of an era. Louis's glorious, history-making ring days were over.

The sadness and pathos made Louis more human and increased affection for him.

The third factor behind Louis's official image after the war was a new racial consciousness, or sensitivity. After the war, references to Louis's color decreased. Racial, alliterative nicknames, save for the familiar "Brown Bomber" and "Dark Destroyer," disappeared completely. White papers rarely identified Louis as a "Negro" and almost never described him as "dusky," "tan," or "dark." References to Louis's race had slowly declined since the beginning of his career. Constant exposure to Louis purged the white press of its obsession with race, as only writing about the same black person again and again could. Because Louis stayed in the news so long, the color of his skin became boring as a descriptive theme. It also seemed less unusual. Unconsciously, white writers identified Louis as a Negro less and less and also stereotyped him less.

The decline in references to Louis's race did not reflect a conscious sense that it was inappropriate to identify him as a "Negro." Writers still identified him as a "Negro" too often for that to be true. On the other hand, white writers clearly did not think it was always necessary to refer to Louis's race. References to his race were infrequent and random, more the result of lingering journalistic practice and writing convenience than racist preoccupation.

The modern, color-blind journalistic style was still a few years away, but Louis had gotten white writers to take his race for granted in their writing styles, to accept the color of his skin. Acceptance of Louis's blackness was no less important than the acceptance of Louis as heavyweight champion. White acceptance of Louis's color made every black person in America less of an outsider.

The almost-total absence of stereotypes reflected a new consciousness. White reporters were becoming more sensitive to the most egregious sterotypes. Before the war, they had emphasized the differences between Louis and themselves by stereotyping him, referring to his color, calling him a "credit to his race" and an "African." After the war, white writers bent over backward to downplay the differences between Louis and themselves. They carefully quoted Jimmy Cannon: "Louis in the years he has held the title has been an exemplary guy, honest in his approach to everything, and as Jimmy Cannon said today, a credit to his race—meaning not the colored race, but the human race." They strained to contradict stereotypes: "[Louis] will be in there thinking from bell to bell." As they had during the war, they bent over backward to identify Louis as an American: "He was a credit not only to his sport but to his people, and since both of these are a part of America, he was a credit to all of us." Shirley Povich remembered:

> It was all a degree of acceptance, then people were becoming more enlightened anyway. The war had something to do with it. Joe Louis had something to do with it. He was able to subordinate the color line with his good, I won't say "behavior" because you don't expect any better behavior from blacks than you do from whites, but with his simple comportment.
>
> Maybe he educated the sports writers to be more tolerant. We became a little more, as I say, enlightened. You always need some factor to change your views, and here was a universally esteemed black athlete, a man of great courage, a man of patriotism, a man of simple honesty, and you think in terms of Louis and you don't think in terms of "black" as much as with other athletes. I think it helped to alert people to the fact that blacks are good human beings.

Povich was right that the war had something to do with it. In the process of collectively defining themselves as different from a racist enemy, Americans defined themselves as racially tolerant. Nazi racism threw a challenge at American racism. Louis's two fights with Max Schmeling and the 1936 Olympics helped white Americans understand that challenge.

The war with Germany confirmed the symbolism of Louis's vengeful knockout of Schmeling in 1938. After the war, white reporters remembered Louis's second fight with Schmeling more than any of his other fights. Whenever reporters recapped Louis's career, they remembered the Schmeling fight, and in symbolic terms. In 1948 Arthur Daley of the *Times* wrote, "Max Schmeling was the lone opponent Louis ever faced who he hated with an all-consuming hatred. . . . Schmeling, returning in triumph to Nazi Germany [after defeating Louis in their first fight], was hailed as the arch-apostle of the doctrine of Aryan superiority over an inferior race. After a while he came to believe it and spread it." Remembering the fight in symbolic terms, Americans remembered Louis as America's representative fighting a Nazi, remembered the outcome as a repudiation of racism.

Louis took advantage of the new race consciousness to speak out. In an autobiographical piece for *Life* magazine, "My Story," published in November 1948, Louis struck out against the stereotypical treatment he had received at the hands of the press:

A lot of the stuff they wrote about me has come to be like gospel truth, because they wrote it over and over, but a lot of it was wrong. They wrote that I was born with the movements of a cat, or a panther and how I was a born killer. I never said it was wrong before because Mr. Roxborough educated me not to get into arguments with writers. The real truth is I was born kind of clumsy-footed. . . . That footwork the writers said was cat-sense was something "Chappie" Blackburn drilled into me.

In a ghosted article for *Salute* magazine, entitled "My Toughest Fight: Prejudice," Louis supposedly said, "There's one fight I've always wanted—that's a crack at jim crow." Through his ghost Louis related his experiences with racism in the army and concluded:

Prejudice is weakening. The good people are softening it up. So we can't stop punching now. We just have to punch faster and harder. That's the only way we can make America a better place for my little boy and girl and all the little boys and girls in our country. I'm going to do my part.

Louis and his managers supervised Louis's ghosts fairly closely. They probably would not have allowed a ghost to write such an article before the war.

The three factors contributing to the establishment of Louis's official image—the genuine affection of white reporters, reporters' warm memories of Louis's glory days as Louis became a pathetic figure in the ring, and a new consciousness about race—were all developments in the second half of Louis's career. The fourth factor behind Louis's overwritten and patronizing official image had been a component of white press coverage of Louis from the beginning of his career. In 1935, white reporters had sensed Louis's potential social significance as the only truly prominent black figure in the mass media. Even when white writers had stereotyped Louis before the war, they had also

praised him for being inoffensive and well-behaved. White reporters had encouraged Louis to continue his good behavior and
assumed that if Louis made a good impression on the white
public, white attitudes toward blacks would improve. The
phrase, "a credit to his race," possessed real meaning for the
writers who used it repeatedly.

White reporters continued to praise Louis's behavior and
ignored his marital and financial difficulties because they thought
Joe Louis's public image was important. And after the war,
white writers began to notice signs that Louis was influencing
race relations. When Louis retired in March 1949, *Life* wrote
of Louis as a

> towering figure. . . . Negroes had great successes in the
> prize ring before him. Some of them were gentlemen, some
> of them were not. It remained for Joe Louis to turn the
> instinctively gentlemanly act into something that brought
> all manner of good to his race.
>
> The color bars have been falling fast since Joe Louis first
> became champion by knocking out Jim Braddock in 1937.
> Since that time Negroes have cracked the major leagues
> and Levi Jackson has become football captain at Yale. If
> Joe Louis had been a roistering good-time Charley like
> Negro heavyweight Jack Johnson before, this might never
> have happened. But Louis's example has helped the Negro
> even outside the world of sport. Dr. Ralph Bunche has be-
> come U.N. mediator for Palestine. Recently a colored
> undergraduate was chosen Queen of the Winter Carnival at
> McGill University. Negroes have been appointed to police
> forces and to post-office jobs all over the North. They owe
> much of their opportunity and prestige as public servants
> to Louis.

This sense of Louis's significance led many white reporters to
describe Louis's various retirements and defeats as the end of an
era. Louis dominated the heavyweight division for fifteen years
and during that time had been the most prominent athlete in
America, with the possible exception of Joe DiMaggio. Louis's
retirement did mark the end of an era—the era of segregation
in American sport. When Louis became famous in 1935, there

were a few black contenders in boxing's lighter weight divisions, and Jesse Owens and Eulace Peacock were making a splash in amateur track. Otherwise, whites did not allow blacks to compete in sport any more than in other areas of American life. Louis assumed such symbolic importance precisely because he was the first black athlete in America to achieve enduring success and win lasting popularity with the white public. When Louis retired in 1951, black athletes dominated boxing and had broken down the first barriers in professional baseball, football, and basketball. Never again would one black athlete be so alone, or so important, as Joe Louis had been.

In boxing, Louis directly influenced black participation almost immediately. Louis inspired black kids all over the country to take up boxing. At the same time, he reassured whites that interracial competition would not cause racial tension and proved that good black boxers could draw white fans. Joe Walcott remembered that after Louis won the heavyweight championship, "Negro heavyweights became not only more acceptable for main bouts, but stylish."

Other sports quickly followed suit after the war. In 1945, end Willy Strode began a brief football career with the Los Angeles Rams. Meanwhile, Bill Willis and Marion Motley starred for the Cleveland Browns of the All-America Conference, a professional league that rivaled the NFL for a few years. The All-America Conference folded, and the Browns joined the NFL.

Northern college football teams had occasionally permitted blacks to play, but before the war southern teams had successfully boycotted those occasional black players. After the war white teammates and public opinion stood behind the black players, and the southern boycotts began to collapse. In 1947 a boycott by Southern Methodist University fell apart, and Penn State's Wallace Triplett and Dennis Hoggart became the first blacks to play in the Cotton Bowl.

The Harlem Globetrotters played a series of annual basketball exhibitions against the all-white NBA champions and performed so well that pressure built on the NBA to allow blacks to join the league. In 1949–50 the league finally gave in.

The most important breakthrough, of course, came in professional baseball. Baseball was far and away America's most popular sport and sold itself as the national pastime. Because of baseball's high visibility, it drew fire for its Jim Crow policy. Jimmy Cannon of the *New York Post* led a campaign against the color line in baseball. On August 25, 1946, Cannon appeared on radio station WJZ and the ABC national radio network with Drew Pearson. Cannon denounced baseball as a "game of prejudice, played and dominated by bigoted men with jim crow for an umpire." Cannon continued, "Having jim crow as an umpire in organized baseball is laughable when you realize what a fine champion Joe Louis has been. As I have always said, Louis is a credit to his race. Naturally, I mean the human race."

In 1945, Branch Rickey, the general manager of the Brooklyn Dodgers, quietly scouted and signed two players from the Negro Leagues. One was a pitcher, John Blanchard. The other was a shortstop with the Kansas City Monarchs named Jackie Robinson. In 1946 Rickey assigned them to the Dodgers AAA farm club in Montreal. Robinson performed spectacularly, winning the batting championship and leading Montreal to the league pennant. Robinson was ready for the major leagues.

In the spring of 1947, Rickey asked Louis, Paul Robeson, and Bill "Bojangles" Robinson to come to Brooklyn to talk with Jackie. As Louis remembered in his autobiography:

> We didn't need to say anything to Jackie. He'd been in the Army, he knew just what to look for. He knew he'd have to be strong and take the shit, or he'd close the door for black people in baseball for Lord knows how many more years.
>
> I felt real good when Jackie said that if it wasn't for me and Jesse Owens, he wouldn't be where he was.

During the season of 1947, Robinson came under constant pressure. He played an unfamiliar position, first base, and got off to a slow start at the plate. His hair started to fall out. The St. Louis Cardinals talked about boycotting their games with the Dodgers if Robinson played, but Commissioner Happy Chandler threatened the Cardinals with suspensions. The Cardinals played. Robinson finished strong, hit close to .300, and helped the Dodgers win the National League pennant. The *Sporting News* voted him Rookie of the Year.

Robinson's success paved the way, and black players began to trickle into the major leagues. In the middle of the 1947 season Bill Veeck of the Cleveland Indians signed outfielder Larry Doby from the Negro Leagues and brought him up to the big leagues immediately. Doby became a star, although initially he did not handle the pressure as well as Robinson and played only part-time. Some franchises, like the New York Yankees and St. Louis Cardinals, did not sign black players for years, but others, including the Dodgers and New York Giants, signed large numbers of blacks.

The black athletes who followed Louis did not get as much press coverage as Louis had at the beginning of his career. They were playing team sports, so they were less likely to receive individual attention. Unlike boxing, baseball, football, and basketball did not have to fill as much dead time between actual competition with publicity about the players' characters. And Joe Louis's success made the successes of Jackie Robinson and other black athletes less surprising, less unusual, and less newsworthy than Louis's own breakthrough had been.

White press coverage of other black athletes generally followed the changed style white reporters used when covering Louis. There was a tendency to identify lesser-known athletes as Negroes in news stories, when the public was less likely to know that the athlete was black, and white reporters occasionally stereotyped black rookies, though the stereotypes faded as the players became familiar figures.

After the Dodgers had clinched the 1947 pennant in Robinson's rookie year, *Time* did a cover story on Jackie Robinson that revealed the new journalistic race consciousness Joe Louis had helped bring about. The writer displayed an awareness and disapproval of the prejudice Robinson faced. The story said that Robinson had to hold his temper on the field in the face of racist taunts and talked about his "long, patient battle." Instead of stereotyping Robinson, the story countered stereotypical notions, quoting Robinson: " 'You know,' he says, 'colored people do not like music or dancing any better than white people . . . the white people just think they do.' " The story even mentioned Robinson's decision to avoid confrontations instead of fighting back against prejudice. In 1935, that had not been an issue for Joe Louis. Sportswriters then were prejudiced themselves and told Louis he had to behave himself.

This change in journalistic style and consciousness resulted in large part from the reaction of white reporters to Joe Louis. No other phenomenon in the society at large can fully explain it. Pres. Franklin Delano Roosevelt's New Deal and the Fair Employment Practices Commission he created during World War II may have helped focus some attention on black problems. But FDR was more form than substance on race relations and tried to submerge the issue in order to win the support of southern Democrats. The continuing black migration northward and a corresponding rise in black political power in the North cannot explain a change in white attitudes—both were just as likely to increase racism as to decrease it. Sensitivity to racism among intellectuals and academics was growing but was still uneven and could not have penetrated the popular culture quickly enough to explain the revolution in white attitudes between 1935 and 1945. Although fighting a racist enemy in World War II may have increased America's awareness of its own racism, Joe Louis was a key factor during the war in bringing that awareness about.

It was no coincidence that in the immediate postwar years sport was the cutting edge of desegregation. Louis had convinced whites of the safety and justice of interracial sports competition. Early in his career, Jackie Robinson himself recognized Louis's importance in desegregating sports. In a column he wrote for the *Pittsburgh Courier*, Robinson said, "I have said many times before that I only hope I can do half as much for my people as he has done." In another column Robinson wrote:

He's been an inspiration to all of us. . . . Joe has made it easy for me and the other fellows now in baseball. I'm sure his example had a lot to do with my breaking into big league ball. I imagine that Mr. Rickey said to himself when considering the idea; "Joe Louis has proven that a Negro can take honors and remain dignified. If we get one like that in baseball, the job won't be hard."

Louis did more than open sports to blacks and lay the groundwork for a new race consciousness in the American media and white public. In 1935, when Louis began making headlines, a Great Depression and the threat of world war had robbed many Americans of their faith in progress. Black Americans felt the national pessimism more deeply than any other group. White Americans ignored the problem of racism in America, and neither whites nor blacks had any reason to assume that race relations would improve. Individual blacks occasionally had penetrated this depressed silence, only to disappear again, like blips on a radar screen. But Joe Louis stayed in the news so long that he not only won white affection, he also became a fixture on the American scene. The pessimism of the Depression years slowly gave way as Americans rediscovered their faith in progress after winning a world war. Part of that new faith in progress was a sense that black achievers, like Joe Louis and the wave of black athletes now participating in other sports, were not isolated blips but permanent signs of a larger pattern.

After the war, coverage of Louis in the black press indicated that blacks thought Louis had influenced white attitudes for the better. An anonymous reporter for the *Baltimore Afro-American* remembered how important it was for Louis to overcome the legacy of Jack Johnson: "Given an opportunity to regain the prestige which was lost to his race through the questionable behavior of a predecessor, Louis has done a magnificent job." Bill Nunn of the *Pittsburgh Courier* wrote an open letter to Louis in 1948, saying that Louis's impact on white attitudes had produced tangible progress for blacks:

> . . . in the wake of your bombing brown gloves came opportunities that had been denied us for so long.
> You made white America realize that Negroes were Americans, too. You let them see that Negroes had feelings

. . . had patriotism . . . had loyalty . . . had decency . . . had a sense of humor.

You shamed White America into realizing that they had to do better by their "forgotten tenth."

You were our representative, Joe . . . and no finer, grander representative could have been wished for. You did the right things.

The black press also remembered the impact Louis had on blacks. In a 1949 editorial, the *Chicago Defender* said:

No one will ever know how much Joe Louis really meant to Negro youth in America. Nevertheless, we are certain that Louis has inspired more of our youth and given them more confidence than any of our leaders no matter how great their prestige. He was a living symbol of greatness which was achieved in the right way and his actions in the ring made him a model of American fairplay.

Because of Louis's symbolic importance, he retained a special popularity with black Americans until the end of his career, even after other black athletic heroes had emerged to replace him. After Louis knocked Walcott out in their second fight, 10,000 black fans met him at the Hotel Theresa in Harlem and tore his car apart. They were celebrating Louis's victory over another black fighter. After the 1947 World Series the *Baltimore Afro-American* began a write-in contest and poll, asking who was the most popular athlete—Louis or Jackie Robinson. Louis got over sixty percent of the vote.

The breakthroughs of Louis and Robinson symbolized a trend toward tokenism in the North. Historian Howard Sitkoff has suggested that all the black "firsts" and the new, postwar assumptions of progress beguiled blacks, snuffing out any stirrings of militancy. The black press certainly was conservative after the war, just as it had been before the war. After the success of Louis and other black tokens, the black press placed an exaggerated faith in the ability of blacks to change white attitudes simply by good behavior and preparation. The black press used Louis as an example of the success awaiting blacks if they behaved well and "prepared" themselves. A *Pittsburgh Courier* editorial said:

> One has to be able to take advantage of opportunity when it knocks and to do even better than expected, as Jackie Robinson did and as Joe Louis and hundreds of others have done. . . .
>
> There is too much of a tendency for people nowadays to give more time to clamoring for opportunity than to preparing themselves for the opportunity when it arrives.
>
> Agitation is all very well, but execution is far more important.

The exaggerated faith of the black press in moral suasion through "good behavior" suggested the limitations of the process Joe Louis had helped to start. Tokenism could only go so far. White Americans may have admired and liked Joe Louis in the abstract, but they still denied the mass of blacks any chance for equal participation in American life.

In the southern press, "good behavior" had a different connotation, and southern reporters liked Joe Louis's behavior for different reasons. William Keefe of the *New Orleans Times-Picayune* described Louis as "the Alabama boy, who now lives in Detroit but who is unspoiled by the prominence and petting he got up there." Fred Russell of the *Nashville Banner* quoted Bob Murphy, a southerner who was an editor with the *Detroit Times*:

> "What I admire most about Joe is that he won't allow himself to be used in any way by certain people in this country who want to stir up trouble. He won't have any part of them. He sticks strictly to business. He wants the admiration of the white people, which, I feel, he certainly has.

Joe Louis or no Joe Louis, blacks would have to demand their rights. But Louis had given blacks hope and helped bolster the confidence necessary to confront white America with its own racism. And because of Joe Louis's influence, whites were more ready to listen.

12

"WE LOVE YOUR NAME"

After his loss to Rocky Marciano, Louis went on a tour of the Far East. The United States was at war in Korea, and he entertained American troops there, as well as in Japan. When he returned, he still entertained vague notions of continuing his boxing career because of his tax bill and because boxing was his only profession. But several boxing commissions made it clear that they would not grant Louis a license to fight in their states in order to protect him from further humiliation and the risk of injury. This official discouragement and Louis's own lack of enthusiasm ended talk of another comeback.

Louis's financial situation was absurd and tragic. He owed the IRS well over $500,000, and his tax bill accumulated interest every day. Besides his $20,000 salary from Jim Norris's International Boxing Club, which had been part of the payment he received for giving up his title, Louis had no sure sources of income. All of his investments had gone sour long before. He had no assets save for the clothes on his back and no home.

Louis scrambled. He was a partner with Billy Rowe in an advertising agency, and he helped Rowe recruit clients. He made commercial appearances, getting traveling and living expenses and occasionally some walking around money. Louis's generosity and humility during his boxing career now served him in good stead. He had friends and casual acquaintances all over the country. He traveled wherever there was a businessman who would pay his expenses, lived in hotels or the homes of friends, made his appearances, shook hands, went to parties. His fame did not provide him with million-dollar endorsements, but it did provide a living. Everywhere people were eager to play golf or go to dinner with Joe Louis, to bask in his reflected glory, to give him things. If Joe Louis didn't pay a bill, who would complain?

This life-style might have been uncomfortable for someone else. Although Louis occasionally tired of the succession of appearances, it was, on the whole, the way he preferred to live. During his boxing career, he had lived a double life. When in training, he was isolated from his wife and many of his friends, from nightclubs and public attention, and followed a rigorous schedule. Constant training thus more than filled any need Louis felt for peace and tranquility. It also prevented him from beginning a regular family life—he married Marva when his career was in full swing, and the Louises did not have any children during the first eight years of their marriage.

Between fights Louis had the world at his feet, and he rushed to make up for what he had missed while in training. He made love to many women, traveled to see his friends, spent money recklessly, played golf, and generally enjoyed his role as one of the world's most public figures. With all the fun and entertainment available to him, it was small wonder that he preferred travel and partying to domestic life.

Louis's preferences, ingrained by years of habit, did not change when his career ended. He still liked to roam, free to play golf, pick up with friends, or make love to a different woman. After his final divorce from Marva in 1949, he had no family to return to, anyway.

The IRS tried to keep up with Louis, but there was little hope that he would ever pay a significant percentage of his tax bill. His hand-to-mouth life-style made the collection of even his current taxes difficult and allowed Louis to live reasonably well despite his tax bill. For several years, the government took what it could. In 1953, Louis's mother, Lilly Barrow Brooks, died of heart disease. Louis felt the loss keenly. His mother had always been a source of stability and a touchstone with his roots. The

IRS underscored the tragedy by taking the $667 that Mrs. Brooks left her son Joe.

In 1956, the government filed two more tax liens against Louis. The new assessments and interest accumulated over the years brought the total of his tax liability to over $1,200,000. The government moved to seize trust funds for Louis's children that his wife Marva had established. The government claimed that Marva had set up the trusts with money that was properly income to Louis and should have gone toward paying his tax bill. The government won its case in federal court.

That same year Louis accepted a $100,000 guarantee to go on tour as a professional wrestler. Newsreel cameras recorded the staged spectacle of Louis, belly bulging over his trunks, receiving several dirty blows from his bad-guy opponent before ending the match with a well-choreographed forearm or right cross. There was one moving aspect of the show. Professional wrestling is a morality play. Louis always played the good guy. In some southern cities the other player was black, but usually Louis's triumphs came over white villains.

Louis's wrestling career ended after a few matches, when Rocky Lee, his 320-pound "opponent," accidentally landed hard on Louis's chest, breaking two of his ribs and bruising the muscles around his heart. Again, solicitous state athletic commissions moved to prevent Louis from hurting himself by denying him a license to wrestle. At least one good thing came out of Louis's wrestling career—he made connections with wrestling promoters who occasionally hired him to referee wrestling matches at $1,500 a crack.

Public sympathy for Louis's financial plight swelled. The media perceived Louis's brief wrestling career as a degrading comedown for the former heavyweight champion of the world, and wrestling dramatized his tax problems. People got the idea that the IRS had cruelly and unfairly driven Louis to make his unsuccessful comebacks in boxing and had now hounded him into wrestling. In truth, the IRS was just doing its job. Louis had already spent hundreds of thousands of dollars that he should have paid in taxes. A government which depended on the voluntary compliance of millions of people to collect its taxes could hardly afford to publicly forgive Joe Louis for such an egregious violation of the tax code just because his boxing career was over or because he was well loved.

Nonetheless, Rep. Alfred D. Sieminsky (D, N.J.) introduced legislation to have Congress forgive Louis's tax bill. The bill did not pass, but the IRS did agree to limit its collections for back taxes to $20,000 a year, an amount that would not even cover the interest on Louis's total bill. In addition, Louis still had to pay taxes on his current income, of course.

The IRS probably settled on the $20,000 figure because Louis still received $20,000 a year from Jim Norris's International Boxing Club. However, a year later the government won an antitrust suit against the IBC, and the courts disbanded the organization. Norris tried to reorganize and continued to pay Louis $20,000 a year until 1959, but eventually the new organization went under as well. Louis's only regular source of income went with it.

On Christmas day, 1955, Louis married Rose Morgan, a black woman who owned and ran a large beautician's business in Harlem. He now enjoyed an even more prosperous life-style out of the reach of the IRS, since he moved in with his wife and the new Mrs. Louis paid the bills out of her income. Louis did not change his habits to accommodate his wife. He still traveled often. When he was at home, he slept and played golf during the day and partied with friends all night. Rose had to run her business, and could not stay out late with her husband. The arrangement suited Louis perfectly. He never intended to tie himself down to just one woman.

Rose Morgan told a reporter later: "I tried to make him settle down. I told him he couldn't sleep all day and stay out all night any more. Once he asked me why not, and I told him I'd worry and wouldn't be able to sleep. So he said he'd wait up till I fell asleep before going out. Well, I stayed up till four A.M.—and then he fell asleep."

Rose's victories were too few and short-lived. Eventually, she tired of getting so little from her husband, and in the summer of 1957 the two agreed to separate. A year later they had the marriage annulled.

Louis returned to the life of an urban nomad, but he did not stay single for long. He met and courted another strong, financially secure woman he could lean on. Martha Malone Jefferson was the first black woman attorney admitted to the California bar and had built a successful criminal practice with her husband, Bernard Jefferson. After seven years of marriage the Jeffersons divorced, amicably enough so that they maintained their law partnership until Bernard Jefferson became a judge of the California Superior Court. On the surface, Martha was smart and tough, and underneath she had a sympathetic streak a mile wide—all traits that would serve her well in a relationship with Louis. She married him in 1959.

Once again, Louis had found a haven from the IRS. He moved into Martha's big house in Los Angeles. She installed a television for him in virtually every room, including the bathroom, and left him alone during the day while she maintained her large law practice.

When not watching television, Louis played golf. He often played thirty-six holes a day and then hit several buckets of balls on the driving range. Golf fit Louis's self-absorption. As a professional athlete, Louis had acquired the habit of working at sports. He had never worked at anything else. He had also experienced the satisfaction of having the work pay off, of becoming a great boxer. Though Louis never became a great golfer, he was a superb amateur who shot in the low seventies. He had already invested most of his ego in boxing, and because of his previous success, he could accept his limitations in his second sport. The peculiar nature of golf offered Louis a personal challenge without forcing him to measure himself against others. Golf offered intrinsic pleasures. It's fun to hit a golf ball hard, and Louis could hit the ball very hard. Golf was not as physically demanding as boxing. Louis didn't have to stay in shape, or take a punch. Golf also satisfied Louis's need for activity at a leisurely pace. It filled the abundance of time which was one of the few things left for this non-contemplative man whose accomplishments had overreached his ambitions at the age of 21.

Louis still traveled frequently, making commercial appearances and refereeing wrestling matches. Boxing promoters paid him small fees to appear at training camps and talk to the press. Martha even set him up in business as a boxing promoter himself, but Louis quickly went broke because he insisted on paying his boxers more than the going rate. When Martha complained, he said, "I was a fighter. I know how tough it is. Pay them good."

Louis never made much money from his sporadic attempts at enterprise, and the IRS still took $20,000 a year for back taxes on top of the normal tax rate. Martha Louis got fed up with the IRS pursuit of her husband, and in the early 1960s finally convinced Commissioner Dana Latham to forget about Louis's back taxes and tax him only on his current income. The IRS never officially forgave Louis his huge tax debt, though, and Louis died owing the government millions.

Martha supported her husband without complaint and also tolerated Louis's continuing fondness for staying out late with friends and making love to other women. She once told a journalist, "If these sort of women like living on the side streets of a man's life, I wish them well. But I am his wife and when I come on the scene, they got to get the hell out."

Martha had to tolerate a lot. In the mid-1960s, Louis began to lose even the loose grip he had kept on his life. His troubles began when a business acquaintance set him up with a New York prostitute. In his autobiography, Louis gave her the pseudonym Marie and claimed that she introduced him to cocaine. In December 1967, Marie gave birth to a baby boy and told Louis that he was the father.

Louis tried to keep the situation from Martha, but Marie's attempts to contact him and his own clumsy hotel-room machinations aroused Martha's suspicions. Eventually, Martha found out about the baby from one of his friends and confronted Louis. Louis had faced the best boxers of his generation without fear, but he ran from Martha, pulling one of his disappearing acts. Martha sought out Marie herself. Knowing that Marie could not take care of the child properly, Martha offered to raise him and convinced Marie to go along. The Louises legally adopted the boy and named him Joseph. The baby bore a strong resemblance to his namesake.

Martha loved children. She had adopted a daughter, Candace, before she met Louis. Streetwise from her experience as a criminal lawyer and sympathetic by nature, Martha struck up a friendship with Marie. Over the years, Martha adopted three more of Marie's babies, John, Joyce, and Janet, even though Louis was not the father of any of them.

Around the time they adopted Joseph, Martha noticed that Louis, who had always been fastidious and a sharp dresser, began to go several days without changing clothes. He played golf only rarely and sat around the house all day. With growing frequency he voiced fears that someone was trying to kill him. The central figure in the fears that consumed the last years of his life was a woman he met between his marriages to Rose Morgan and Martha, in early 1958.

There is no doubt that this woman existed and that Louis had a tempestuous affair with her that lasted at least through the 1960s. But because Louis himself was the only source of the accounts of their relationship and because he told the stories when he was mentally ill and severely delusional, it is difficult to sort out what actually happened. In a 1978 autobiography written with Edna and Art Rust, Jr., an uncertain project because of Louis's mental illness, Louis and the Rusts gave the woman the pseudonym Annie Mitchell. In the autobiography Louis said that when he met her, Annie told him that one of her lovers had shot and killed her husband. Ignoring this indication of trouble to come, Louis took up with her. Louis said that Annie introduced him to hard drugs by giving him a surprise injection in his rear when he had his back turned to her, a story that is very hard to believe. At any rate, Louis was hooked, and he got in deeper and deeper with Annie. She often traveled with him. Louis began to suspect that she was dealing drugs for the Mafia and using his companionship as a front. In his autobiography Louis said that two FBI agents talked with him and confirmed his suspicions. The agents told Louis that they were watching Annie and warned him that he was involved in a dangerous situation.

According to Louis's autobiography, the meeting had its desired effect, and he left Annie for good. But years later, in the midst of paranoid delusions, Louis told friends that Annie and the Mafia had tried to get him to appear in a pornographic movie. Louis also claimed that Annie's Mafia connections had told him to stay away from her. For some reason, perhaps because he had been unable to stay away, Louis was afraid that Annie's Mafia friends were trying to kill him.

Louis no doubt exacerbated his delusions about Annie by continuing to use cocaine. On a business trip to New York in 1969, he collapsed with abdominal pain. He later told several different people that he had taken some bad cocaine that morning. His doctors were properly discreet, but Louis's problems could not be hidden for long. He would not eat food that Martha had not prepared, fearing some unknown poisoner. Martha had to travel with him, packing a hot plate and canned soups so she could cook for Louis in their hotel rooms. His most persistent fear was that Annie's Mafia friends were trying to gas him. He taped over air-conditioning and heating ducts and smeared mayonnaise on cracks in the ceiling in a futile attempt to block the gas. He thought strangers were following him. He had trouble sleeping, and when he did sleep, he kept his clothes on and piled pillows and furniture around the bed, forming a makeshift cave to protect himself against his own imagination.

Martha took him to several doctors, including a longtime family friend. Neither the doctors nor Martha could chase Louis's demons for long or convince him to seek medical treatment. Desperate, Martha Louis finally lured her husband to their summer home in Colorado. A Colorado statute authorized the probate courts to hold someone for involuntary medical treatment at the request of the immediate family. Joe Louis Barrow, Jr., then working in Denver, signed the commitment order on behalf of the family.

Pursuant to a court order, on May 1, 1970, three deputies from the Denver Sheriff's Department and a liaison officer of the probate court came to the Louises' summer home to escort Louis to the Colorado Psychiatric Hospital. Martha Louis had hoped that the deputies would act swiftly and discreetly. Unfortunately, she had arranged to be out of the house, and in her absence Louis successfully stalled. While the deputies waited, uncertain what to do, Louis insisted on calling the White House. An operator told Louis he could not speak to President Nixon but could talk to one of Nixon's aides. Louis hung up and called the local newspapers to schedule an impromptu press conference. Refusing to acknowledge that he was sick, Louis told the deputies, "I want everybody to know what you are doing to me."

When reporters and cameramen arrived, Louis calmed down. By then it was too late; the news of Louis's forced hospitalization for mental problems got out. The family naturally did not reveal the extent of his illness. Press coverage was brief, vague, and sympathetic.

Colorado law required Louis to undergo three months of treatment. Early on, his doctors determined that Louis's problems were not the result of "organicity"—any physical damage to his brain from his boxing career—and began to treat Louis using psychiatric therapy. Louis made some progress and developed some trust in his attending physician, Dr. Martin. Colorado law provided that the courts could extend his hospitalization for another three months if it was medically advisable. Dr. Martin thought Louis should continue his treatment but was so encouraged by his progress that he gave Louis permission to leave the hospital on weekends.

Ash Resnick, an old friend, urged Louis to come to Las Vegas. Resnick ran Caesars Palace Casino, which had welcomed Louis with open arms for years, giving him a free suite and money to gamble with at the tables. It was a way to help Louis, and Louis's presence in the casino was good for business. Louis always promptly lost the money back to the casino, anyway. He enjoyed the atmosphere of big money and the chance to play celebrity.

There was a problem with going to Las Vegas, though. Once out of Colorado, Louis would be out of the jurisdiction of that state's courts and could not be forced to return to the hospital in Denver against his will. Dr. Martin and Martha thought Louis could be trusted to return for treatment voluntarily. The Louises moved back to Caesars Palace.

For a while Louis faithfully returned to Denver during the

week for treatment. But then Dr. Martin had to interrupt the therapy to go into the hospital himself for minor surgery. Louis lost faith in Martin and refused to return to Colorado again. He suffered a full relapse and retreated into his paranoid fantasies. He even accused his wife of being part of the conspiracy against him and saw his forced hospitalization as part of a Mafia plot.

The people around Louis tried to make the best of a bad situation. Caesars Palace formalized its arrangement with Louis, set him up in a large house with a swimming pool, and paid him $50,000 a year to be a "greeter." Louis spent most of his evenings in the casino, betting with house money when action at one of the tables slowed down. He signed autographs and played golf with special guests.

Except for a rare paranoid outburst at a total stranger in the casino, Louis was patient with the public and hid the symptoms of his illness. When he talked about his fears with Martha and with friends, they ignored him or tried to joke him out of his mood. His delusions came and went; he was generally able to function and often seemed like his old genial, gentle, and care-free self. He quit using cocaine, though he took up the more common vices of drinking and smoking in his fifties.

Throughout the 1970s Martha adopted Marie's children. Martha scaled back her law practice and spent a lot of time with the kids. Louis lived his last years in the midst of a big, bustling, young family. He was the same person with the family he was with strangers in the casino. Save for his fits of paranoia, he was friendly on the surface, pleasant to spend time with, humble and accepting. Which was enough, unless you wanted him to be a husband or a father. He made no attempt to tailor his schedule so that he could spend time with the children, staying up late in the casino and waking up late. Louis's own words from his autobiography revealed his carelessness: "Sunday morning, bright and early, Martha's getting them together to go to Sunday School. The boys are in the church choir. Sometimes I even get there if I don't get home too late from Caesar's Palace the night before."

In October 1977, at the age of sixty-three, Louis suffered a severe heart attack. While hospitalized, he suffered a cerebral hemorrhage. Frank Sinatra paid all of Louis's medical expenses. For the rest of his life Louis had difficulty speaking and was confined to a wheelchair.

He still managed to attend Caesars Palace functions. On Saturday night, April 11, 1981, Louis went to the Larry Holmes–Trevor Berbick heavyweight championship fight at Caesars. As friends wheeled him into the sports pavilion, individuals in the crowd stood up, trying to get a glimpse of the great champion. Some began to applaud, and soon 4,000 people were standing and cheering. The next morning, Sunday, April 12, at 9:45 A.M., Louis collapsed at home and died of a massive heart attack.

The press reaction to Louis's death revealed that his public image had changed little since his retirement. After World War II Louis's boxing skills visibly declined, and the truth about his disastrous finances started to sink in. In shaping Louis's public image at the end of his career, the white press mixed pathos with respectful memories of Louis's boxing skills, affection for him as a person, and a sense of his social significance.

The public events in Louis's life after he left boxing intensified the theme of pathos in his public image. By the mid-1950s the press and public had finally realized the full extent of Louis's staggering tax liability. Virtually every obituary, column, and editorial written after Louis's death mentioned his financial problems.

Louis's health problems and his job as a greeter at Caesars Palace—which many writers seemed to regard as little better than a degrading sinecure tainted by its connection with gambling—added to the perception of Louis as a pathetic figure. Shirley Povich of the *Washington Post* wrote: "At the finish, Joe Louis was more than broke; he was a broken man. He'd been in that wheelchair for more than four years, and was getting life-support from the generosity of the gamblers who run the Vegas casinos, a breed in which sentiment sometimes runs deep. His role was as a greeter." Donald Kaul of the *Des Moines Register* wrote, "He was a gentleman, a great fighter, and in his later years, a pathetic figure. . . . [He] ended his days working as a glorified doorman at Las Vegas gaming houses."

Dave Kindred, also of the *Washington Post*, reacted sadly when Caesars Palace, with Martha Louis's approval, arranged to have Louis lie in state in the Caesars Sports Pavilion. On the Thursday after his death, thousands of mourners filed into the pavilion to view Louis's body, lying in a copper casket in the middle of a boxing ring, surrounded by a military honor guard. Kindred wrote, "Just when you thought the Joe Louis story could get no sadder, they put him dead in a boxing ring in a tin warehouse."

Such reactions lacked perspective and would have been alien to Louis. He was happy in Las Vegas and did not think of his circumstances as pathetic. He was not the type of person who worried about justifying his life in terms of achievement, who measured his self-worth in terms of a regular job and money in the bank. Even if he had, his success in boxing would have been more than enough. He had far outstripped the most grandiose dreams of any boy growing up in the Detroit ghetto during the Depression. Nor would Louis have ever thought that there was anything wrong with working for a casino. He accepted the world as he found it. He did not think his job with Caesars was charity, but if there was an element of charity in it and an element of cashing in on his past success, so what? When he retired, Louis didn't think he should have to work. He fully intended to live off his fame and popularity. He expected people to give him things, to treat him as special. They always had during his boxing career.

Several days after his father's death, Joe Louis Barrow, Jr., told Dave Kindred,

> Being at Caesars doesn't bother me at all, because my father loved it here. He enjoyed his job as a greeter, he enjoyed having people come up to him for autographs, and he enjoyed being part of the public environment. The only thing that bothers me is when people impose their values on his environment. It may not be the life you like, or the life I like, but it was his life. He loved it. People who talk about him as a freak without dignity don't know Joe Louis. I hate to see people demean him for his life here when it clearly made him happy.

The need to see Joe Louis as a pathetic figure may have fit a more general need of liberals to see all blacks as victims. The liberal assumption when dealing with victims is that *they* would be like *us* if *they* had the choice, but the society that *we* have created does not give *them* a choice. So the writers assumed that Joe Louis must have been disappointed to do such demeaning work. The *Boston Globe* editorialized, "We are haunted by the suspicion that other people got more enjoyment out of the champ's life than he did." And, so went the dogma, it wasn't his choice to work as a greeter; it was our fault that he had to do it. Bob Greene, a syndicated columnist, wrote:

> By necessity, the obituaries skimmed over the last years of Louis' life—the years after he had been heavyweight champion. Those are the years people prefer to forget about, but in a way they were the most telling of Louis' years. Because in this country we are very good at creating heroes. When we are finished with them, though, we are never quite sure what to do with them.

Similarly, white reporters assumed that Louis would have saved his money and paid his taxes if he had had the choice, if he had gotten good financial advice, if the people around him hadn't taken his money. The *Atlanta Constitution* editorialized, "Joe Louis was the symbol for everything this country stands for, and yet he became a victim of a mean-spirited few who took him for every penny he earned in the ring." The truth was that Louis had spent or given away all his money without a thought for the future, and he had one hell of a good time doing it. Louis himself had no delusions about what would have happened if he had it all to do over again. When a friend suggested that if he had fought in the 1960s, he would have earned far more money, Louis said cheerfully, "Wouldn't make no difference. I'd still end up broke."

Not only had Louis been the victim of thieves, according to the press, but some writers suggested that the IRS had treated him unfairly by demanding that he pay his taxes. In a syndicated editorial column, sportswriter Ray Fitzgerald of the *Boston Globe* said that the government repaid Louis for his two charity bouts at the beginning of World War II by "yanking Louis around when the war was over and hounding him for income-tax money that he didn't have." A *Baltimore Afro-American* editorial read: "Outside the ring, Joe got rabbit punched because he couldn't defend himself against those who out-counted and out-smarted him. Even Uncle Sam, to whom he gave in every way he knew how, including Navy and Army charity bouts, hounded him for back taxes he could never get the money to pay."

To see Louis as he really was required more complex judgments. Louis had his contradictions: he was tolerant, accepting, and friendly with everyone on a casual level, but he was too casual with the people he loved most; he was a hardworking, disciplined athlete who never worked at anything else in his life; he preserved a sense of self and carried himself with dignity in trying circumstances, but he was not embarrassed to rely on other people for money in his later years. By willfully seeing Louis as a victim of thieves and the mean-spirited IRS, white writers glossed over the most difficult part of Louis's life history. During his career he had chosen to spend as much as he could, even borrowing against future purses to do it. He did not plan or save for his future; such thinking was alien to him. And he assumed that American society would provide for him, would always like and admire him, because he was the greatest boxer in the world and had always played the game. To treat Louis as a free human being responsible for his own actions might be to see him as exploiter rather than exploited, a harsh judgment that might smack of racism.

It was easier to write about Louis as a favorite victim. At his death journalists described him in the same warm clichés that they had used during his career. Some of the praise of Louis as a person was sincere, and some of it was tinged with the traditional condescension. A front-page obituary in the *New York Times* read:

There was no Joe Louis behind any facade. He was the same slow-spoken, considerate person in a close social group as he was to the vast crowds that surged in on him to clutch his every word when he was at the apogee of the boxing world. A simple dignity was characteristic of Louis, who never pretended that his sharecropper origins in Alabama were more than humble.

While Louis's public image remained basically constant, the historical context, which had so influenced the development of his image, changed. In the late 1940s and early 1950s Louis began to lose his unique significance as a symbol for all blacks when other black athletes—Jackie Robinson, Joe Walcott, Satchell Paige, Don Newcombe, Sugar Ray Robinson, Larry Doby, Roy Campanella, Monte Irvin, Willie Mays—joined him in the white media. In 1954, three years after Louis retired, the Supreme Court handed down its historic decision in *Brown v. Board of Education*, striking down school desegregation as unconstitutional. Shortly thereafter Rosa Parks refused to move to the back of the bus, Martin Luther King, Jr., led a boycott of the Montgomery, Alabama, bus lines, and the most active phase of the civil rights movement began. The civil rights movement culminated in national legislation banning most forms of overt segregation, eliminating the most obvious restrictions on black voting and requiring affirmative action to correct the effects of past discrimination.

As American society became more aware of its own racism and as many blacks became famous in sports, politics, and the arts, the white media slowly came to accept black celebrities who spoke out against racism and refused to conform to stereotypes. A growing black militancy and rising white consciousness fed each other. In such a context, Joe Louis's image as inoffensive and popular with whites seemed dated and less worthy of respect.

During his career Louis did not speak out against racism. He did make mild appeals for equal opportunity and actively opposed segregation in the army during and after World War II, but he was always careful to avoid offending whites. His black managers consciously tailored his public image that way. No other strategy was possible during the 1930s and 1940s.

Louis's silence and seeming conservatism were more than good public relations, however; they were his personal style. He was no politician. Though he certainly resented the racism of white America, he was tolerant and accepting of white individuals, and it was not in him to be bitter or righteously indignant. He did not have the initiative or vision to challenge social institutions. Alabama and the Detroit ghetto had drummed into him too strong a sense of his own educational shortcomings. He did not think it appropriate to be much more than the heavyweight champion of the world.

So his silence continued after he retired and even during the civil rights revolution of the 1950s and 1960s. Occasionally, white reporters sought his reactions to the activities of more militant black athletes. Louis revealed himself as a gradualist and an integrationist, certainly not uncommon attitudes for blacks of his generation. When Cassius Clay announced his conversion to the Black Muslim faith and changed his name to Muhammad Ali, Louis told the white press:

> I'm against Black Muslims, and I'm against Cassius Clay being a Black Muslim. I'll never go along with the idea that all white people are devils. I've always believed that every man is my brother. I was born a Baptist and I'll die a Baptist. . . . The way I see it, the Black Muslims want to do just what we have been fighting against for 100 years. They want to separate the races and that's a step back at a time we're going for integration.

When some black athletes talked of boycotting the 1968 Olympic Games in Mexico City, Louis disapproved, suggesting that examples of black achievement would do more good than a protest.

Such conservative sentiments, his failure to play an active role in the civil rights movement after he retired, and his public image as a "credit to his race" cast Louis as an Uncle Tom to some people who lacked a sense of history. No doubt many were disappointed in Louis because his bankruptcy cast him as a pathetic, weak figure.

Louis certainly was no radical—he was too tolerant, and he loved spending money too much for that—but he was no Uncle Tom, either. He occasionally expressed regret that he did not have the drive or the talent to be a black leader. He told one reporter, "Sometimes I wish I had the fire of a Jackie Robinson to speak out and tell the black man's story." And though he recognized that he was not personally suited to lead, there was no doubt where his sentiments lay. During the civil rights demonstrations in Little Rock, Arkansas, journalist Barry Nagler went to visit Louis in Harlem. Nagler rode the elevator with a well-dressed black man who was telling a companion that he did not care whether the demonstrations in the South were successful or not, that they would not affect his life in New York. Nagler was shocked. When he got to see Louis, Nagler asked Louis what he thought about what the man in the elevator had said. "He's dumb," Louis responded.

The perception of Louis as an Uncle Tom did not run deep. His sins were of omission. And though it was hard for some, especially the young, to realize how much Louis had meant to the black cause in a different era, most of the survivors from Louis's time remembered. Muhammad Ali's complex reaction to Louis was an example. In the early 1960s Louis criticized Ali not only for his conversion to Islam but also for his boxing skills. Ali's dancing style ignored all the fundamentals of boxing that Louis had worked so hard to master. "Can't throw a punch when he's movin' like that. Shouldn't pull his head back to get outa the way of a punch." Perhaps stung by this criticism and certainly haunted by the specter of Louis going broke, Ali called Louis an Uncle Tom and vowed he "would never end up like Joe Louis." Yet in 1976, when he was training for his rematch with Ken Norton, Ali asked Louis up to his camp for ten days. At the end of Louis's stay, Ali tried to give him $30,000.

As an athlete, Ali respected Louis enormously. Ali knew that Louis was the only real obstacle between him and his claim that he was "the greatest of all time." After appearing with Louis on television, Ali told Louis about a dream in which he had knocked Louis out. Louis glared at Ali and said, "Don't you even dream it."

As a black champion, Ali was the conscious heir to Louis's symbolic role. Louis had been Ali's childhood hero when every Louis victory over a white man had somehow avenged the racism of America, had been a real, physical repudiation of white supremacy. Ali always sought the same significance for his career, though he often had to look outside of the ring to do it, because virtually all of his boxing opponents were black men, too. When a reporter reminded Ali of earlier statements that he didn't want to wind up like Joe Louis, Ali said:

> I never said that, not that way, anyhow. That's demeaning. Look at Joe's life. Everybody loved Joe. He would have been marked as evil if he was evil, but everybody loved Joe. From black folks to red-neck Mississippi crackers, they loved him. They're all crying. That shows you. Howard Hughes dies, with all his billions, not a tear. Joe Louis, everybody cried.

Few reporters even mentioned the Uncle Tom accusations from the 1960s when they wrote about Louis after his death. White or black, they were virtually unanimous in saying that Louis had advanced the cause of civil rights. However, one black reporter, syndicated columnist Carl Rowan, reacted angrily to this praise. Rowan wrote:

> We have seen a classic example of white people telling Black people who their heroes and villains are supposed to be—but in the process revealing anew what sort of Black person they really like.
>
> One white sportswriter wrote that "No black man meant more to Black men than Joe Louis, with the possible exception of Martin Luther King Jr." This is an absurdity. . . .
>
> White people who would never compare the achievements of Jack Dempsey or Rocky Marciano with those of Jonas Salk or Franklin D. Roosevelt glibly tell us that an uneducated boxer was the most meaningful of Black men. . . .
>
> I do not intend to demean Joe Louis in any sense. He was one of my boyhood heroes. . . .
>
> But even at 16 I could distinguish between Louis and Booker T. Washington. Joe was a remarkable athlete, but he was limited in both intellect and education by the atrocious bigotry under which he grew up. He was no threat to the "system"; unwittingly he would nurture it, for the

media could rave about how Joseph Louis Barrow rose against the odds and thus make white America forget how many millions of Louis' contemporaries got mutilated by the "system."

Rowan's thinking paralleled that of some upper-class blacks in the 1930s who had looked down on Louis's achievements and wished that the first black hero had been an intellectual or a politician. Rowan forgot what Louis had meant to most blacks in the 1930s, when American racism was implacable and a black man winning in any competition against whites was a revolutionary.

Other black writers remembered. Conservative black sociologist Thomas Sowell told readers of the *Los Angeles Times* that he cried at Louis's death:

> It is hard to re-create for a new generation the world in which Joe Louis first appeared, or his role in changing that world for blacks in general. But to those of us who are black and old enough to remember that era, Louis had an importance that went far beyond sports. . . .
> What made Louis a unique figure was not simply his great talent as an athlete. He appeared at a time in American history when blacks were not only at a low economic ebb—but were also the butt of ridicule. . . .
> In this kind of world Joe Louis became the most famous black man in America. What he did as a man could reinforce or counteract stereotypes that hurt and held back millions of people of his race. How he fared in the ring mattered more to black Americans than the fate of any other athlete in any other sport, before or since. He was all we had. . . . Joe Louis was a continuing lesson to white America that to be black did not mean to be a clown or a lout, regardless of what the image-makers said. It was a lesson that helped open doors that had been closed for too long.

It is true that during his career Louis avoided offending whites, and as a result Louis was not a difficult figure for whites to love. But when Louis began his career, it didn't matter whether blacks were militant or inoffensive—white society did not give blacks a chance to step outside their roles as servants or laughing buffoons. In such a situation there was no chance that whites would accept a militant black boxer or give him a chance to win the heavyweight title.

As it was, it took years before the white public came to accept and respect Louis fully. During that time Louis was under incredible pressure. Not only did he have to establish himself as a dominant athlete to get a shot at the heavyweight title; he also had to prove that blacks could compete on equal terms with dignity and without exacerbating racial antagonism. Louis accepted that responsibility and performed so well that he became a challenge to segregation, the challenge that began to crack the system. When whites accepted Joe Louis, they accepted a black man at the height of his strength. They also implicitly accepted the possibility that other blacks might do as well. In the face of such an achievement, such a historic impact on American social attitudes, Louis's failure to take strong stands after he retired was staggeringly irrelevant.

On Friday, April 17, 1981, people started to line up at 8:00 A.M. in front of the Caesars Palace Sports Pavilion for a eulogy to Joe Louis. Over 3,000 attended the services. Sammy Davis, Jr., sang *For the Winners*. Frank Sinatra, who had been a loyal friend to Louis for years, said a few words. Then the Reverend Jesse Jackson rose to give the eulogy. Standing at a podium in the center of the Caesars Palace boxing ring, with Louis's copper casket before him, Jackson said, "This is not a funeral, this is a celebration. Funerals are untheological. We are honoring a giant who saved us in a time of trouble."

His voice falling to a whisper to draw his listeners in, then rising with emotion, Jackson continued:

Often we tred on godlike descriptions as we describe our relationship with Joe. With Joe Louis we had made it from the guttermost to the uttermost; from slaveship to championship. Usually the champion rides on the shoulder of the nation and its people, but in this case, the nation rode on the shoulders of the hero, Joe. . . . When Joe fought Max Schmeling, what was at stake was the confidence of a nation with a battered ego and in search of resurrection, and the esteem of a race of people.

In ways that presidents and potentates never could, Joe made the lion lie down with the lamb. The black, brown, and white—the rich and the poor were together, and none were afraid. With fist and character the predicate was laid for snatching down the cotton curtain.

Jackson recalled what Louis had meant in the 1930s:

God sent Joe from the black race to represent the human race. He was the answer to the sincere prayers of the disinherited and dispossessed. Joe made everybody somebody. . . .

Something on the inside said we ought to be free, something on the outside said we can be free.

Joe, we love your name. To all the witnesses gathered here, you leave and tell the story. Turn out some more editions—Extra! Extra!—the way they used to do.

Jackson thrust back his shoulders and rose to his full height. "We all feel bigger today because Joe came this way. He was in the slum, but the slum was not in him. Ghetto boy to man, Alabama sharecropper to champion. Let's give Joe a big hand clap. This is a celebration. Let's hear it for the champ. Let's hear it for the champ!"

The audience started to clap, and Jackson urged them on. "Express yourselves, be glad, he lifted us up when were down, he made our enemies leave us alone, he made us feel good about ourselves." The audience was standing now. "Wave to Joe now, give the champion a wave." Three thousand people put their arms in the air and slowly waved.

Jackson had found the appropriate mood to mark the passing of an icon of American popular culture. And Reverend Jackson was the appropriate speaker. Three years later, when he became the first black man to run for the presidency of the United States, Jackson was continuing something that Joe Louis had begun. He carried a part of Joe Louis with him as well. When he was born in 1941, his parents named him for the heavyweight champion of the world—Jesse Louis Jackson.

EPILOGUE

On September 24, 1935, Joe Louis needed only four rounds to knock out Max Baer, the former heavyweight champion still generally considered the best white fighter in the world. Several days later Louis took his new bride Marva home to Detroit. On Sunday, September 30, they went to the Calvary Baptist Church with Louis's mother. A white reporter, sent to cover the event by editors who had always ignored the colored side of town, estimated that 2,200 Negroes crammed into the church and 5,000 more waited outside just to get a glimpse of the first black hero.

The reporter had difficulty describing the unfamiliar scene. He misheard Pastor J. H. Maston's name and quoted the sermon and the response of the congregation in dialect that was a mix of observation and preconception. In his story for the *New York World Telegram*, he misspelled a word because a black man spoke it.

Pastor Martin shouted, "He's doing more to help our race than any man since Abraham Lincoln."

"Amen to that, brother."

"He don't smoke."

"Amen."

"He don't pour no red-hot likker down his throat."

"No, sir. Amen to that."

"He fights clean and he shall stand before Kings. That's what the Bible say."

"Amen to all that. Amen."

NOTES

In these notes, I have not attempted to document primary sources, which are generally identified sufficiently in the text. Virtually all of the newspaper quotations from 1935 to 1941 are from the Joe Louis scrapbooks, housed in the Michigan Historical Collections on the campus of the University of Michigan, Ann Arbor. My purpose here is to acknowledge debts to other writers and to point interested readers toward valuable secondary sources.

Chapter One:
"LET YOUR RIGHT FIST BE THE REFEREE"

The account of Roxborough and Black's first meeting with Jack Blackburn is from a UP interview with Blackburn that appeared in the *Honolulu Advertiser*, June 18, 1936. For background on Roxborough, Black, and Blackburn, see Gerald Astor, ". . . *And a Credit to His Race": The Hard Life and Times of Joseph Louis Barrow, a.k.a. Joe Louis* (New York: E. P. Dutton & Co., Inc., 1974), pp. 32–36, 39–41 (hereafter Astor); Joe Louis with Edna and Art Rust, Jr., *Joe Louis: My Life* (New York: Berkley Publishing Co., 1981), pp. 26–27, 31–33 (hereafter Rusts). In interviews Truman Gibson (hereafter Gibson interview) and Barney Nagler and Harry Markson (hereafter Nagler and Markson interview), described Roxborough as cultured and polished and Black as shrewd and tough. Gibson said of Blackburn, "When he drank, [he] was wholly unnatural."

Blackburn told the story about his run-in with Jack Johnson often. See Rusts, p. 63. For initial black prejudice against Louis because he was light skinned, see Roi Ottley, *New World A-Coming* (Cambridge, Mass.: Riverside Press, 1943), p. 187 (hereafter Ottley). Blackburn's negotiation with Roxborough and Black is from Astor, pp. 43–44. For accounts of Louis's early training with Blackburn, see Astor, p. 41; Rusts, pp. 33–34; Barney Nagler, *Brown Bomber* (New York: World Publishing, 1972), pp. 36–37 (hereafter Nagler). The hot-blood story is from Astor, pp. 42–43. Blackburn remembered his early worries over Louis's lack of a killer instinct in the UP interview. Blackburn's speeches to Louis about Jack Johnson and throwing fights are from Rusts, p. 33. Blackburn's "you can throw two, you can throw three" speech and the story of the meeting with Roxborough and Black are from Astor, pp. 41–43. Blackburn's final advice to Louis is from the UP interview.

Chapter Two:
BEGINNINGS

For the barriers against sports participation in early nineteenth-century America, see John A. Lucas and Ronald A. Smith, *Saga of American Sport* (Philadelphia: Lea and Febiger, 1978) pp. 127–28 (hereafter Lucas and Smith); Foster Rhea Dulles, *A History of Recreation: America Learns to Play* (New York: Appleton-Century-Crofts, 1965) pp. 4–5 (hereafter Dulles). For the religious barriers to sport, see Lucas and Smith, pp. 3–8, 59, 70–71, 87–88; Dale A. Somers, *The Rise of Sports in New Orleans, 1850–1900* (Baton Rouge: Louisiana State University Press, 1972) p. v (hereafter Somers); Robert H. Boyle, *Sport—Mirror of American Life* (Boston: Little, Brown and Co., 1963) pp. 5–7 (hereafter Boyle); John R. Betts, *Organized Sport in Industrial America* (unpublished Ph.D. dissertation, Columbia University, 1951), p. 687 (hereafter Betts). For the influence of immigrants bringing new games and breaking down strict American sabbath observance, see Lucas and Smith, pp. 139–46; Boyle, pp. 17–18; Betts, pp. 26–28. For industrial and technological developments aiding the growth of sport, see Betts, pp. 106–108, 137–53, 681–83; Somers, pp. v–vi; Richard D. Mandell, *Sport: A Cultural History* (Columbia University Press: New York 1984), pp. 182–84 (hereafter Mandell); Lucas and Smith, p. 127; John Rickard Betts, "Sporting Journalism in Nineteenth-Century America," *American Quarterly*, spring 1953, p. 40 (hereafter Betts article). For the emergence of a new industrial, bureaucratic culture, see Robert H. Wiebe, *The Search for Order 1877–1920* (New York: Hill and Wang, 1967), passim (hereafter Wiebe); Somers, pp. vii–ix.

For the upper-class beginnings of American sport, and the development of horse racing, yachting, country clubs, track and field, baseball, and college sport with upper class sponsorship, see Lucas and Smith, pp. 149–247; Betts, pp. 67–106, 119–29. For the motivations of urban reformers and progressives, see Wiebe, pp. 164–96; Mandell, pp. 188–89; Betts, pp. 309–14, 340–47.

For the influences of British culture and social Darwinism on the growing pro-sports ideology, see Lucas and Smith, pp. 137–38, 291–94; Betts, pp. 183–92. For the communications revolution, see Mandell, pp. 184–85. For accounts of Richard K. Fox and the growth of the *Police Gazette*, see Betts article, pp. 50–51; William Henry Nugent, "The Sports Section," *American Mercury*, March 29, 1929, pp. 334–35 (hereafter Nugent). For the importance of sports coverage in the New York newspaper wars and the growth of yellow journalism, see Betts article, pp. 52–56; Nugent, pp. 336–38.

For the growth of lower-class participation in the sports boom, see Mandell, pp. 189–90; Betts, pp. 319–31. For attacks on sport, see Mandell, p. 181; Lucas and Smith, pp. 167–68. For the explosion of sport in the golden twenties, see Lucas and Smith, pp. 306–17; Boyle, pp. 37–43; Betts, pp. 422–52. For the overwhelming sports coverage during the era, see Jerome Holtzman, ed., *No Cheering in the Press Box* (New York: Holt, Rinehart and Winston, 1974), p. 17 (hereafter Holtzman); Nugent, passim. For the role of radio and the movies in popularizing sport, see Lucas and Smith, p. 309; Boyle, pp. 40–41.

For the influence of sports heroes on American culture, see Somers, p. xi. For the appeal of sports heroes, and their new role, see Mandell, p. 191; Lucas and Smith, pp. 294–96.

For the early history of boxing, see generally Sam Andre and Nat Fleischer, *A Pictorial History of Boxing* (New York: Bonanza Books, 1981); Betts, pp. 50–52, 129–33, 207–11. The newspaper quotes from Horace Greeley and the *New York Daily Times* are from the Betts article, p. 44. For the pattern of increasing segregation in sport from the 1880s on, see Mandell, p. 194; Lucas and Smith, pp. 267–85; Somers, p. 286.

For a superb full biography of Jack Johnson, see Randy Roberts, *Papa Jack: Jack Johnson and the Era of White Hopes* (New York: Free Press, 1983) (hereafter Roberts). For a full study of Johnson's public image, see Al-Tony Gilmore, *Bad Nigger! The National Impact of Jack Johnson* (Port Washington, N.Y.: Kennikat Press, 1975) (hereafter Gilmore). John L. Sullivan's denunciation of Tommy Burns for breaking the color line is quoted in Gilmore,

p. 27. Johnson's explanation for his relationships with white women
is from his autobiography, *Jack Johnson: In the Ring and Out*
(London: Proteus Publishing Ltd., 1977), p. 65. His habit of taping
his penis is from Gilmore, p. 14. The letter from the worried black
reader appeared in the *New York Times*, May 11, 1910. The rest
of the press quotes are from Gilmore, pp. 41, 107, 109, 98, 99, 124,
respectively. The accounts of Johnson's private life, his prosecution
for violating the Mann Act, and his escape to Europe are entirely
from Roberts, pp. 138–85. The quote from Asst. Atty. Gen. Harry
Parkin is from Roberts, pp. 177–78.

Johnson's claim that he threw the Willard fight is from his autobiography, pp. 155–60. My conclusion that Johnson let himself be
knocked out is from film of the fight in the Library of Congress.
For an account of the 1960s pro-Johnson fashion, see Roberts, pp.
228–29.

Grantland Rice's quote is from Gilmore, p. 137. Randy Roberts
has also produced a superb biography of Jack Dempsey, *Jack
Dempsey: The Manassa Mauler* (Baton Rouge: Louisiana State University Press, 1979), from which the remainder of this chapter was
drawn.

Chapter Three:
"NEW YORK AIN'T READY FOR HIM"

The Mushky Jackson quote is from Astor, pp. 64–65. The figures
on Louis's early purses and the description of his early spending
habits are from Rusts, pp. 36–42. The ratings of Louis and his opponents are from Bert Randolph Sugar, ed., *The Ring Record Book
and Boxing Encyclopaedia* (New York: Ring Publishing Co., 1981).

Jack Blackburn's cynicism about New York and Louis's own
memory of negotiations with Jimmy Johnston are from Rusts, p. 43.
Nagler's account of Roxborough's call to Jimmy Johnston is in
Nagler, pp. 42–43. The description of boxing's discrimination against
blacks and Barney Nagler's comment about Jimmy Johnston are
from the Nagler and Markson interview. The story of the creation
of the 20th Century Sporting Club is from Nagler, pp. 43–44, and
Astor, pp. 76–78. The background material on Mike Jacobs is from
Astor, pp. 66–76. For accounts of Jacobs discovering and signing
Louis, see Astor, pp. 78–80; Nagler, 44–46; Rusts, pp. 45–47. Louis's
description of Jacobs as unprejudiced is from Rusts, p. 134. His
memory of Jacobs's recruiting pitch is from Rusts, pp. 46–47. The
background on Primo Carnera is from Astor, pp. 86–96.

Chapter Four:
"SOMETHING SLY AND SINISTER"

For a brief account of the New Deal's treatment of blacks, see John Morton Blum, *V was for Victory* (New York: Harcourt Brace Jovanovich, 1976), p. 181 (hereafter Blum). The quotes from Red Burman, Bob Pastor, Shirley Povich, and Don Dunphy are from interviews with the author (hereafter Burman interview, Pastor interview, Povich interview, and Dunphy interview). For an indication of the scant newspaper coverage of blacks during the 1930s, see the *New York Times Index*. The story of Father Divine is from Ottley, pp. 88–99. The impressions on press coverage of the 1932 Olympics are from reading the *New York Times, Chicago Tribune*, and *Los Angeles Times*. Roi Ottley's description of Louis's initial shyness around whites is from Ottley, p. 199. The story of the Klan threats against Dr. Joseph Bier is from the Nagler and Markson interview.

Truman Gibson's skepticism about any earlier consciousness of Louis's role as a racial ambassador is from the Gibson interview. For Roxborough's background, see Astor, pp. 32–36. The quote from Louis about the black toy dolls is from Rusts, p. 36. Harry Markson's famous watermelon story is from the Nagler and Markson interview. The quote from John Hope Franklin about black identification with Ethiopia is from his landmark survey of black history, *From Slavery to Freedom*, 5th ed., (New York: Alfred A. Knopf, 1980), p. 422.

The description of the Carnera fight is from a frame-by-frame analysis of film of the fight in the Library of Congress. Carnera's dialogue is from Rusts, p. 55. Louis's eloquent description of the thrill he felt after the Carnera fight is from Joe Louis, as told to Meyer Berger and Barney Nagler, "My Story," *Life*, November 8, 1948, p. 148.

Barney Nagler's memories of Grantland Rice are from the Nagler and Markson interview. The description of King Levinsky's fear of Louis is from Nagler, p. 58. Jack Blackburn's promise to quit drinking if Louis knocked out Levinsky in one round is from Rusts, p. 59. The description of the Levinsky fight is from film in the Library of Congress. Levinsky begging the referee to stop the fight is from Rusts, p. 59. For background on Paul Gallico and Gallico's own memories of his career as a sportswriter, see Holtzman, pp. 61–80.

For background on Max Baer, see Astor, pp. 111–15. For the considerable southern newspaper coverage of Louis, see Alexander Joseph Young, *Joe Louis: Symbol* (unpublished Ph.D. dissertation, University of Maryland, 1968), p. 8 (hereafter Young); A. O. Edmonds, *Joe Louis* (Grand Rapids: William B. Eerdmans Publishing Co., 1973), p. 33 (hereafter Edmonds). The story of Louis's courtship of Marva Trotter and his "No Jack Johnson problem here" quote are from Rusts, p. 64. The story of Louis's nonchalance at the weigh-in is from Astor, p. 117. The account of the wedding ceremony is from Rusts, pp. 65–66. Joe Humphrey's introduction of Louis and Baer and Clem McCarthy's radio play-by-play of the knockout are from sound recordings in Ted Patterson's private collection (hereafter Patterson collection). Baer's quote about getting executed is from Astor, p. 119. Shirley Povich's quote about the "prejudice of the American scene" is from the Povich interview.

Chapter Five:
"THE FINGER OF GOD"

For background on Max Schmeling, see Astor, pp. 131–34. The account of Schmeling's mission to reassure the American Olympic Committee about American participation in the Berlin Olympics is from Schmeling's memoirs, published in German—*Errinnerungen* (trans. Karin and Alden Mead) (Frankfurt: Verslage Ullstein GMBH, 1977), pp. 322–34 (hereafter Schmeling's memoirs). Schmeling's impressions while watching Louis train and watching the fight with Uzcudun are from Schmeling's memoirs, p. 324. Harry Markson's description of the Uzcudun fight is from the Nagler and Markson interview. Uzcudun falling over when he finally tried to take a shower is from Astor, p. 123. Louis's training routine for Retzlaff is from Rusts, p. 74. The description of the Retzlaff fight is from film in the Library of Congress.

For Louis's frank account of his stay in Hollywood, see Rusts, pp. 74–76. The description of Louis's life-style while he was out of training was gleaned from a combination of many sources. Colvin Roberts, a Chicago businessman who was a good friend of Louis, shared his vivid memories of going out with Louis in an interview (hereafter Roberts interview). Truman Gibson had a deep understanding of Louis's outlook on life and steered me to Colvin Roberts and to Ted Jones, Louis's accountant, who told me about Louis's spending habits and his attitudes toward women (hereafter Jones interview). I also drew heavily from the Rusts, Astor, and Nagler books, as well as the Nagler and Markson interview. Billy Conn, an opponent and a good friend of Louis's, also shared his memories of what it was like to be with Louis and how Louis spent money (hereafter Conn interview).

Schmeling's memories of getting laughed at by American reporters and of his first meeting with Hitler are from Schmeling's memoirs, pp. 326–34. For accounts of Louis's overconfident and insufficient preparations to fight Schmeling, see Rusts, pp. 76–79; Astor, pp. 128–31; Nagler pp. 66–67; see also John Roxborough's interview with W. W. Edgar, describing Louis's overconfidence and poor training, in the *Detroit Free Press*, June 21, 1936.

The quotations from Nazi papers are translations by Alden Mead. The description of the prefight instructions and the fight itself are from film in the Library of Congress. The quote from Edwin C. Hill's radio coverage of the fight is from a recording in the Patterson collection. Schmeling's fear that Louis was trying to foul him intentionally and his decision to go for the knockout are from a Schmeling interview with Paul Gallico in the *Saturday Evening Post*, "This Way I Beat Joe Louis," August 29, September 5, 1936, and from Schmeling's memoirs, pp. 350–53. His memories of the crowd yelling "Kill him" are from Schmeling's memoirs, p. 353.

Harry Markson's story about lunch at Dinty Moore's is from the Nagler and Markson interview. The reaction of top Nazi officials to Schmeling's victory was reported in the American press. The account of Schmeling's triumphant return to Germany and his meeting with Hitler is from Schmeling's memoirs, pp. 358–65.

Chapter Six:
". . . AND NEW HEAVYWEIGHT CHAMPION OF THE WORLD"

For Louis's grief over his stepfather's death, see Rusts, p. 86. Louis described his nervousness before the Sharkey fight in Rusts, p. 87. The account of the Sharkey fight is from press coverage and a sound recording from the Patterson collection. For a description of Jacobs's negotiations with Joe Gould, including background on Gould and the story of Roxborough's abduction, see Astor, pp. 146–49; see also Rusts, pp. 88–89, 91–92, 97–99; Nagler, pp. 82–84. Eddie Simms's dialogue with Arthur Donovan is from Rusts, p. 91. The account of the Pastor fight is from press coverage and Rusts, pp. 94–96. Bob Pastor's claim of foul play is from the Pastor interview.

Blackburn and Louis's hard work on tour before the Braddock

fight is from Rusts, pp. 100–101. Lake Geneva's prejudice is from Rusts, p. 102. For background on Jim Braddock, see Astor, pp. 151–56. George Nicholson's warm memory of Braddock is from Astor, p. 156. Blackburn's plan to have Louis take it easy in sparring drills is from Rusts, p. 104. The account of the Braddock fight is from Library of Congress film. Blackburn's brief speech to Louis before the fight is from Nagler, p. 86. Blackburn's instructions to Louis during the fight are from Rusts, pp. 107–108, and Nagler, p. 86. Braddock's brave threat to his manager is from Astor, p. 158.

Chapter Seven:
"IN A FOOTNOTE AT LEAST"

The reasons for Louis's new contract with Mike Jacobs, his eagerness for a rematch with Schmeling, and his confidence that he could beat Schmeling, are from Rusts, pp. 115–16. For Schmeling's account of the negotiations and his memory of the crowd cheering him before the Louis-Farr fight, see Schmeling's memoirs, p. 416. For Hitler's foreign policy in 1937–38, see Alan Bullock, *Hitler: A Study in Tyranny* (abridged edition) (New York: Harper and Row, 1971), pp. 204, 233. For Jacobs's attempts to defuse the threatened boycott, see Rusts, p. 138; Astor, p. 168. Louis's meeting with FDR is from Astor, p. 169; Nagler, pp. 92–93.

Schmeling's sense of a change in the American atmosphere and the account of his reception in New York are from Schmeling's memoirs, pp. 401, 423–24. Roxborough's quote on Louis's enthusiasm for training is from the *New York Journal and American*, June 16, 1938. Shirley Povich's quote is from the Povich interview. Schmeling's feeling that the prefight publicity had gotten out of hand and his appreciation of Louis's role as a symbol are from Schmeling's memoirs, p. 424.

Louis's activities on the day of the fight are from Rusts, pp. 129–30. Louis walking into the commission's office for the weigh-in and the weighing-in itself are from a Universal newsreel in the National Archives. Louis's memory of arriving at Yankee Stadium is from Nagler, p. 95. The prefight scene at the stadium is from press coverage. The scene in Louis's dressing room is from Rusts, pp. 129–30.

Schmeling's nervousness, the barrage he took from fans on the infield, his loneliness in the ring, and the boos for the former champs introduced from ringside are from Schmeling's memoirs, pp. 426–27. Clem McCarthy's radio coverage is from a sound recording in the Patterson collection. Referee Donovan's prefight instructions and the description of the fight itself are from film in the Library of Congress. Max Machon's instructions to Schmeling during the fight and his fear that the Americans would allow Louis to maim Schmeling are from Schmeling's memoirs, p. 428.

Schmeling's postfight radio statement is from a sound recording in the Patterson collection. German Ambassador Dieckhoff's visit to Schmeling in the hospital is from Schmeling's memoirs, pp. 431–32.

Chapter Eight:
BUMS OF THE MONTH

Jacobs's monopoly over boxing, his Carnival of Champions, and his merger with Madison Square Garden are from Rusts, p. 120. The story of Jacobs's shedding of his secret partners in the 20th Century Club is from the Nagler and Markson interview. Jacobs's settlement of his contract with Joe Gould is from Astor, p. 149. The negotiations preceding the Louis–John Henry Lewis fight and Louis's decision to go for a quick knockout are from Rusts, pp. 134–38. The description of the Roper fight is from film in the Library of Congress.

For background on Galento and for the prefight publicity antics of Galento and Joe Jacobs, see Astor, pp. 199–220. Barney Nagler's recollection of the things Galento said to Louis before the fight and the way Louis cut Galento are from the Nagler and Markson interview. The account of the Pastor fight is from the Pastor interview.

The accounts of both Godoy fights and the Paycheck fight are from film in the Library of Congress. Louis's respect for his Bum-of-the-Month opponents is from Rusts, p. 149. Red Burman's memories of his fight with Louis are from the Burman interview. The story of Arthur Donovan getting drunk before the Buddy Baer fight is from the Nagler and Markson interview. The account of the Baer fight is from press coverage.

The background on Billy Conn is from the Conn interview. Shirley Povich's claim that Louis first used the "run but can't hide" line before the Pastor fight is from the Povich interview. Conn's comments about the prefight publicity are from the Conn interview. Louis's extra effort to get his weight down before the Conn fight is from Rusts, p. 153.

The background on Don Dunphy, his conversation with Louis at the Conn weigh-in, and his policy of being color blind are from the Dunphy interview. The account of the Conn fight is from

Library of Congress film and Rusts, pp. 153–54. The advice of
Conn's handlers and trainer and his explanation for the amount of
punishment he withstood are from the Conn interview.

The ABC National Urban League radio program is from the
Library of Congress's sound recording collection. Barney Nagler's
memory of the warm feeling that white reporters had for Louis is
from the Nagler and Markson interview.

Chapter Nine:
"SOME BLACK MOTHER'S SON"

The introductory paragraph, as well as much of the rest of this
chapter, is heavily dependent on Lawrence W. Levine, *Black Culture and Black Consciousness: Afro-American Folk Thought from
Slavery to Freedom* (New York: Oxford University Press, 1977)
(hereafter Levine). The folk song, "He Don't Know my Mind" is
from Levine, p. xiii.

Louis's memory of the early attention he got from black fans is
from Rusts, pp. 44–45. His routine at the Harlem Opera House and
the scene at his training camp for the Carnera fight are from Rusts,
pp. 49–52. For the celebration after Louis's victory over Carnera
and the near riot at the Savoy ballroom, see Astor, pp. 102–105. The
excerpt from Maya Angelou is from *I Know Why the Caged Bird
Sings* (New York: Random House, 1969), pp. 110–15.

Sociologists Drake and Clayton are quoted in Edmonds, p. 93.
The overwrought quote from Louis about drinking bringing out
"the objectionable traits in people" is from the *Chicago Defender*,
September 7, 1935. The quotation from Levine is on p. 433. The
quotation from Charles S. Johnson is from his book *Growing Up
in the Black Belt: Negro Youth in the Rural South* (Washington,
D.C.: American Council on Education, 1941), p. 246. E. Franklin
Frazier's quote about vicarious aggression is from his book *Negro
Youth at the Crossroads* (Washington, D.C.: American Council on
Education, 1941); 1967 Schocken Books edition, p. 179 (hereafter
Frazier). The two songs with images of white fighters on their
knees ("Bob Pastor was on his knees" and "Joe Louis hit him so
hard . . .") are from Levine, p. 436.

Paul Oliver's quote about the special appeal Louis had to blues
singers is from Paul Oliver, *Aspects of the Blues Tradition* (New
York: Oak Publications, 1970), pp. 146, 149 (hereafter Oliver). The
form and exultant tone of the early blues about Louis is from

Oliver, pp. 148–63. "Joe Louis Is the Man" is from Oliver, pp. 151–52. For the list of blues about Louis and their lyrics, see Oliver, pp. 152–56.

Gunnar Myrdal's one-room schoolhouse is from *An American Dilemma*, 20th anniversary ed. (New York: Harper & Row, 1962) p. 903 n.b. Martin Luther King, Jr.'s story about the condemned man calling Louis's name is from *Why We Can't Wait* (New York: Harper & Row, 1964), pp. 110–11. Richard Wright is quoted in Edmonds, p. 99. For Malcolm's boxing career, see *The Autobiography of Malcolm X* (New York: Grove Press, Inc., 1964), pp. 23–24 (hereafter Malcolm X). The disproportionate numbers of blacks who filled boxing gyms after Louis became successful is from the Nagler and Markson interview.

Lena Horne's reaction to Louis's loss to Schmeling is from Horne and Schickel, *Lena*, p. 75, quoted in Levine, p. 434. Schmeling's memories of Harlem that night are from Schmeling's memoirs, pp. 355–56. Jack Johnson's bragging is from Ottley, p. 195. The other incidents after Louis's defeat are from the *Chicago Defender*, July 4, 1936. Powell and Ottley's newspaper columns after the loss to Schmeling are from the *New York Amsterdam News*, June 27, 1936.

For Malcolm X's description of the "Sugar Hill Negroes" in Boston see Malcolm X, p. 41. The middle-class black girl's ambivalence is from Frazier, pp. 190–91. Romeo L. Dougherty's column is from the *New York Amsterdam News*, October 5, 1935. For the full lyrics to "King Joe," see Oliver, p. 160. The ABC National Urban League radio program is from the sound recording collection in the Library of Congress. For a fuller treatment of the white reaction to black adulation of Louis, see Edmonds, pp. 87–93. The final quote about the changing mood in black America is from Levine, p. 438.

Chapter Ten:
JOE LOUIS: AMERICAN

For Louis's reaction to Pearl Harbor, his draft classification, and his decision not to apply for a deferment, see Rusts, pp. 156, 158. The summary of Louis's financial situation is from the Gibson and Jones interviews and Rusts, pp. 156, 165. The planning of the Navy Relief Fund charity fight is from Rusts, p. 156.

The Broadway column about Louis's charity fight highlighting the bigotry of the navy is from the *New York Daily News*, January 8, 1942. Blackburn's failing health before the Baer fight is from

Rusts, p. 157. The description of the prefight scene is from press coverage. Wendell Willkie's speech is from a sound recording in the Patterson collection. The description of the fight is from a videotape at the Museum of Broadcasting in New York. Baer's statement that he couldn't have beaten Louis that night is from a sound recording in the Patterson collection. The staged induction scene is from a Universal newsreel in the motion picture collection of the National Archives. Shirley Povich's memory of the new appreciation for Louis is from the Povich interview. The editorial praising Louis is from the *Chicago Tribune*, January 11, 1942. Paul Gallico's article on Louis appeared in the June 1942 issue of *Reader's Digest*.

The summary of Louis's many appearances in newsreels at the beginning of the war is from a review of the Universal and Paramount newsreel collections in the National Archives motion picture collection. The account of the Boxing Writers Association awards dinner is from Nagler, pp. 127–28. For Louis turning down the army's offer of a commission, see Rusts, p. 158. For Louis's unusual training routine before the Simon charity fight, see Nagler, pp. 129–30. The story of Louis's speech at the Navy Relief Society dinner is from the Nagler and Markson interview. The speech itself is from a sound recording in the Patterson collection. The radio broadcast of the Louis-Simon fight is in the Library of Congress's sound recording collection.

Louis's frequent introduction as "the first American to kayo a Nazi" is from Edmonds, p. 84. For a brilliant account of official attempts to "sell the war," and of American impressions of their enemies, see Blum, pp. 15–53. Chandler Owens's pamphlet "Negroes and the War" is from Blum, pp. 194–95. The Army Signal Corps film "The Negro Soldier" is in the National Archives motion picture collection. For a comprehensive account of armed forces policies toward blacks during World War II, see Ulysses Lee, *United States Army in World War II, Special Studies Volume 8, The Employment of Negro Troops* (Washington, D.C.: Office of the Chief of Military History, 1966) (hereafter Lee). The account of Stimson's policy recommendations to FDR, and FDR's approval, is from Lee, pp. 75–76. For the army's attempts to placate blacks with the promotion of Davis and the appointment of Hastie and for Hastie's difficulties getting anything done, see Lee, pp. 79–81.

The account of Randolph's threatened march on Washington is

from Blum, pp. 185–88. For the limited effectiveness of the FEPC, see Blum, pp. 197–99. For a full account of the Detroit race riot, see Blum, pp. 199–207. Hastie's resignation is from Lee, pp. 171–74. The letter to Gibson is in the National Archives, box 221 in the files of the Office of the Assistant Secretary of War, Civilian Aide to the Secretary; subject file—NAACP, 1940–47.

For Louis's reaction to Blackburn's death, see Rusts, pp. 161–62. For his maturation in the army, see Rusts, p. 166; Astor, pp. 229–30; Nagler, p. 140. Louis's assignment to Fort Riley and his relationship with Jackie Robinson are from the Gibson interview and Rusts, pp. 163–65. The story of the aborted Louis-Conn wartime charity fight is from Astor, pp. 215–17. The story of Conn's fight with his father-in-law and of Louis kidding him about it are from the Conn interview. Louis's debt to the IRS is from *Yank* magazine, June 5, 1942; Astor, p. 216. Truman Gibson's memory of Louis's spending habits is from the Gibson interview.

For an account of Louis's attempt to set Marva up in Kansas City to have the baby near him, see Rusts, pp. 166–67. I don't know if the film *This is the Army* is available in a library—I saw it at a film festival. For Louis's stay in Hollywood, see Rusts, pp. 168–69. For Marva's singing career, see Rusts, pp. 172–73. The account of Louis's morale tours is from the Gibson interview. For Louis's decision to fight Jim Crow on army bases, see Rusts, p. 170. For an account of the incident at Camp Sibert, see Nagler, p. 138; Rusts, p. 170. For his experiences with discrimination abroad, see Rusts, p. 171. For Louis's marital problems and attitudes, see Rusts, pp. 170, 174. For the army's practice of breaking up black combat units and assigning them to labor details, see Lee, pp. 475–77.

Al Laney's column praising Louis is from the *New York Herald-Tribune*, October 11, 1944. Margery Miller's book was *Joe Louis: American* (New York: Current Books, Inc., 1945). For her version of Roxborough's background and his dream, see pp. 26–28; for her symbolic accounts of the Schmeling fights, see pp. 65–73, 97–108; for her description of Louis's impact on white attitudes see pp. 180–81. Truman Gibson's letter to John J. McCloy is in the National Archives, in the files of the Office of the Assistant Secretary of War, Civilian Aide to the Secretary, along with S. G. Henry's reply memo. The proposed bribe to get Louis out of the service is from the Gibson interview. For a fuller account of black protest during the war, see Blum, pp. 207–20.

Chapter Eleven:
SWAN SONG

For accounts of Louis's indebtedness, see Nagler, p. 148; Rusts, p. 181. Ted Jones explained the differences in the tax code after the war during the Jones interview. The account of Jacobs's preparation of Louis's tax returns and Jacobs's plan to defer Louis's tax bill are from the Gibson interview. For Louis's falling out with Black and his contract with Marva, see Rusts, p. 178. For his decision to keep Roxborough as a manager and to sign with Marshall Miles, see Rusts, p. 178; Nagler, pp. 145–46. For the training routines of Conn and Louis, see Rusts, pp. 179–80.

The account of the Conn weigh-in is from newsreels in the National Archives motion picture collection. The prefight scene was drawn from press coverage; Harry Balogh's introduction is from a sound recording in the Patterson collection; the description of the fight is from film in the Library of Congress. Conn's realization that he just "didn't have it" is from the Conn interview. The postfight dressing room scene is from press coverage.

For the division of the Conn purse, see Nagler, p. 148; Rusts, p. 181. For the reconciliation with Marva, see Rusts, pp. 179, 183. The account of the Mauriello fight is from film in the Library of Congress. The postfight meeting with Governor Dewey is from newsreels in the National Archives. Mauriello crying after the fight is from press coverage. For Miles's unsuccessful plan to save the money from the Mauriello purse, see Nagler, pp. 149–51; Astor, pp. 239–40.

For an account of the South American tour, see Rusts, pp. 184–85. For the negotiations leading up to the first Walcott fight and for background on Walcott, see Astor, pp. 242–43. For Louis's difficulties training and for an account of the fight, see Rusts, pp. 188–89. Harry Balogh's announcement of the decision is from a sound recording in the Patterson collection. The postfight scene in Louis's dressing room is from press coverage. For Louis's decision to retire for the first time, see Nagler, pp. 160–61. For an account of the European tour and for Louis's continuing marital problems, see Rusts, p. 192. For Louis's difficulties training, an account of the second Walcott fight, and referee Fullham's impatience with the boring fight, see Rusts, pp. 193–94.

Louis's negotiations with Madison Square Garden and the Kilpatrick memo are from Astor, pp. 247–48. The account of the negotiations with Voiler and Hearst, and later Norris and Wirtz, are

from the Gibson interview. For Louis's lack of remorse over dis-
placing Jacobs, see Rusts, p. 197. For the final divorce between
Louis and Marva, see Rusts, pp. 194–95, 197.

The accounts of the tax audit and the creation of the Joe Louis
Corporation are from the Jones interview. Gibson's attempt to nego-
tiate an offer in compromise is from the Gibson interview. The
account of the Charles fight and its aftermath is from press coverage.
For the negotiations leading up to the Marciano fight and for an
account of the fight itself, see Rusts, pp. 207–209. The locker room
scene is from press coverage.

The *Life* magazine article in which Louis lied about the extent
of his investments was Joe Louis, as told to Meyer Berger and
Barney Nagler, "My Story," *Life*, November 8, 15, 1948. Harry
Markson's affection for Louis is from the Nagler and Markson inter-
view. Shirley Povich's statement about the growing acceptance of
Louis is from the Povich interview.

For the breakthrough of black athletes after World War II, see
Ocania Chalk, *Pioneers of Black Sport* (New York: Dodd, Mead
and Co., 1975), pp. 110; 233–35. For Louis's meeting with Branch
Rickey and Jackie Robinson, see Rusts, p. 186. For the story of
Jackie Robinson's entry into big-league baseball and for a study of
the press coverage black big leaguers received during the late 1940s
and early 1950s, see Jules Tygiel's superb book *Baseball's Great
Experiment* (New York: Oxford University Press, 1983).

Chapter Twelve:
"WE LOVE YOUR NAME"

My account of Louis's life after he left the ring is heavily dependent on Barney Nagler's excellent book *Brown Bomber*, which
primarily focuses on the development of Louis's mental illness.
Nagler had the cooperation of Martha Louis when researching his
book and accumulated a wealth of detail about Louis's life after he
left the ring.

For Louis's grief at his mother's death, see Rusts, p. 213. For the
government's seizure of the trust funds for Louis's two children
and for Mrs. Brook's bequest to her son, see Nagler, p. 194; Astor,
p. 261. For an account of Louis's wrestling career, see Astor, pp.
262–63, and newsreels in the National Archives.

Rose Morgan's description of her marriage to Louis is from Gay
Talese, "Joe Louis: The King as a Middle-Aged Man," *Esquire*,
June 1962, p. 93 (hereafter Talese). For his courtship of Martha

Jefferson, see Rusts, pp. 221, 224–25; Nagler, pp. 6–8. For Louis's life with Martha, see Nagler, p. 196; Talese, pp. 92–93. For his golfing habits, see Talese, p. 93. For Louis's attempt to become a boxing promoter, see Nagler, p. 201. Martha Louis's comment about the other women in her husband's life is from Talese, p. 94. For the development of Louis's illness, his relationship with "Marie," the adoption of Marie's children, his hospitalization, and his employment at Caesars Palace as a greeter, see generally, Nagler, passim; Rusts, pp. 234–51.

For Louis's few public comments and activities concerning race relations during the 1960s, see Astor, pp. 270–73. The story of Louis's reaction to the black man who expressed indifference to the demonstrations in Little Rock is from the Nagler and Markson interview. For an example of Muhammad Ali's attempt to find the symbolic significance for his own career that Louis's career had, see Muhammad Ali with Richard Durham, *The Greatest: My Own Story* (New York: Random House, 1975), p. 400, where Ali describes George Foreman, a black opponent, as the representative of "White America, Christianity, the Flag, the White Man. . . ." Ali's generosity to Louis in 1976 is from Rusts, pp. 248–49. Jesse Jackson's funeral oration is from press coverage.

INDEX